CHRISTOPHER HAMPTON:
DRAMATIC IRONIST

To John Thaxter, with thanks for helping to raise the curtain on my theatrical career.

BEN FRANCIS

CHRISTOPHER HAMPTON: DRAMATIC IRONIST

AMBER LANE PRESS

Published in 1996 by
Amber Lane Press
Church Street
Charlbury
Oxford OX7 3PR

Tel: 01608 810024

Printed and bound in Great Britain by
Bookcraft Ltd, Midsomer Norton, Bath, Avon

A CIP record for this book is available from the British Library

ISBN: 1 872868 19 3

CONTENTS

ACKNOWLEDGEMENTS

Writing a book is somewhat like launching into space, and if one doesn't have guidance, one is likely to get hopelessly lost. I would like to express my gratitude to everyone who helped keep this book on course. My thanks are due to Christopher Hampton himself, his secretary Margaret Camplejohn, his associate Norma Heyman, and his agent Tom Erhardt. I am also grateful to my mother, who translated from the French for me and did the indexing, my father, Brian Louis Pearce, Mike Walker, Barbara Parker, Roderick Millar, Jenny Scott, Peggy Butcher, David Sivier, the staff of the Theatre Museum in Covent Garden, and Charlie Glynn, Graham Cooper and Steve Bryan at the British Film Institute. I am also indebted to Sophia Kingshill and Kenneth Dean for translating Norwegian for me. I would also like to thank Judith Scott of Amber Lane Press for her encouragement and patience and her many suggestions.

Ben Francis
Twickenham, 1996

PREFACE

> Asking a working writer what he thinks about critics is like asking a lamp-post what it thinks about dogs.
>
> *Christopher Hampton*

A preface to a literary study usually begins by explaining why another book on an overworked subject is needed. In this case, however, no explanation is required. Christopher Hampton has been writing plays and film scripts for over twenty years and yet no full-length study has appeared in Britain before. He may have pinpointed the reason for this himself when he said that he made a deliberate effort not to restrict himself to a narrow set of obsessions, but rather to exercise different areas of his mind for each play. He can encompass such diverse genres as the drawing room comedy (*The Philanthropist*) and the broken marriage drama (*Treats*), as well as reconstructing eighteenth-century France (*Les Liaisons Dangereuses*), Egypt in the 1950s (*White Chameleon*), the struggles of two major French poets (*Total Eclipse*) and the tribulations of a group of expatriate writers in wartime Los Angeles (*Tales from Hollywood*).

Hampton says: "People have often asked, but I see no connection between my plays whatsoever except for the fact that I wrote them. I try to approach each subject in a way appropriate to it. I have no particular style." This versatility could well make him unpopular with the school of criticism that believes all writing to be a form of disguised autobiography. He does not go over the same ground obsessively and this makes it difficult to trace his development or to pick out his dominant themes. He concentrates more on creating formal designs in his plays than on the spontaneous outpouring of emotion and he doesn't draw attention to himself as an artist. This doesn't mean that he doesn't put his personality into his work but he rarely makes his personal feelings the subject matter.

Perhaps the dramatist most like Hampton among his contemporaries is Tom Stoppard. Both are passionate about language and have a concern for form and both tend to use literary sources as a starting point. But Hampton never followed Stoppard into the area of comic surrealism. Nor does he, like Frayn, Ayckbourn or Pinter, draw on any recognisable class or regional milieu. And unlike Hare or Brenton he does not (except in *Savages*) deal directly with political issues.

To understand Hampton fully it is necessary to see him in the context of other European writers who have been his main influence. In an interview with Barry Norman in 1966 his response to the suggestion that he might one day be knighted was that he was more interested in being elected to the Académie Française. He admires the lucid objectivity of the French writers of the eighteenth and nineteenth centuries. The theatre critic Michael Billington called him "a classicist in an age of romantics" and "an ironist with compassion", a description that is also applicable to Flaubert. Hampton and Flaubert both see that life is full of tragic ironies but they refuse to react with cynicism or contemptuous detachment. As Horváth, the main character in *Tales from Hollywood*, observes: "After all, civilisation depends, does it not, on our awareness of the sufferings of others?"

Hampton doesn't fit into any of the trends of postwar British theatre: he has neither formed a movement nor followed one. He has become the sort of playwright that each play needed him to be. But we shouldn't overlook a chameleon simply because it is so good at blending into the background.

CHAPTER ONE

WHEN DID YOU LAST SEE MY MOTHER? (1966)

> I was considered, you know that word, when they don't really like you but think you might not go away, promising.
>
> *Tales from Hollywood*

The plot of *When Did You Last See My Mother?* came to Christopher Hampton in fifteen minutes and it took him six weeks to write. He was eighteen at the time and about to go up to Oxford. The script was left in a drawer for two years until he submitted it to OUDS (Oxford University Dramatic Society) student drama festival. It was rejected initially but was then brought in as a replacement when the organisers realised that one of the two plays they had chosen would be too expensive to produce. When the star of the second play went down with appendicitis *When Did You Last See My Mother?* was left as the only work to be staged in the festival, with Hampton playing the leading role of Ian. In an interview with the *Essex County Standard* in 1974 he said: "I suppose that was one of the reasons why I wrote the play—a huge bravura part. I thought I'd never get a part as good as that again."

Hampton had already started acting as a schoolboy at Lancing, where he and fellow pupil David Hare had appeared in Robert Bolt's *A Man for All Seasons*. He went on to star in Goethe's *Iphigenie auf Tauris* (in German), playing the female title role as his voice had not yet broken.

When he was in the sixth form Hampton went with a school party to see Peter Brook's 1962 production of *King Lear*, which deeply impressed him. He was later to work with three members of the cast: Paul Scofield, Alec McCowen and Irene Worth. After university he lost his early ambition to act and has not done so since.

After OUDS had staged *When Did You Last See My Mother?* Hampton was approached by various literary agents offering to represent him. He asked Elizabeth Sweeting of the Oxford Playhouse for advice and she told him that the only person worth considering was Peggy Ramsay, who had a reputation for encouraging talented young playwrights, among them Joe Orton and Edward Bond. Hampton sent her a copy of his play and she invited him to come and see her at her London office. "I was 20 and terrified of her," he told a journalist on the *Evening Standard* Magazine in 1988. "When I went to see her she plunged into her handbag, brought out a fistful of fivers and said: 'Do you need some money, dear?' I declined it, but I never knew if it was a test or not, if I'd passed or failed."

Ramsay sent the script of *When Did You Last See My Mother?* to the Royal Court Theatre, where it languished in the out-tray until Robert Kidd, at that point an ASM, found it and decided that he would like to direct it. The play was presented on 5 June 1966 in a Sunday night 'production without décor'. The Royal Court did not tell Hampton that this was Kidd's first show as a director, but then Hampton did not admit that he had never seen any of their productions before. The two men were to enjoy a long and fruitful working relationship that ended only with Kidd's death, after a long struggle with pancreatic illness, at the age of 37 in 1980.

When Did You Last See My Mother? owes something to the influence of John Osborne's *Look Back in Anger.* Hampton even names one of his protagonists Jimmy, as if in open tribute to Jimmy Porter, though the characters are not alike. It is Ian in *When Did You Last See My Mother?* who is nearest to Osborne's anti-hero, both of them being driven by self-loathing and spite.

But Hampton's first play differs from *Look Back in Anger* in one important respect: the central relationship is homosexual and unconsummated. Ian is in love with Jimmy (who is bisexual) and tries to dominate him but, unlike many of Hampton's manipulators—Braham in *The Philanthropist* or Dave in *Treats*, for example—he has a conscience. He starts an affair with Jimmy's mother but ends it after tacitly admitting to her that he is in love with her son. When she subsequently dies in a car crash he is racked with guilt because he feels her death may have been suicide. Jimmy also feels responsible as the last time he saw his mother they had had a row. What he doesn't know is that she had driven to Ian's flat afterwards. Ian is unable to explain to him what had really happened and "When did you last see my mother?" is the question that Jimmy never asks.

Even with this first play we can see some of the obsessions that were to recur throughout Hampton's later work: sexual manipulation, cruelty, apathy and loneliness. His characters are often weak, dishonest and unreliable. Early on in *When Did You Last See My Mother?* Ian describes how he went to a lecture in Paris where everyone left during a slide show. He says that he walked out before the end too and imagined the look of desolation on the lecturer's face when she turned round to find she had been deserted. But at the end of the play he admits that he hadn't sneaked out of the lecture at all. He had stayed to the end and saw the lecturer get into her car, quite unconcerned about what had happened. He says that he lied because it was an aesthetically pleasing thing to do.

Hampton's characters often lie about their experiences, either to deceive or simply to appear entertaining. Celia in *The Philanthropist*, Dave in *Treats* and Valmont and Merteuil in *Les Liaisons Dangereuses* all play this game.

When Did You Last See My Mother? has not dated well and the original published text is now out of print. Ian's heavy-handed sarcasm seems rather cumbersome, as when he says, for example: "I'm surprised you deign to rub shoulders with an under-privileged pauper like me. Why don't you go and live with someone rich so that you can co-exist in the style to which you are accustomed? Like that collapsible haggis you were with this evening. You could sleep with her as well. (*He adds, as an afterthought.*) Of course, you could always sleep with me, but Mummy wouldn't like that, would she?"

The sneering irony is overdone and soon becomes wearing, as indeed it does in *Look Back in Anger* too. Hampton would later eschew Osborne's haranguing approach, preferring a more coolly measured and even-handed style. But both writers have an acute awareness of the way language shapes experience. Osborne's characters use words to fight through the apathy that surrounds them, though they often become increasingly bitter in the process. Hampton's characters use language more cunningly, to manipulate others and to hide from themselves the sense of their own futility. But his play is bleaker than Osborne's. *Look Back in Anger* ends on a note of reconciliation but in *When Did You Last See My Mother?* the central relationship is broken for ever. Ian lapses into a state of total apathy, a condition that also afflicts Don in *The Philanthropist* and Able in *Able's Will*.

Hampton has always acknowledged his debt to Osborne as someone who was responsible for "giving one the notion that it was possible to have a serious career as a playwright".

A review of *When Did You Last See My Mother?* in the *Observer* praised the play as "an astonishingly mature probe into the loneliness and self-pity of adolescent homosexuality, cleverly avoiding the old ghastly clichés". It transferred to the Comedy Theatre for a short run before going on to Broadway and this success earned Hampton the epithet of 'promising newcomer'. A student playwright was a novelty that the press seized on and he was subjected to a series of fatuous interviews. He got rather fed up with all the fuss but when he complained about this to a woman from the producer Michael Codron's office assigned to look after him during interviews she pointed out that many writers struggled for years for such recognition. But, as he said to one interviewer during this period, he didn't want to be celebrated as the youngest professional playwright in Britain: one day he wished to be remembered as the oldest.

At this stage of his career Hampton was not committed to writing plays full-time. He told the critic Barry Norman that he would be concentrating on writing fiction in the future. He had already written a novel about public school life and although the manuscript had been rejected he had received a £50 advance for a second book. This work was never completed and the first novel never found a publisher. Many years later Peggy Ramsay rang to tell him that there had been a fire at her office. "There's bad news and there's good news," she said. "The bad news is that a lot of my archive has been destroyed by this fire but the good news is I think your novel went up as well."

In an interview with Robert Butler in the *Independent on Sunday* in 1993 Hampton explained why he had stuck to writing plays. "I do think it's a much more difficult form," he said. He has always found technical challenges stimulating.

As part of his degree in modern languages Hampton spent a year in France and Germany and while he was abroad he wrote the first draft of his next play, *Total Eclipse*, which had been commissioned by Michael Codron. He returned to Oxford for his final year and Robert Kidd and the Royal Court's Artistic Director, William Gaskill, visited him in his rooms. Hampton told them that he had a new play and that Codron had backed out of producing it because of the expense of its large cast and many scene changes. They listened while he read the play through. After a thoughtful pause Gaskill agreed to put it on. (Hampton clearly had better luck than John in *The Philanthropist* who reads out his play for two acquaintances, only to blow his brains out five minutes later.)

In a similarly casual way Hampton became the Royal Court's first resident dramatist with an offer that seems to have been made on the spur of the moment. A few weeks before finals Gaskill asked him what he wanted to do after leaving university. Hampton said that he had no idea, to which Gaskill replied, "Well then, I suppose you'd better come here," shrewdly reckoning that by creating the role of resident dramatist the Arts Council would probably agree to cover the cost of the salary, which they duly did. Hampton took up his post in 1968, having come down from Oxford with a First.

The idea of Hampton as the one of the shapers of the Royal Court's artistic policy is a slightly incongruous one. Ever since their controversial production of *Look Back in Anger* in 1956 the directors had been determinedly steering their theatre away from what they saw as the middle-class outlook of English drama, yet they were proposing to employ a man who had been educated at public school and Oxford as their first writer-in-residence. Even so, they recognised a gifted writer when they saw one and they were always willing to create opportunities for new talent. If Hampton was sometimes taken aback by the viciousness of the artistic opinions expressed by some of his colleagues, he nevertheless served them well, both in artistic and commercial terms. (The trend continued when David Hare—from the same public school and a graduate of Cambridge—took over as his successor in 1971.)

At the end of his first year at the Royal Court Hampton had a firm offer of a teaching post at Bristol University. But Gaskill pressed him to stay on and he did—with a 20 per cent pay cut. As he didn't much relish the idea of working in an atmosphere of jealousy, back-biting and destructive promiscuity he decided he would be better off in the theatre than in academia. (His low opinion of the academic life is evident in *The Philanthropist* and his dramatisation of *The History Man*.)

Hampton describes *When Did You Last See My Mother?* as a dry run for *Total Eclipse*. Both plays focus on a squalid and violent homosexual affair but *Total Eclipse* far outshines the earlier play with its sharp wit and economy of writing. With his second work he was to find his own voice and show just how much he had learned in only two years.

CHAPTER TWO

TOTAL ECLIPSE (1968)

> Out in the desert there was a statue of Memnon that was sometimes heard to sing: but only as the sun went down. I could tell that was how it would be.
>
> *White Chameleon*

Hampton estimates that *Total Eclipse* has now received more productions than any other of his plays. "Enthusiastic strangers have told me how much the play means to them in Utah and in Tokyo," he says in the introduction to the collected edition published in 1991.

In exploring the relationship between two poets, albeit from another culture and from a different age, Hampton was able to ask himself the questions most writers ask at the beginning of their careers: what does it mean to be a writer and what could one reasonably hope to achieve? His subjects in *Total Eclipse*, the symbolist poets Verlaine and Rimbaud, struggle with these questions too and reach entirely different conclusions. Verlaine remains a poet and becomes guardian to Rimbaud's work while Rimbaud gives up writing at the age of nineteen and goes to Africa to work as a building consultant.

For reasons that he felt unable to explain Hampton deliberately reduced the literary debate in the play to a minimum, concentrating on the lives that the poets chose to live rather than their work. Although he was concerned about the effect literature has on the world he didn't want this to be the only theme of the play. The decision about whether one should go on writing or not is a question that only directly concerns writers but the choice of how to live one's life, whether to believe in something or believe in nothing, is one that everyone has to face.

When *Total Eclipse* was broadcast as a radio play in May 1969 Hampton wrote an article in the *Radio Times* outlining why he had found the lives of the two poets so interesting: "Their tragedy was that the solutions they chose . . . though radically different, were equally unsatisfactory. But the decisions they both made, Rimbaud's rejection of a solipsistic universe, and Verlaine's refusal to abandon his delusion, placed them among the first modern representatives of a long established and distinguished company—the heroes of failure."

What fascinated Hampton most was the way Verlaine and Rimbaud acted out in life the debate that was raging in his own head about the usefulness of art.

Total Eclipse is a play that continues to obsess him. So far there have been four published versions of the text, two English and two American, and he admits that there may be yet more to come. As Dorothy Parker said of her poems: "I'm always chasing Rimbauds."

Hampton was determined to stick to the known facts as much as possible and only the last scene, where Verlaine meets Rimbaud's sister, was invented. Much of the factual material came from the biography *Arthur Rimbaud*, published in 1961. When the author, Enid Starkie, met Hampton she asked him whether he had plundered her book; he remembers that she "seemed delighted when I admitted that I had".

Act One of *Total Eclipse* opens with the first meeting of the two writers in Paris in 1871. Verlaine invites Rimbaud to call on him and is astonished to discover that so gifted a poet is only sixteen. The impecunious Rimbaud stays for several weeks at the house of Verlaine's in-laws, where Verlaine is forced to live, and turns out to be a thoroughly obnoxious character. He is deliberately foul-mouthed, steals household ornaments, which he tries to sell back to the family, and has an aversion to all forms of hygiene. He delights in ugly behaviour just as he writes offensive verse, in order to shock and provoke. In spite of the embarrassment he causes, Verlaine allows him to stay and the two men soon become lovers. Rimbaud urges Verlaine to leave his wife, Mathilde. The offer he makes can be summed up by the old Goon Show joke: "Let me take you from the squalor you live in to the squalor I live in." He proposes an alliance where both can take what they want from the other until they get bored. He doesn't believe in love: "I mean it doesn't exist. Self-interest exists. Attachment based on personal gain exists. Complacency exists. But not love. It has to be re-invented."

Rimbaud is the first in a long line of ruthless sexual exploiters in Hampton's work. (Ian in *When Did You Last See My Mother?* is too guilt-ridden to fit into this category.) These characters are often clever, cunning and highly articulate but they always end up being defeated by their own callousness. Even when they appear to escape punishment their victory is a hollow one. Dave in *Treats*, Merteuil in *Les Liaisons Dangereuses* and Howard Kirk in *The History Man* all deny their own deepest needs and find themselves isolated from humanity as a consequence.

Verlaine and Rimbaud are opposites in almost every respect. The older poet is married, bourgeois, a failed radical, and a weak and indecisive man while the other is a strong-willed visionary, filled with self-disgust and with a kind of contemptuous pity for the people around him. It is Rimbaud's confidence in himself, and his recognition of Verlaine's weaknesses, that allows him to manipulate the action. Unlike most of Hampton's other weak heroes, though, Verlaine is capable of violence. He punches Mathilde in the face when she criticises Rimbaud, in spite of the fact that she is eight months pregnant. Oscar Wilde's aphorism about the power of women—"The tyranny of the weak over the strong. It is the only tyranny that lasts"—applies equally well to Verlaine, though he does not realise it.

> VERLAINE: If strength involves brutality, I prefer to be weak.
> RIMBAUD: With you, weakness involves brutality as well.

Verlaine's self-hatred can be judged by the story he tells Rimbaud about his family. His mother kept the remains of her three miscarriages preserved "ominously enough" in alcohol. He envied the foetuses their serenity and one day, in a drunken black depression, he smashed the jars. But his attempt to shock failed completely; his mother put the foetuses back in new jars and never mentioned the matter. "That's when I get violent," he says. "When I see things as they really are." He believes in the usefulness of art but he doesn't see the point in his own life and, when it comes down to it, he wishes he were dead.

Rimbaud's violent streak is more controlled. At the end of Scene Five in the first act he asks Verlaine if he loves him, then tells him to put his hands on the table, palms upward, and stabs them with a knife. The wounds in Verlaine's palms are like stigmata and, in hurting him in this way, Rimbaud seems to be mocking Christ as well. This act is entirely unprovoked although he had warned Verlaine what to expect earlier in the scene.

> VERLAINE: I don't like hurting people.
> RIMBAUD: Then don't. And if you do, do it coolly, and don't insult your victim by feeling sorry for him afterwards.

Rimbaud issues a final ultimatum: Verlaine must choose once and for all between him and Mathilde. As Scene Six brings the first act to a close Verlaine has still not made up his mind. He now has a baby son and Mathilde is eager for them all to emigrate to Canada to make a fresh start. But however much he feels the pull of family and duty he is unable to resist the alternative that Rimbaud represents.

At the beginning of each act Verlaine's voice is heard in the darkness, quoting from 'The Foolish Virgin and the Husband from Hell', a section of Rimbaud's poem 'Saison en Enfer'. This describes the relationship as Rimbaud imagines it from Verlaine's point of view: "His kindness is enchanted. I am its prisoner."

As Act Two begins we see that Verlaine has made his choice. For the next two years Rimbaud and Verlaine move from one set of cheap lodgings to another in London and Brussels. Their relationship is one of persistent quarrels, recriminations and bitter partings.

> VERLAINE: You came back here with me because you wanted to, and because you needed to.
> RIMBAUD: Well now, that's quite original for you, even though you have made your customary mistake.
> VERLAINE: What's that?
> RIMBAUD: Getting carried away by an idea because it's aesthetically plausible rather than actually true.

The mistrust of aesthetics, the suspicion that art can only achieve its effects by distorting and simplifying human nature, re-emerges in Hampton's next play, *The Philanthropist*.

Rimbaud is reluctant to express any clear views on the nature of art but in Act One he does reveal something of his aesthetic values when he chases the poetaster Aicard with a sword. Aicard is reading a poem he has written entitled 'Green Absinthe':

> AICARD: "Oh! Drunkard, most contemptible of men . . . "
> RIMBAUD: Shit.
> AICARD: (*His voice cracking*) "Degraded, fallen, sinful and obtuse . . . "
> RIMBAUD: It is! Authentic shit!
> AICARD: "Degraded, fallen, sinful and obtuse,
> You scruple not to beat your wife and child . . . "
> RIMBAUD: For trying to deprive you of the juice.

This reaction to bad poetry is even more extreme than Alceste's in *Le Misanthrope* and Aicard's doggerel is indeed so dreary one can appreciate Rimbaud's drunken desire to kill him. Yet it is interesting to note that Aicard's poem is 'true' in one respect: he has drawn an accurate picture of Verlaine, whose weakness for green absinthe makes him set fire to his wife and throw his son against a wall. However, as Horváth says in *Tales from Hollywood*, literature has to do with more than being right. Rimbaud begins to doubt that there is any truth worth expressing. He describes his growing disillusionment: "And I found I had tormented myself and poked among my entrails to discover something that people do not believe, or do not wish to believe, or would be foolish to believe. And with the lyricism of self-pity, I turned to the mirror and said Lord, what shall I do, for there is no love in the world and no hope, and I can do nothing about it, God, I can do no more than you have done, and I am in Hell." He claims that he is too intelligent to be happy as if happiness is necessarily an illusion and the truth too terrible to be borne. He also despises people but, like Celia in *The Philanthropist*, his fear is that other people will see him as he sees them.

His swings between hope and despair are a reflection of a myriad personality which drives him to become a different person for every experience in life. It is this aspect that makes him and the other symbolist poets the precursors of the modernist writers who were interested in the fragmentation of self and frequently used different poetic voices to achieve their effects. Instead of trying to give an impression of harmony, modernism often strives for bizarre conjunctions of different styles and moods to create a sensation of conflict and Rimbaud too explores this contradictory nature of the personality: "I knew what it was like to be a model pupil, top of the class, now I wanted to disgust them instead of pleasing them. I knew what it was like to take communion, I wanted to take drugs. I knew what it was like to be chaste, I wanted perversions. It was no longer enough for me to be one person, I decided to be everyone. I decided to be a genius. I decided to be Christ. I decided to originate the future." But later on he announces his new artistic credo: "Harden up. Reject romanticism. Abandon rhetoric. Get it right." He is trying to see the world as it really is instead of being carried away by false sentiment and spurious bursts of emotion.

Rimbaud uses hashish to achieve a "derangement of the senses" instead of developing artistic techniques as a way of getting into his subconscious. Many artists of this period were addicts, which may explain why many of them failed to maintain their initial promise. Hampton doesn't judge his characters but neither does he glamorise the squalor and corruption of addiction. Writers like André Gide and Jean Genet managed to inflate their reputations by glorifying life in the gutter but Hampton is not swayed by any *nostalgie de la boue*. Even at the age of twenty-two he had no youthful wish to shock.

Under the influence of what might be either drink or drugs, Rimbaud tells Verlaine a fairy tale. The story is of a man on a remote southern island who can create wonderful things by using a magic ring. The man gives the ring to a woman but she throws it in the sea. Everything the man has made disappears and he realises that he will be alone for ever. This story could be seen as a metaphor for Rimbaud's loss of the gift of creation. It also shows his desire for "heat and violence of landscape", which he feels he needs to live life more fully.

One of the underlying reasons for the many arguments between the two poets is that while Verlaine declares his true feelings for his lover and praises his poetry as the work of a genius, Rimbaud will not reciprocate. "Pre-marital junk" is the only artistic judgement he can bring himself to make of his partner's work. Verlaine tries to convince himself that they cannot live apart but Rimbaud denies it.

VERLAINE: You apologized. You begged me to come back. You said it was all your fault. You said you loved me. You said it would be all right in the future. You said you were crying as you wrote. I could see your tears on the paper.
RIMBAUD: Well, I didn't have any money, did I? That was before I thought of pawning your clothes.

It is this remark that drives Verlaine to shoot at Rimbaud. The earlier stabbing incident was calmly and cruelly premeditated but the shooting is the ridiculous reaction of a hysteric deranged by love and wounded vanity. Rimbaud's response is to go to the police. Robert Cushman in the *Observer* remarked: "Rimbaud stabs Verlaine in the hand, and enslaves him more effectively. Verlaine shoots Rimbaud in the hand, and Rimbaud shops him." This is not quite fair on Rimbaud, who only acts when he fears that he is going to be shot again, and he does try later to get the charges dropped, but Cushman has spotted that Rimbaud is the more ruthless of the two.

Verlaine is arrested, tried and sent to prison for two years. As a former political activist he had always feared that he might be put away and had dreaded the possibility of losing his liberty but he now finds peace. The disciplined prison regime liberates him from his self-destructive impulses —something which the freedom of the Commune had failed to do— and with a renewed faith in God he is able to regain his emotional strength.

After his release in 1875 he goes to the Black Forest to see Rimbaud again. When they meet he is shocked to learn that Rimbaud has given up writing.

RIMBAUD: The world is too old, there's nothing new, it's all been said. Anything that can be put into words is not worth putting into words.
VERLAINE: The truth is always worth putting into words.
RIMBAUD: The truth is too limited to be interesting.
VERLAINE: What do you mean? — Truth is infinite.

Verlaine says that while he was in prison he came to know God and to ask for forgiveness. He wants to bring Rimbaud back to Christ but he soon finds his new-found faith being undermined.

RIMBAUD: Then, here in the wilderness, I offer you an archetypal choice—the choice between my body and my soul.
VERLAINE: What?
(*Long silence*)
RIMBAUD: Choose.
VERLAINE: Your body.
(*Silence.*)

> RIMBAUD: See, the ninety-eight wounds of Our Saviour burst and bleed.

Rimbaud tells Verlaine that he no longer has any sympathy for him; he plans to stay in Germany for a little while longer before leaving Europe altogether. Verlaine is distraught and begs him not to go. Rimbaud punches him hard a couple of times "carefully and methodically". He then walks away, this time for good.

Despite the failure of their final meeting Verlaine may have left his mark. In the last scene of the play, set in 1892 and seventeen years after his final separation from Rimbaud, Verlaine is a drunken wreck in a seedy cafe in Paris. We get a clear impression that his life has become more and more wretched. Isabelle arrives with the news that her brother has died of a tumour on the knee (a disease that Verlaine explains he also has and which, ironically, will kill him too four years later). Isabelle is consoled by the knowledge that Rimbaud had been confessed by the hospital chaplain and Verlaine is genuinely moved to hear that, after all his bitter, blasphemous attacks on God, he had died in a state of grace. He says to Isabelle: "That must be a great comfort." This is the only line in all of his work that Hampton stipulates is to be delivered without irony.

Isabelle wants to suppress some of Rimbaud's earlier poetry as she considers it to be indecent and profane but Verlaine refuses to do this. Rimbaud, who wanted to be so many different people in life, has been turned into different people after his death, in the carefully arranged memories of those who loved him. Verlaine's Rimbaud is the passionate advocate of a new poetry while Isabelle's is a good Catholic and a loving brother. Neither of these pictures is wrong, but neither is complete in itself.

Verlaine argues that Rimbaud's conversion is all the more striking precisely because he had written such blasphemous work in the past. However, his own sliding in and out of religious faith shows that he is as indecisive about God as he is about people. He and Rimbaud, like Baudelaire before them, seem to belong to that school of French poets who lived in violent revolt against religion but died reconciled to it. But then no earthly remedy could reach the despair that they had known. As Rimbaud says to Verlaine after stabbing his hands: "The only unbearable thing is that nothing is unbearable." In other words, mankind is incapable of feeling deeply enough about anything. Man can, in his infinite indifference, shrug off even the most horrific of experiences. Maybe this is "the death which causes repentance" that Verlaine speaks of in his opening soliloquy. To have a heart that has cut itself off from all affection is a sort of living death; by accepting God Rimbaud is rejecting the idea that nothing matters and is thereby escaping apathy before it claims him entirely. Only when he has lost his faith in human action is he able to regain his belief in an overwhelming metaphysical solution.

Perhaps it comes as no surprise that Rimbaud should return to religion in spite of the abuse he had always heaped upon it. He compares himself to a prophet and contrasts a corrupt humanity with a transcendent reality. Originally this transcendence was to have been provided by his poetry but when he discovers that he can't create heaven on earth he realises that the only way to find a purpose in life is to believe in a transcendence after death.

Rimbaud's overpowering ambition is remarkable but because he cannot change the world with his poetry he renounces writing altogether. Perhaps this is the total eclipse of the title: the obliteration of his talent by some unseen force from within himself. Hampton reinforces the imagery with his references to the sunset. Verlaine meets both Rimbaud and Mathilde at sunset, just before the light is blotted out. Sunset is associated with old age and death and the fading of beauty and talent (as in *Sunset Boulevard*) so impermanence is suggested even with these initial meetings. But for just a few brief moments, as the sun goes down, its suffused light casts a warm glow on everything it touches. Perhaps too the eclipse refers to the total darkness that engulfs Verlaine at the end of the play when he is left with nothing more than a fantasy Rimbaud to sustain him.

After Isabelle has left, Verlaine recalls his first meeting with Rimbaud: "It was a long time ago. But I remember the first time I saw him. That evening in the Mautés' main room. When we walked in, he was standing with his back to us, looking out of the window. He turned round and spoke, and then I saw him, and I was amazed how beautiful he was. He was sixteen."

But we cannot trust his memory. He was alone when he first saw Rimbaud but he had been accompanied by a friend when he had met Mathilde a couple of years earlier and found her at the window silhouetted by the sunset in the same room in her father's house. Like Rimbaud she was just sixteen years old. In his mind his wife and his lover have become fused into the one love of his life, his "great and radiant sin". Now he is totally alone. Rimbaud is dead and Mathilde has long ago obtained a divorce and will not let him see their son. He dreams that Rimbaud comes in and, instead of stabbing his hands, he kisses them. As the play ends Verlaine is a solitary figure in a gradually diminishing pool of light. The sunset from the beginning of the play has vanished and there is only the darkness which finally absorbs him.

The *Sunday Times* criticised the play's ending as one of "excruciating sentimentality" but in an article in the Autumn issue of *Theatre Quarterly* in 1973 Hampton argues that he intended to show how Verlaine had turned a painful truth into a beautiful illusion: " . . . this scene was *meant* to show the false and sentimental way in which Verlaine remembered the relationship". It seems that in truth Rimbaud had more or less forgotten him:

> VERLAINE: Did he . . . I don't suppose he ever mentioned me.
> ISABELLE: No.
> VERLAINE: It was a long time ago.

When the critic Nicholas de Jongh interviewed him in 1970 Hampton said that one of the themes of *Total Eclipse* is the death of romanticism: "I admired the fact that Rimbaud really wanted to do something different and revolutionary and idealistic. He couldn't. And I thought I could change the world by wonderful writing. There seemed no reason why I couldn't do it but I found there is a big gap between what you say and what you want to say."

Historically there is no clear explanation of why Rimbaud gave up writing at such a young age, and the play doesn't attempt to simplify the complexities of his genius. When he looks straight at the world he finds nothing there to inspire him so he loses confidence, not only in his own talent but in the validity of art altogether. Verlaine clings to art as something that can transcend ordinary life and make it radiant while Rimbaud is the more modern figure in his contempt for romanticism and his suspicion that art, like everything else, is futile. Indeed, his decision to work in Africa chimes in with the emerging school of thought that art itself should forget about eternal truths and stick to solving social problems. Rimbaud the idealist and Verlaine the romantic both fail to make life live up to their ideals.

Total Eclipse opened at the Royal Court on 11 September 1968 to a lukewarm reception. Critics complained that the play was slow and heavy-going. Some also felt that the dialogue was anachronistic and the use of contemporary slang inappropriate. Derek Malcolm and Milton Shulman both picked out the phrase "get a grip of your knickers" as being particularly objectionable and Hampton cut this from the 1981 version of the text.

Robert Kidd once again directed and cast John Grillo as Verlaine and Victor Henry as Rimbaud. Henry, who had played Ian in *When Did You Last See My Mother?*, was an actor whose reputation for unruly behaviour put Rimbaud in the shade. He had a habit of asking people to punch him, and provoking them until they did so. He spent several years in a hospital bed, having been knocked down by a hit-and-run driver who was never caught. Although his brain was still functioning he was never able to speak again, despite the specialist help that Hampton and Kidd paid for, and he died in 1985. Simon Callow, who played Verlaine in the 1981 revival, wrote Henry's obituary for the *Evening Standard*, and Hampton dedicated the 1991 edition of the text of *Total Eclipse* to him and Robert Kidd.

During the play's 1968 run the Lord Chamberlain's office lost its power to censor plays. Up to this time the complete text of all dramatic works had to be submitted in order to gain a licence to perform. Failure to comply with any changes that were demanded could lead to fines or imprisonment. Kidd and Hampton were quick to restore some of the cuts that they had been forced to make. They had originally been told that the language had to be toned down. Verlaine was not allowed to say, for example, "I wouldn't like to mislay my balls" or Rimbaud to explain " . . . how I took upon me the sins of the world and became Christ without the benefit of a virgin birth". When Rimbaud tells Aicard that giants had once rid France of untalented poets by "pissing on them from a great height" the phrase was queried and then allowed to stand with the anxious proviso: "No action to accompany this line". Hampton recalls: "For years people had been running at closed doors, using their heads as battering rams; now the doors were open and all my generation had to do was saunter through them."

Total Eclipse was broadcast on Radio 3 on 1 May 1969 with Derek Godfrey as Rimbaud, Kenneth Cranham as Verlaine, Rosalind Shanks as Mathilde and Gwen Watford as Isabelle, and was produced by Ronald Mason. It was seen on BBC television on 10 April 1973, directed by Peter Gregeen, with Ian Hogg as Verlaine, Joseph Blatchley as Rimbaud, Sarah Craze as Mathilde and Avril Elgar as Isabelle.

The ever astute Peggy Ramsay helped the play on its way to America, as Hampton explained in an interview in the *Sunday Correspondent* in 1990: "I was in her office when a theatre in Washington DC called to enquire about another of her client's plays. 'Oh,' she said, 'you don't want to do *that* play, dear. He's never got it right. Never solved the ending. I'm here with Christopher Hampton. Why don't you talk with him and do his play?' And that's how the first American production of *Total Eclipse* came about."

The revival at the Lyric, Hammersmith in 1981, directed by David Hare, was received with more enthusiasm than the first production had been. Hampton did not change the structure of the play in any way but he considerably tightened up some of the scenes. A couple of the minor characters, such as Cabaner, the musician who composes a cantata to a meat pie, were dropped, and some of the others, like the poet Carjat, appear less often. The moment where Carjat finds that Rimbaud has used one of his poems as toilet paper did not survive. Hampton also left out most of the references to Verlaine's political activity, though he did keep the story Verlaine tells about setting out drunk one evening to assassinate Napoléon III but failing to do so. The effect of this anecdote is to cast doubt on Verlaine's credibility as a true revolutionary.

The 1981 version of *Total Eclipse* was broadcast on Radio 3 on 23 May 1993, produced by Alison Hindell and starring David Haigh as Verlaine, Richard Lynch as Rimbaud and Maggie O'Neill as Mathilde.

Hampton is at his best when he is being unsparing and in *Total Eclipse* he makes no concessions to easy sympathy. The temptation to make Rimbaud more picturesquely decadent, as opposed to portraying him as hard and callous, or to show less of Verlaine's sentimental brutality, has been resisted. Instead we see two men whose despair renders them incapable of coming to terms with the world as it is. Rimbaud, who had believed that he could forge a new language, sees that men are rotten with selfishness and either cannot or will not face up to the futility of their lives. His search for beauty leads him only to recoil at men's cruelty and apathy, not least at the savage cowardice of Verlaine.

Today Rimbaud is a cult figure. The European Film Federation estimates that they get more scripts about him than on any other subject. The idea of the destructive young genius is an appealing one so a myth has emerged that the mark of the true artist is a tendency towards violence and excess. But in *Total Eclipse* the scenes where Rimbaud behaves outrageously are treated comically. Hampton's hero is simply someone who looks directly at life, unable to hide behind trivialities. With both poets we are presented with two complex, credible and entirely individual artists in search of ultimate meanings.

Often the most interesting arguments one can have are with oneself, not necessarily to convince but to explore. Hampton said that to write about two such opposed characters had triggered a "fruitful internal debate". When he began writing *Total Eclipse* he was in sympathy with Rimbaud but by the time he had finished it he had come to respect Verlaine. The fact that he found it worthwhile to write the play at all is, in a sense, the only argument he puts up against Rimbaud's view of the futility of art. We can be glad, though, that up to now he has sided with Verlaine.

CHAPTER THREE

THE PHILANTHROPIST (1970)

There are times when I feel like a character in a farce by Molière.

Carrington

After a relatively easy time with his first two plays, Hampton ran into difficulties with his third, The Philanthropist. He completed it in August 1969 but the Royal Court then got a bad case of what he referred to as "commissioner's droop". William Gaskill liked the piece and wanted to direct it, but only if he could get Alan Bates for the lead. Lindsay Anderson thought the work was frivolous. Robert Kidd, Hampton's regular director, had by now been fired for, as he claimed, "having received better reviews than he deserved". The manuscript was booted around from one director to another for several months until Kidd, who had been working for Granada Television, was allowed to return.

The Philanthropist finally reached the stage on 3 August 1970, with Alec McCowen in the main role of Philip, a lecturer in philology at Oxford, and a supporting cast including Jane Asher, Penelope Wilton and Dinsdale Landen. In contrast to the large cast of *Total Eclipse*, with its many locations, T*he Philanthropist* has only seven characters and just one set: Philip's rooms at Oxford.

The opening night was very hot and one patron passed out early on in the second act and so Hampton found it appropriate that it was with the profits from this play that air-conditioning was finally installed in the auditorium. On 7 September the production transferred to the Mayfair Theatre, where it ran for three years, becoming the Royal Court's most successful straight play. It won both the Plays and Players/London Theatre Critics Best Play Award and the 1971 Evening Standard Drama Award for Best Comedy. McCowen won the 1970 Variety Club Best Actor Award for his performance.

The accolades were well-deserved for *The Philanthropist* is a masterpiece of sophisticated comedy: what appears at first to be a series of casual witty conversations is in fact a model of thematic unity where nearly every line contributes to the overall effect. The play is subtitled 'A Bourgeois Comedy' —quite a provocative thing to offer to an audience in an era when popular radicalism was at its zenith. The Royal Court was not usually associated with carefully constructed plays where well-educated people dissect one another over pre-dinner drinks.

A common pattern for a bourgeois comedy—Coward's *Private Lives*, for example, or Lonsdale's *On Approval*—is for two mismatched couples to change partners during the course of the action. In *The Philanthropist* Hampton presents one established couple, Philip and Celia, who are engaged to be married, and four single people, Braham, Araminta, Don and Liz. Araminta makes an obvious play for Braham but he snubs her and turns his attention to Celia, perhaps in order to get back at Philip whom he feels has insulted him. As Braham isn't available Araminta sets about pursuing Philip. However, the plot of *The Philanthropist* does not resolve itself like most comedies where, after a series of accidents or misunderstandings, all or most of the characters finish up with the right partners. Philip, Celia, Braham and Araminta are all left without a stable relationship and only Don and Liz would seem to have any kind of future together.

The Philanthropist is a sort of companion piece to *Le Misanthrope*, a fact which Hampton acknowledges by taking as his epigraph a line from Molière's masterpiece: "C'est que jamais, morbleu! les hommes n'ont raison" ["But, good heavens! mankind is never right."] When Braham says that he once saw a play about a man who hated humanity we can assume he is referring to *Le Misanthrope*. He shows that he is a philistine at heart when he dismisses the work of the Comédie Française as "terrible camp old rubbish".

One doesn't have to know Molière's play to appreciate *The Philanthropist* but Hampton's main characters all have their counterparts in *Le Misanthrope*. Celia, Philip's fiancée, is like Célimène, the society flirt. The scene where Celia amuses the other dinner guests by inventing tales about her colleagues' attempts to seduce her recalls the bitchy comments Célimène makes about her suitors to a couple of society fops. Celia has a verbal spat with Araminta, her main female rival, just as Célimène has a duel of words with Arsinoë, Molière's religious hypocrite.

The characters in *Le Misanthrope* who represent sane virtue, Philinte and Eliante, are transformed into Don and Liz. Don, although he functions as a moral mouthpiece when he puts down the arrogant and untalented author Braham, is, by his own admission, overwhelmed by apathy. And Liz demurely listens while Braham pontificates. Liz never speaks throughout her one scene, indicating, as Hersh Zeifman points out in the *International Dictionary of Theatre Plays*, that virtue is silent while vice is allowed to run riot. Only at the end of the play, when Philip mentions to Don that he hopes to strike up a relationship with Liz, is it revealed that she has seduced Don in a night of passion that had lasted into most of the next day as well. Hampton once said, doubtless tongue-in-cheek, that his seven characters were based on the seven deadly sins. This remark is helpful up to a point; Araminta is obviously Lust, and Don is Sloth. But most of the other characters seem to have at least three or four of the major vices.

In *The Philanthropist* Hampton borrows Molière's method of defining the leading character's personality by one dominant trait. In most of Molière's plays that trait is a vice (as in *Le Malade imaginaire* or *L'Avare*) but Hampton gives his protagonist Philip a virtue: "compulsive amiability". Molière's Alceste has "no taste for idle chatter" and is sick of society's hypocrisy while Philip is unable to feel anything akin to moral rage or indignation. As he says: "My trouble is, I'm a man of no convictions. At least, I think I am." Alceste loses Célimène because she cannot face his uncompromising honesty, whereas Philip loses Celia because she cannot bear his almost overpowering unassertiveness. The untalented Oronte is offended by Alceste's honest criticism, but the two writers in *The Philanthropist*, Braham and John, are offended by Philip's unwillingness to criticise anything, which they take to be patronising or subtly insulting. Alceste finally vows to go into the desert rather than put up with society, while Philip finds himself lost in an interior wilderness of his own. Yet in their own way both Alceste and Philip are admirable; Alceste may be unyielding in his strictness but he provides a healthy antidote to the shallowness around him and Philip's guilelessness is endearing compared to the duplicity of his friends.

Hampton realised that, in the atmosphere of the late 1960s, a figure like Alceste and his "abrasive candour" would be welcomed at the university. After all, the main hobby of the characters in *The Philanthropist* is being critical of other people. But in the mistrustful academic environment everyone takes offence at Philip's desire to be inoffensive. Celia thinks he is weak, the predatory Araminta is infuriated by his tactlessness and Braham thinks that he is being deliberately rude. But Philip is sincere. Unlike most of Molière's characters, he is fully aware of what his defining trait is: "I mean, I mean that the basic feature of my character is an anxiety to please people and to do what they want, which leads to, that is, which amounts to a passion, and which is, in fact, so advanced that I can only describe it as . . . terror." He illustrates this by telling a story of what happened to him while he was a teacher in Hong Kong. He used to give money to a beggar who would then insist on cleaning his car. One day, finding that he hadn't anything smaller than a ten-dollar note, he tried to drive off before the beggar could reach him. The beggar jumped away from the car and fell awkwardly, and Philip was too embarrassed to stop. The beggar never went near him again. Philip sees the incident as one of the most humiliating things that ever happened to him.

That someone could even conceive the idea that he was unkind is too much for him. Philip's problem is that because he is a man who wants to be liked by everyone he is in danger of eradicating his own personality so as to leave nothing that people can object to. And this is what so infuriates Celia, who describes him as "a pudding, wobbling gently". Yet, although he is unable to feel any strong antipathy to anyone, Philip is not fundamentally bland. His philanthropy may be based on a kind of terror but it is none the less a genuine recognition of our common mortality. "For instance, it's easier to like people if it occurs to you that they're going to die," he says. "It's difficult not to like a man if you can envisage his flesh falling from his bones."

The Philanthropist is full of such images of death, the most striking of which occurs in the opening scene. John, an unsuccessful playwright, is reading aloud his play to Philip and Don. As the scene begins John is nearing the end of his read-through and has reached the moment where one of his characters is explaining why he is about to kill himself. The speech is addressed to two people and ends with the words "I think both of you are responsible for this." The scene ends with him putting a gun into his mouth and pulling the trigger just as his fictional character does. Whether this gesture is a deliberate act of suicide or a momentary lapse into carelessness is left ambiguous. But John seems to be saying that he holds Don and Philip responsible for his state of mind. But, apart from upsetting Philip, his death appears to achieve nothing. The only direct consequence is that Philip has to throw out his blood-spattered Picasso print. Even the picture John destroys is only a reproduction.

The shock of John's death reverberates throughout the play all the more because it is hardly referred to again, but it serves as an unspoken reminder to the other characters, if only they would pay attention, of the spectre of their own death. In the next scene Don treats the incident as an accident, thus denying it any meaning. He can't resist joking about it just as he can't resist joking about the fact that it is November the 5th and a machine-gun wielding colonel in drag has assassinated the Prime Minister and nine members of the Cabinet.

The torpor that hangs over them all and permeates the University as an institution is symptomatic of the political sloth of the nation as a whole. Individuals are apathetic, institutions are sluggishly run and the only politically active person is a homicidal lunatic. Celia recognises the underlying stagnation that surrounds her:

> PHILIP: You're not going to tell me Professor Burrows made a pass at you?
> CELIA: Ah, no, well I've made an interesting discovery about Professor Burrows. Professor Burrows is actually dead.

Celia bitchily suggests that Professor Burrows is mechanically wound up by his wife before he gives his lectures.

It is not only academia that is in this necrotic state: literature and death are intertwined throughout the play. In Act Two we hear that a famous author has been murdered by a terrorist group called FATAL (Fellowship of Allied Terrorists Against Literature—a joke that unnervingly prefigures the Salman Rushdie affair). The fashionable novelist Braham, however, is only dead from the neck up. His opinion of writing as "a kind of subsidized masturbation" reveals the extent of his moral decay. His life and his art are both solipsistic acts of self-gratification and are of no relevance to anyone else. (He is so irrelevant that, as he is piqued to discover, FATAL don't bother to put him on their death list.) We can see how far standards have declined since Molière's time: Braham is successful and a darling of society, whereas Oronte's bad poetry is privately derided by everyone. But Braham regards art as useless and has come to despise his former political radicalism as well. He knows that what he writes will have no bearing whatsoever on what the world thinks so he is content to exploit his talent as a marketable product. As Carlos, the revolutionary in *Savages* says, "Blessed are the complacent: for they shall never mourn."

With Braham Hampton accurately identified the Thatcherite mentality before it became fashionable. Braham announces that his next novel will be about a social worker who "gives up the comforts of moral superiority for the harsh realities of high finance". One needn't take him seriously of course, and Don delivers a crushing put-down of him when he observes: "He's one of those writers who've been forced to abandon the left wing for tax reasons." But Don has encountered a far more definite rejection of art. He tells everyone the story of James Boot (known to his more jovial colleagues as Jack), one of his literature students, who locked himself in his room to try and solve all the political problems of the world. Don is quite impressed with Boot's opinions on art: "Wordsworth, he said, with some passion, had nothing to do with anything, and his work, like all art, was a lot of self-indulgent shit which had no relevance to our problems and was no help at all to man or beast. I must say, the way he put it, it sounded quite convincing."

Boot rejects art but cannot think of a political act that achieves anything either. After burning his books and setting fire to the college he is committed to an institution where he is reduced to a state of catalepsy.

Don is not much more active than Boot. He tells Philip that he ambles through life and declares himself to be "more than half in love with easeful sloth". (The original line of Keats's poem reads, of course, "half in love with easeful death".) Once more the connection between spiritual and physical death is subtly underlined. Don shuts himself up in his rooms to listen to classical music while keeping his mind a total blank. The music is no longer an artistic experience for him but a smokescreen behind which he hides his indifference to the world.

One of the reasons we can sympathise more with Philip than with Don is that he still tries, though usually unsuccessfully, to communicate with other people. He sees that words can create unforeseen difficulties. He tells Celia about the first girl he was ever in love with. Just as they were about to go to bed for the first time he told her that he was a virgin. The girl said that "she wasn't going to be a guinea-pig for anyone". "So there it was," says Philip, "a whole relationship doomed by a random word-association." His character, with its mixture of sympathy and incomprehension, also shows in his attitude to literature. He is the only person in the play who genuinely seems to read for pleasure but his honesty is undermined by his lack of aesthetic standards, as he readily admits: "I've enjoyed every book I've ever read for one reason or another. That's why I can't teach literature. I have no critical faculties. I think there's always something good to be found in the product of another man's mind. Even if the man is, by all objective standards, a complete fool. So you see I'd like a play however terrible it was."

His love of words and his penchant for word-games, however, show that he is more than just a cold-hearted pedant. At the end of the play he thinks of a new anagram: 'Imagine the theatre as real,' which can be re-arranged to read 'I hate thee, sterile anagram'. And the statement is symbolic. Although he is no longer satisfied by such idle pleasures he has nothing to replace them.

As is bound to happen in a society based on deception, the people around him don't believe that Philip is as innocent and straightforward as he seems. As a result he tends to be misunderstood, as when he tries discuss Braham's use of language with him.

> PHILIP: That's something else. Your use of paradox. You've got it down to a fine art, it's a reflex action. You've digested that it's an extremely simple and extremely effective technique.
> BRAHAM: You are being insulting!

It doesn't occur to Philip that Braham might feel threatened by this exposure of his literary tricks. People keep seeing devious motives in his simple desire to please. He can think of no polite way to refuse Araminta when she makes a pass at him but their night together is a complete failure. Hampton makes a joke at their expense when he specifies that music from Mozart's *Abduction from the Seraglio* should be used at the end of Act One as Araminta is coaxing a reluctant Philip into the bedroom and that Act Two should open with

Purcell's ode 'Welcome, welcome, glorious morn', at the start of what turns out to be the worst day of Philip's life.

The only way Philip can avoid repeating his experience with Araminta is to tell her the truth—that he doesn't find her attractive—though he is upset when she takes offence at this. Celia, understandably enough, doesn't believe him when he explains all this to her. She mistakenly thinks he is being cunning. She also thinks that he lacks firmness (which, in a different context, was Araminta's complaint).

Philip and Araminta represent two sides of love and their names reflect this. Philip's name is based on 'philos', the Greek word for love of mankind. He is also, of course, a philologist, which means a lover of words. His opening word at the beginning of Scene Five is simply "Love", which contrasts with the single word Araminta utters in the preceding scene: "Passion". Her name is French, dating from Molière's era, and sounds like 'amorous'. She has a reputation for being promiscuous but she admits she has never been in love. Philip's trouble is that he loves mankind but finds it difficult to communicate with individuals. But as Auden says in his poem '1st September, 1939', people don't want to be loved collectively but to be loved alone.

The intensity of Philip's loneliness shows that he is certainly capable of feelings, but he can't connect successfully with other people. Araminta will sleep with anyone and Philip will talk about anything. They persist because they fear isolation. When Celia breaks with Philip he asks her not to leave but to stay and talk. She asks what they could talk about and burst into tears when he replies "Anything". It upsets her to feel that whatever she said it wouldn't matter to him because all he wants is company.

Araminta remembers that she was once locked in a room for three weeks by a madman who burnt most of her clothes. Philip later says that all the rooms that he can recall being in were empty. The only person happy when alone in a room is Don for whom idleness is a way of life. (Jack Boot spends weeks alone in his room at college and now cannot move in his room in his asylum.) All these experiences alone in rooms indicate the loneliness that all these characters fear may be waiting for them. This isolation is underlined by their laughter. One of the first stage directions indicates that Philip "laughs merrily and alone". Don laughs alone over John's death, Celia laughs when she tells Philip he has no sense of humour and Braham laughs at the memory of how he upset a journalist with his opinions on art. There is little shared laughter. Celia's invented catalogue of failed seducers presumably meets with a good reception, and Braham's calculated outrageousness causes some amusement, but often where Don sees comedy Philip sees tragedy, where Celia sees humour Philip sees malice, and where Philip sees wit John sees condescension. They can rarely make their senses of humour coincide.

According to Don people cannot face the futility of their lives and so they cope by deluding themselves in one way or another. He explains that there are two sorts of people in the world: those who live by what they know to be a lie and those who live by what they falsely believe to be the truth. His philosophy echoes that of Dr Relling in *The Wild Duck* (which Hampton was to translate in 1979), who believed that everyone must find a 'life lie' to maintain themselves. Don lives by a lie that he is "a teacher of English" when all he does is to repeat the same lectures to each new intake of students. He prides himself on coming to terms with his own uselessness.

Another of Don's ideas disturbs Philip even more:

> DON: I have this theory which I think is rather attractive. I think we're only capable of loving people who are fundamentally incompatible with us.
> PHILIP: That's horrible.
> DON: But attractive.

And yet the idea seems to have some validity in Philip and Celia's case. Celia loves Philip's kindness but cannot bear his passivity. Philip loves Celia's vivacity but can't understand why she is so malicious. Don's theory seems to be proved although he doesn't seem to trust it himself. "But, I mean, trying to make elegant patterns out of people's hopelessness doesn't really work," he says. "It's only a frivolous game." This could express Hampton's distrust of aesthetics. It is only Philip, with his fundamental decency, who manages to avoid letting these games run his life. According to Don, the couple's fundamental incompatibility is that Celia lives by a conscious lie while Philip thinks that he knows the truth. Celia maintains her existence by hoping that not everyone is like her, i.e. malicious, while Philip believes that everyone is like him, i.e. incapable of malice. It seems that what Don is saying is that Celia needs to believe she is unique in her malice; she can't bear to think that her friends say such unpleasant things about her as she says about them. As he observes, she must live by the lie "because her vanity demands it". Celia had said earlier that "lies are usually that much more interesting than the truth".

Philip is the only one who subscribes to the concept of objective truth (Celia accuses him of being literal-minded) whereas most of the others are more interested in creating amusing stories. Don enjoys playing around with ideas to see what sort of shapes they make but Philip sees how awful life would be if those theories were valid.

With the exception of Philip, Hampton's characters in this play constantly judge events by aesthetic standards. "I suppose in the Tory Party that's the kind of thing that passes for aesthetics," says Don of the November the 5th assassination of the Cabinet. And when Celia asks Philip to explain what Araminta was doing in his room she adds, "Try to make it as entertaining as possible." One can quite literally judge Celia's tales of her unsuccessful seducers by literary standards, as they are indeed fiction. Philip is genuinely puzzled when something he says is judged by how it sounds rather than by what it means:

> PHILIP: I haven't even got the courage of my lack of convictions.
> DON: Oh, I wish I'd said that.
> PHILIP: Why?
> DON: I don't know, it sounds good.
> PHILIP: That's not really why I said it, believe it or not.

Here we can see Hampton resuming his internal debate on the nature of art and its effect on the world. In *The Philanthropist* both the writers reject their calling, John by death and Braham by selling out. But perhaps the play is saying not that art is useless but that it must share Philip's concern for truth if it is to become more than an idle game. Art must not distort truth by imposing a simplifying pattern on life. When Hampton appeared on *Desert Island Discs* in 1996 he said, speaking of his film *Carrington*, that over-simplification was the cause of many of the world's problems.

He continues his meditation on the nature of art in *The Philanthropist* by exploring the distinction between classicism and romanticism. Celia mocks the romanticism of one of her tutors who, she pretends, tried to seduce her. She claims that she spilt sherry in his lap. "I said I thought he'd better go and change his trousers before the next tutorial or his pupils would think he'd been at the Swinburne again." She also taunts Philip when he starts talking about death: "Let us eschew lyricism. Don't you think? I think lyricism should at all costs be eschewed." She treats Philip as if he had "been at the Swinburne" in the sense of indulging a wild and fanciful melancholy.

Araminta, explaining her nymphomania to Philip, says that she is a "classic case" and that because her uncle raped her when she was twelve this rather took "the romance out of things". Don tells us of Braham's divorce: "Their whole relationship was soured by her failure even to attempt suicide, which he apparently regarded as unforgivable. He likes to think of himself as a Romantic." But in this play neither classicists nor romantics have the monopoly on truth. As Molière says, mankind is never right.

Philip can master words but he cannot master people. In the programme notes to *The Philanthropist* Hampton included the passage from Lewis Carroll's *Through the Looking Glass* where Humpty-Dumpty explains to Alice that when he uses a word it means what he wants it to mean. But Philip is more like the White Knight than Humpty-Dumpty. When he recites a bit of nonsense verse it is from the song that the White Knight sings to Alice shortly before they part:

> But I was thinking of a plan
> To dye one's whiskers green
> And always use so large a fan
> That they could not be seen.

By this time Philip has lost Celia (the name is an anagram of Alice) and he is describing himself as a man who is hiding from other people.

The play's closing moments show the extent of Philip's desperation. As is the case in many of his plays, Hampton makes the end mirror the beginning. When Philip calls Don on the phone it would be appropriate for him to quote from the final speech of John's play that we heard in Scene One, to say that he held Don and Liz responsible for the state he was in and to tell them that he was going to do something "to remind you that if you won, I lost, and that nobody can win without somebody losing". Instead he tells Don that he is "about to do something terrible". When he puts the phone down he picks up what appears to be a gun, pauses for a moment and lights a cigarette with it. This action echoes John's probable suicide in Scene One but turns it round so that our expectations are confounded. But if we remember that in Scene Two Philip had told Braham that he had given up smoking because of his fear of lung cancer, we could interpret his resumption of smoking as a form of notional suicide. Death is certainly the theme of the music that Hampton chooses as Philip makes his final exit, which is the aria 'Ich freue mich auf meinen Tod' ['I look forward to my death'] from Bach's *Cantata No 82*, 'Ich habe genug' ['I have enough'].

But there is an element of hope. The stage directions specify that Philip goes out "leaving the door open". After all the isolating experiences the characters have had in lonely rooms Philip has made a gesture that means that for him the room will no longer be a place where he hides from the world. When the door opens at the end of Sartre's play *Huis clos* none of the characters feels able to leave the room; they are doomed to spend eternity together. Unlike many of Hampton's other characters (Ian in *When Did You Last See My Mother?*, Able in *Able's Will*) Philip is not totally defeated. He goes out to meet Don and Liz, determined not to renounce human contact or to give in to his own uselessness.

The critical reception to the play was enthusiastic although some reviewers misunderstood some aspects of it. (One thought that Philip had been named after Philip Larkin.) But nearly everyone agreed on its wit and intelligence.

Harold Hobson in the *Sunday Times* declared that it was "intellectually stimulating, touchingly sympathetic and gloriously, gloriously funny". It ran for three years at the Mayfair Theatre in London and when Alec McCowen and Jane Asher went with it to Broadway their roles were taken over by George Cole and Frances Jeater, who both also starred in the radio adaptation that was broadcast in 1976. A televised version had been screened the year before with Ronald Pickup and Helen Mirren. There was a revival in 1985 at the Chichester Festival Theatre (with some textual cuts) and this revised version was later seen at Wyndham's Theatre in 1991 with Edward Fox and Sarah Berger.

The university was to become a popular setting for plays and novels in the 1970s. Tom Stoppard's *Jumpers*, Simon Gray's *Butley*, Malcolm Bradbury's *The History Man* (which Hampton was to adapt for television in 1980), Michael Frayn's *Donkey's Years*, David Lodge's *Changing Places* and Tom Sharpe's *Porterhouse Blue* are all examples of this trend. *The Philanthropist* does not deal with departmental politics like *The History Man* or with complex philosophical problems like *Jumpers* (though Stoppard once cited "I'm a man of no convictions, at least I think I am" as his favourite line in modern English drama). Instead Hampton's academics stand in for the leisured moneyed aristocrats that Molière wrote about.

The Philanthropist was Hampton's last play as the Royal Court's Resident Dramatist (a position that was then taken over by his friend and assistant David Hare) although his next two plays were also produced there. He later said: "The play was disgracefully successful, so much so that I've always felt I left under something of a cloud." It is quite possibly his best work and only the 1981 version of *Total Eclipse* comes close to rivalling it. Both are a testament to man's loneliness and the near impossibility of love but they deal with this theme in a way that is unsparing but not despairing. Rimbaud can find God and Philip can leave his room. The witty dialogue and almost faultless construction of *The Philanthropist* serves Hampton's purpose—to show a man whose dilemma is that in order to be liked, as he wants to be, he must be less likeable. If anyone needs proof that comedy is more than "a frivolous game" then they need only see this play.

CHAPTER FOUR

SAVAGES (1973)

> Naturally, it distresses me that people are wasting their energies killing each other all over the world, and of course I'm sorry thousands of Indians starve to death every year, but I mean that's their problem, isn't it?
>
> *The Philanthropist*

Savages is Hampton's only original play to be inspired by a topical event. The author Norman Lewis published an article entitled 'Genocide in Brazil' in the *Sunday Times* in 1969, describing the systematic slaughter of Brazilian Indians over four centuries. When Hampton was profiled on ITV's *South Bank Show* in 1989 he explained that he went to Brazil to research his play and found that the whole country was in a state of crisis and the Indians were not the only ones being exploited. This discovery is also made by West, Hampton's central character in *Savages*, his fourth play for the Royal Court Theatre.

In his article Lewis wrote about the bombing of the Cintas Largas tribe in 1963, which was carried out on the orders of a manager employed by Arruda & Junqueira, a rubber extraction company. The people were massacred during the feast of the 'Quarup', a ceremony where the creation myths of the tribe are re-enacted. The ill-fated 'Quarup' makes up one strand of the drama.

The play opens with a bare stage that is lit only by burning torches. West enters and recites a poem he has written based on an Indian myth about the creation of fire. As he is speaking the Indians enter from the wings and the auditorium and take the torches away one by one. At intervals during the performance they reappear and are seen performing marriages, dancing and wrestling, and decorating the posts that symbolise their ancestors, At the end of the play, as the ceremony of the 'Quarup' reaches its climax, the village is bombed from the air. The two pilots of the plane then land in the village in order to burn the bodies.

There was a great deal of discussion at the Royal Court about the role of the Indians in the play. The director, Robert Kidd, originally wanted to cut them out altogether; Hampton argued against this but agreed that without specialist knowledge it would be difficult to show the tribal ceremonies realistically. However, they were able to consult an anthropologist who had lived among the Amazonian Indians and he helped them to stage some authentic rituals. In his introduction to the published text Hampton thanked him for his assistance but declined to name him in case this caused him difficulty with the Brazilian government.

Lindsay Anderson, one of the Royal Court's Associate Directors, argued that two scenes where a member of a death squad describes his part in a massacre were superfluous. Hampton didn't object when the scenes were conflated but he was upset when the section was cut altogether after the play later transferred to the Comedy Theatre.

Hampton didn't write any dialogue for the Indians, except for one, who has a small speaking role, but conveys their lives through the choreographed ritual scenes. It could be argued that this decision was a mistake as it deprives them of a voice and makes them unduly passive.

The two central characters in *Savages* are Alan West, an urbane English diplomat with liberal views, and Carlos Esquerdo, a young Brazilian revolutionary. West is kidnapped and held captive by Carlos and his associates, who are demanding that twenty-five political prisoners be freed in return for his release. These two men carry the main political arguments in the play. Hampton also makes them both poets, which allows him to explore the relationship between art and politics.

A series of flashback scenes shows how West becomes increasingly aware of the Indians' plight. He starts by investigating a land deal in the Mato Grosso and discovers how the people are being driven out of their own territory. It is a narrative of almost unbelievable evil as whole tribes are wiped out by shooting and bombing or the distribution of blankets infected with smallpox and sugar laced with arsenic. One of the epigraphs that Hampton gives for the play is taken from André Gunder Frank's *Capitalism and Underdevelopment in Latin America*: "The 'Indian problem' in Latin America is in its essence a problem of the economic structure of the national and international capitalist system as a whole."

While West is being held hostage Carlos tries to explain how capitalism operates in Brazil. "Capitalism, there's a quaint old word," is West's response. "Don't hear it nearly so often nowadays. I remember when I was much younger, I was posted in Venice, at the Palazzo Dario. Used to hear a lot about capitalism in those days, and I used to think this is where it started and this is what it is: a lot of sinking palaces."

Carlos dismisses West's view as "far too romantic" and says that in order to understand the true nature of capitalism one only has to look at Brasilia. This was designed as a city for the people but they are not allowed to live there; they are bussed in to work from the slums some twenty miles away.

Some critics felt that Carlos was idealised as a revolutionary hero but Hampton is careful to expose his callous streak. When West tells him of a homosexual friend who was raped and murdered by a death squad he is unsympathetic. Like Brecht in *Tales from Hollywood*, his concern for the masses is balanced by his indifference to the fate of the individual. He attacks West for not facing up to reality and dismisses his compassion as "romantic, bourgeois sentimentality". He mocks West's concern for "those poor naked savages" and reminds him of the Brazilian children who are starving to death. He sees West as a typical representative of the old European order. The Englishman's surname is symbolic and Carlos makes a joke about its significance:

> WEST: Why did you pick on me?
> CARLOS: For poetic reasons.
> WEST: (*surprised*) What do you mean?
> CARLOS: We liked your name.

But both men are aware that although the Western civilisation built on colonial imperialism is now crumbling it is being usurped by something even more rampantly venal. And although Carlos is scornful of West's political position West certainly has no desire to defend everything that has been done by his country.

Carlos quotes rather self-consciously from Camus and Fanon as if to prove his credentials and in order to impress West with his erudition but he is saved from being a mere propagandist by a sardonic freewheeling intelligence that will not allow him to swallow the party line unquestioningly. This attitude brings him into conflict with his superior officers, however, who decide that he needs to be sent to Cuba to be re-educated. He also admits to a fondness for American girls and their "wonderful mixture of alertness and ignorance" and he defines capitalism as "the process whereby American girls turn into American women". (This line has been included in the *Oxford Dictionary of Quotations.*)

When they are not discussing politics the two men talk about poetry, a subject they are both passionate about. Carlos reads some of his verse to West:

> Send for the censor and secret police.
> Rejoice and be exceeding glad.
> Smear the electrodes and sharpen the knives.
> Ye own the salt of the earth: but if the salt have lost his market value,
>   invest in real estate.

West's reaction is equivocal.

> WEST: (*hesitantly*) Yes. I mean, it's a little bit more direct and er crude than what I'm used to.
> CARLOS: Yes, well, you see, we haven't time for all your old European bourgeois subtleties.

West is like Verlaine in his belief in art as something transcendent, while Carlos is more like Rimbaud (although nowhere near as talented) in his desire to have a direct impact on the world. The fact that West is a better poet than Carlos might suggest that a writer's self-obsession could be justified, but we are left to draw our own conclusions.

Martin Esslin observed in his review of *Savages* in *Theatre Quarterly* that West and his sort are threatened with extinction no less than the Indians. West's brand of cultured melancholy has no place in a world where one is expected to extol the virtues of free enterprise and sing the company song. In the days of global corporate idiocy, however, it might be argued that people like West are not to be dismissed as an outmoded bourgeois luxury but should be viewed as a vital force against the yahoo philistinism of market economics. The situation is reminiscent of the scene in the third act of *Uncle Vanya* (which Hampton adapted for the Royal Court in 1970, with Scofield in the title role), where Astrov rails against the senseless destruction of the surrounding countryside by people too lazy or greedy to care for it.

West realises that he can do little to help the Indians directly but he seeks to preserve their culture by producing a body of poems using material drawn from their myths and legends. Hampton sifted through the thousand or more legends that he found recorded in Alexander's *Mythology of all Ages* and Lévi-Strauss's *Mythologiques—Le cru et le cuit* and *Du miel aux cendres* in order to find the stories that would best suit his central character's melancholy stoicism. West's general, rather romanticised, view of the Indians is that they were living in a state of pre-lapsarian bliss before they were exposed to Western influences, but his poetry hints at a darker, more pessimistic culture. For instance, one of the legends that he uses comes from the Arekuna tribe and describes a boy coming from the house of the sun to play music to the villagers. Although the music is beautiful everyone who listens to it dies, and so the villagers attack him and burn him to death.

> And sometimes in the evening we have music
> Strange and beautiful as the boy from the house of the sun
> And sad as his dying.

In another story, from the Xerente tribe, a boy is enticed up to heaven by a star. Then he hears strange music and sees the dance of the dead.

> And now it is known
> That although the stars smile down and speak of the beauty of heaven
> There is no rest and no joy in the field of the dead.

It was Hampton's original idea to have the poems recorded and played during the scenes featuring the Indians, but he was persuaded by Paul Scofield, who created the role of West in the original production, that it would be more dramatic for him to speak the verse directly to the audience. The poetry is a necessary part of the play as it carries a depth of sorrow that is not expressed in the other scenes and gives us an idea of the Indians' culture.

The play's other epigraph is taken from *L'Origine des manières de table* by Lévi-Strauss, who claims that Sartre's concept "Hell is other people" ["L'enfer, c'est les autres"] is not right, and says that if we could only acknowledge that "Hell is ourselves" ["L'enfer, c'est nous-même"] then we would have learned a lesson in humility. Tribal cultures can teach us not to blame other people when the world goes wrong.

Throughout the play Carlos assures West that he will be released soon but eventually time runs out for both of them. We are not shown the negotiations between the guerrillas and the British government but in Scene Twenty-one the hide-out is attacked. Carlos reluctantly shoots West and moments later is himself gunned down by the authorities.

Although we see a lot of West and Carlos they are not fully developed and we don't feel deeply involved when they die. The supporting characters too are rather stereotypical. Mrs West, who appears in just two scenes, is a catty housewife. Major Brigg, who once worked for the Indian Protection Agency until he saw the service go rotten with corruption, is a gin-swilling British Army type. There is an English anthropologist, Miles Crawshaw, whom Hampton uses as a mouthpiece to present us with large, often undigested chunks of information about the Indians and their culture. And the Reverend Penn, who runs a mission for the Indians, is a standard example of insensitive American zealotry. (It could be said that Hampton rather spoils his case by giving Penn and his wife the stock comic names of Elmer and Maybelle.)

In an interview in *Theatre Quarterly* Hampton objected to one critic calling the scene with the Reverend Penn "sub-undergraduate" and defended his characterisation: "Actually there *are* people like the missionary and they *are* locking Indians up and giving them bubble-gum philosophy." He was also bemused by the divided response to the play. "Half the critics had said it was a 'witty' play about kidnapping and the other half said it was a propaganda piece . . . At the centre, which he [Ronald Bryden in *Plays and Players*] said was the best part, was the play about West and Carlos. What he really objected to was that it was this way round, and he would really rather have seen an all-out propaganda piece." In other words Bryden was complaining that Hampton had written a better play than he ought to have done.

Harold Hobson congratulated him for hitting out at the left while Irving Wardle accused him of glamorising Carlos. Some critics said that he had oversimplified the political positions of the two main characters while others complained that they were not sufficiently clear. However, the play went on to become a joint winner of The Plays and Players/London Theatre Critics Best Play Award and won the Los Angeles Drama Critics Circle Award for Distinguished Playwriting.

With *Savages* Hampton was attempting to present a subject with a much broader scope of action than he had previously tackled. The different strands of the play set out to achieve different things: the arguments between Carlos and West give us the wider political view; the scenes where West meets other Westerners such as Major Brigg and the Reverend Penn highlight what is happening to Brazil; and the sections with the Indians tell us about their culture. Martin Esslin identified Hampton's method as "contrapuntal" and praised his control, defending the play from those critics who thought the work undisciplined. But it is not so much a question of what type of play Hampton was writing—a political polemic or a lament for a lost culture—the difficulty is that the characters are subordinated to the plot. They represent various viewpoints but don't have a separate spontaneous existence.

Hampton later recalled, in an interview in the *Guardian,* his difficulty with political plays and English audiences. " . . . the moment Carlos began reading the political manifesto you could feel the stalls freezing over. There's something about the English that resists getting involved in politics: a peculiarly English apathy, and enormous indifference to everything, and that's something I've always written about." His use of the character of Carlos to criticise West's obsession with a handful of tribespeople can possibly be taken as a representation of a certain distrust in his own personal interest in the Indians. It is as if he wants to write about them but can't bring himself to deal with the subject directly so he speaks through Carlos in order to remind the audience that the Indians are not the only people suffering in Brazil. This unease with his own material prompts him to divide the play into discrete chunks but in doing so the drama suffers from a loss of narrative momentum.

Peter Shaffer, in his play *The Royal Hunt of the Sun*, presents Spain's destruction of the Incas in the sixteenth century as symbolic of the West's destruction of itself; we see Pizarro become sick with himself as he grows ever more greedy for gold. Perhaps the remoteness of the events Shaffer was dealing with allowed him more freedom with his material. It was possibly a fear of being condescending that meant that Hampton could not bring himself to invest the Indians with the same allegorical significance that Shaffer gives to the Incas. But this fundamental uncertainty weakens the play. West in particular is the embodiment of this flaw. Hampton deliberately avoids turning him into a tragic hero—it is, after all, a story of imperialist abuse of the third world—but the consequence of this decision is a loss of focus. As has often been said, drama has to grasp the universal through the particular: it is impossible to create an abstract tragedy. What is missing is a metaphysical dimension to West's suffering, a sense that his ordeal leads to a deeper self-knowledge. In the end we learn a great deal about the evil nature of capitalism but rather less about the evil nature of man.

Savages opened at the Royal Court on 12 April 1973. As well as Paul Scofield, the cast included Tom Conti as Carlos, Michael Pennington as Miles Crawshaw and Geoffrey Palmer (later seen in a cameo role in the film *The Honorary Consul* as a British diplomat) as Elmer Penn. The play transferred to the Comedy Theatre on 20 June and went on to Broadway and Los Angeles. In 1975 a televised version went out on BBC1, with Richard Pasco as West and Michael Kitchen as Carlos, and two years later it was broadcast on Radio 3 with Ian Holm as West and Tom Conti and Michael Pennington in their original stage roles. Also in the cast, as Mrs West, was Anna Massey, later to star in Hampton's adaptation of Anita Brookner's novel *Hotel du Lac*.

Hampton has produced very little that is overtly political. In 1969 he was one of nine authors, including Edward Bond and Heathcote Williams, to write for *The Enoch Show*, a satire on the racial attitudes of the politician Enoch Powell that was staged as a Sunday night performance at the Theatre Upstairs at the Royal Court. He was also ready to criticise Communist policy; in 1979 he translated *The Prague Trial*, a transcript of the trials of some Czech dissidents, including Václav Havel. He also compiled *A Night in the Day of the Imprisoned Writer,* an anthology of pieces that were directed by Harold Pinter for a fundraising performance in aid of the families of writers in prison all over the world, sponsored by PEN in 1981.

Like Pinter, Hampton can more successfully tackle political issues when he writes about personal relationships. Apart from *One for the Road*, Pinter's later, more overtly political plays—*Mountain Language* and *Party Time* for example—don't have the same impact as plays like *The Birthday Party*, which, by its very indirectness, has much wider implications about the nature of power. Hampton's perception of how people abuse each other, and their essential indifference to the wider world, is more subtly brought out in chamber pieces like *The Philanthropist* and *Les Liaisons Dangereuses*.

Savages is to Hampton what *Mrs Warren's Profession* was to Shaw and *The Pillar of the Community* was to Ibsen: a play that sprang from a deep desire to criticise society, pursued with a dramatist's intelligence and skill, but not drawing on the more personal emotions that were to fuel their best plays. The passion in *Savages* is a passion without hysteria, but it is strangely impersonal and fails to plumb the depths of true tragedy.

CHAPTER FIVE

TREATS (1976)

> Why do you suppose we only feel compelled to chase the ones who run away?
> — Immaturity?
>
> *Les Liaisons Dangereuses*

Hampton's version of *A Doll's House* opened on Broadway in 1971 and, as he observed in his introduction to *Treats* in the 1991 collected edition of his plays, it had "caught the crest of the Women's Liberation wave". He decided that "in retrospect there seemed something disturbing about this fashionable endorsement". The sound of Nora finally slamming the door on her patronising husband was intended to provoke nineteenth-century audiences into examining their own prejudices.

Hampton felt that by the 1970s Ibsen's play had become "the last word in social orthodoxy. And yet, as everybody knew, there were still just as many women trapped in unsatisfactory, restrictive and degrading relationships". He wanted to write a play where a woman "would slam the door and come back". This idea, together with a persistent mental picture he had of a half-furnished room, formed the two starting points for *Treats*. His purpose was to expose the "apathy and lack of warmth" in modern life. "The country seems to me in a pretty perverse state at the moment," he said in an interview in the *Guardian* at the time that the play opened. It was in that same year, 1976, that Margaret Thatcher was elected to lead the Conservative Party, but even before she became Prime Minister and uttered her famous statement that there was no such thing as 'society' Hampton had recognised that Britain was becoming lethargic and uncaring. The characters in *Treats* are not concerned with society either. They are totally self-absorbed and the notion of adhering to anything as serious as a religious, political or artistic ideal doesn't enter their heads. Few plays have caught so well the callousness of an era that has seen apathy raised to the status of ideology.

Treats has two epigraphs and both refer to the world as a place where very little seems to make sense. The first is 'I wonder . . . who wrote the book of love', the title phrase from the song 'Book of Love' by the Monotones. (Hampton specifies a different song from the 1950s or '60s to be played in the breaks between each scene and this song is played at the close of the first act.)

The second epigraph is taken from the famous scene at the end of *Casablanca* where Rick tells Ilse that "the problems of three little people don't amount to a hill o' beans in this crazy world". Rick chooses to sacrifice love for duty but the characters in *Treats* are incapable of such a noble gesture, and if the outside world is crazy then none of them seems to have noticed.

Hampton effectively deals with the moral decay of society by scarcely mentioning it. Instead he shows us three people who are preoccupied with their own relationships to the exclusion of all else, and he emphasises the depersonalised contingency of their lives by placing them in a sparsely furnished room throughout the action.

The play has a rigidly symmetrical structure. Of the total of nine scenes, there are three where all the characters are on stage together, three involving two of them and three where there is one person alone on stage. The "mathematical rigours" of the play's construction gave Hampton the most trouble when he was writing it and his design has one major disadvantage: the solo scenes are not strong enough to hold our attention during the long pauses when nothing much is happening.

In Scene One we see Ann and Patrick in their sitting room. Ann is leafing through a copy of *Vogue* while Patrick listens to the third movement of Bruckner's Fourth Symphony. His use of headphones hints at his emotional isolation. He tells Ann that Bruckner was so pleased to have his work performed that he tried to tip the conductor. He finds this anecdote endearing, which suggests that he himself is an agreeable but unworldly figure. Because of the headphones he doesn't hear the sound of breaking glass as Dave, Ann's former partner, breaks into the flat.

Dave goes to the record-player and turns it up to full volume and, when Patrick pulls off the headphones in pain, punches him on the nose. He then proceeds to threaten Ann, who tells him to go away, while Patrick, as soon as he has emerged from behind the sofa, tries to sort out the dispute amicably.

Within the first few minutes Hampton has clearly established the personalities of all three characters. Patrick is an amiable but ineffectual blunderer, Dave is an uncouth bully, and Ann is sharp-tongued and has a disastrous taste in men.

It is Ann's misfortune to be attracted to a man like Dave, a misogynist who enjoys physically and mentally torturing women. The stage directions on his first entrance indicate that he is "possessed of a kind of malignant energy". We are led to believe that he is capable of feeling—he breaks down in tears in the first scene—but, as we see later, his emotional outbursts are entirely faked.

Like Philip in *The Philanthropist*, Patrick is solid and dependable but timid. But while Philip longs for human company Patrick seems content with his own blandness. In a rare moment of self-awareness he says: "I'm an incurable optimist, that's the misery of it". In Scene Six Ann complains that Patrick's lack of emotional insight blinds him to her needs and renders him invulnerable.

> PATRICK: I mean, you're everything *I* want . . . But what *you* want . . . I don't think I could ever . . .
> ANN: (*Much warmer*) What do you mean?
> PATRICK: You know . . . maybe I've misunderstood . . . I just wanted to make it clear . . . (*He breaks off, gropes around in his pocket, produces a keyring.*) I'd better leave your key.

Here Patrick fails to see that he had a chance to save the relationship. Just as he is beginning to show some genuine feeling, which is what Ann craves, he holds back and wastes the opportunity. The music at the end of this scene is 'Why Do Fools Fall in Love?' by Frankie Lymon and the Teenagers.

Dave is quick to recognise Patrick's weak points, which he works on mercilessly in order to manoeuvre him out of the way. This sums up his whole approach to life: divide and rule. Friendship between people is dangerous to him because it unifies them, but in a world where everyone lacks commitment he has no trouble picking them off one by one. He doesn't bother to disguise his contempt for others and he takes a malicious delight in their suffering. La Rochefoucauld's aphorism "There is something about the misfortunes of our friends that is not displeasing" is echoed by Dave's remark that "there is no more subtle pleasure than to see your best friend fall off the roof". At one point he tells Patrick how he managed to impress a woman in an argument with her lover about the Jesuits by pretending to be passionate and committed while the other man mumbled and hedged.

> DAVE: The contempt she felt for that poor bastard was something beautiful to behold. Of course, she was very stupid. I married them off in the end. I sometimes wonder how often and in what terms they speak of the Jesuits.
> PATRICK: Is this by way of being a warning?
> DAVE: Only indirectly.

As in much of Hampton's work the human relationships he portrays in *Treats* are based on aesthetic judgements rather than true feeling. Dave is a foreign correspondent for a leading newspaper but he is cynical about his work. He has just returned from Cyprus where he was reporting on the Turkish invasion but he offers no political insights. His only concern was to return without "a bullet up my Khyber". He uses his linguistic skills only to belittle and humiliate people.

ANN: He used to save up clumsy sentences I'd said, and repeat them to me when we got home.
PATRICK: You told me.
ANN: Well, I'm telling you again, it's relevant, isn't it?
PATRICK: Yes, I know, I'm not saying you told me, I don't want to hear it again, I'm saying you told me, I know about it and I can see why you said it.
DAVE: Your sentences aren't too elegant either, are they?

Ann and Patrick also making a living from language—they are both translators—but neither has Dave's quick talent for facile wordplay. Ann eventually gives up her job, having come to the conclusion that Dave was right to dismiss her work because none of the businessmen who employed her were saying anything worth hearing.

The only time that Dave betrays any insecurity himself, apart from at the very end, is when he asks Ann how good Patrick was as a lover and she replies "no worse than you". The stage directions state that Dave is "momentarily shaken" at this point and then quickly recovers. He doesn't seem to enjoy sex particularly but like Howard Kirk in *The History Man* and Valmont in *Les Liaisons Dangereuses* he needs it as a weapon to gain and maintain power over women.

It is difficult to see why Ann puts up with Dave's behaviour and when Patrick asks her why she stayed with him for so long she doesn't answer. In the *Guardian* interview Hampton explained that the play is about people who don't know what they want so they stick to what is familiar, which is similar to T. S. Eliot's statement to the effect that in the choice between evil and blankness at least by choosing evil we know that we exist.

After Ann has thrown Patrick out Dave comes round one afternoon on the pretext of returning his rug to her flat. He offers to make love to her on the rug and she agrees. But before she has finished undressing Dave slaps her hard across the face. He then leaves, telling her that she can contact him at the hotel where he is staying if she wants him. Having established that she is willing to have sex with him he rejects her so as to prove that he still has the upper hand. He had said that sex would be "a little treat" but Ann realises that treats are the last thing she is going to get from Dave, who is incapable of any act of disinterested kindness.

The next scene shows Ann alone, breaking down in tears, and finally reaching for the telephone to call Dave. In the final scene Dave and Ann are living together again in the flat. The dog they once had, which Ann had given away, has been retrieved and can be heard barking offstage. Like Patrick in the opening scene, Dave is listening to music with the headphones on. His choice is significant: it is 'God', a song that John Lennon wrote shortly after the Beatles broke up. The lyrics describe how Lennon no longer believes in the Bible or Buddha, or anything except himself and his marriage to Yoko Ono. Dave just believes in himself. He appears to have got what he wanted but he is living in a void. He has decided that any attempt to make sense of the chaos of life is like "trying to dig steps in the side of the whirlpool". He prefers "dancing in the ruins".

Dave is still listening to the music when he hears the sound of breaking glass. It is Patrick, forcing his way into the flat. He says that he has come to talk to Ann and finally, after she has bandaged his bleeding hand and Dave has given him a glass of brandy, he comes out with what is really on his mind.

> PATRICK: Are you going to get married?
> DAVE: You're joking.
> PATRICK: I just wondered.
> DAVE: Look, in a couple of years' time or sooner or anyway sometime we shall probably make a very unpleasant mess of each other's lives and that'll be the end of it.

Patrick asks Ann if this is what she really wants but she just screams abuse at him. He leaves and Ann follows him. Dave looks in terror at the door that has slammed and for only the second time in the play he shows some genuine emotion. But Ann comes back. She goes up to him, smiling. Dave looks away from her, coldly. Neither of them speaks.

This ending is ambiguous. Maybe the door slamming is an ironic reflection of *A Doll's House*. Nora, who leaves everything behind—her children, her husband, her home and her status in society—strikes a blow for independence. Ann is in a destructive relationship and has nothing to lose by going, one would think, but she chooses to stay. Maybe she has learned how to stand up to Dave and beat him at his own game.

Some critics shared Hampton's scepticism about the supposed new equality for women but others felt that he had made Ann, and therefore by implication all women, too masochistic. It could be said that Ann had more options open to her than to stay with Dave or go with Patrick, but there are many people, and not just women, who will stick with a situation they are not happy with rather than face the unknown.

Hampton's stated aim was to irritate and he found it "rather bracing" to read by far the worst press notices that he had ever received. There were complaints that the play was slight and trivial, and it is true that *Treats* hasn't got the depth of *Total Eclipse* or *The Philanthropist*, but in fact his critique of society is subtler, if less urgent, than in *Savages*. He never directly tackles the subject of contemporary aimlessness. He deliberately hints at large political events (Franco's impending death and an angry demonstration on the street below the flat) only to refuse to examine them. This device is effective but it limits the scope of the piece; to show three characters who are cut off from society does not necessarily indicate that the whole society is decaying. And, as those characters are not given to introspection, we can only guess at what they feel by what they do. This makes the play curiously diffuse in its impact; its implications have to be teased out from underneath the text. *Treats* is in fact almost Pinteresque in its sense of invaded territory. Many of Pinter's plays concern a power struggle between an intruder into a home and that home's owners. The intruder sometimes wins, as in *Old Times*, and sometimes loses, as in *The Caretaker*. In *Treats* Dave is the intruder and although he seems to win by effectively disposing of Patrick, he loses the balance of power to Ann. Hampton told the *Guardian*: "Working with actors over these years, I've learned that I've provided them with too much material—made a play too explicit. With this play, I wanted the bones, I wanted to present a flatter surface, and I wanted the audience to work harder."

It is not unusual for playwrights to create enigmas but Hampton offers no obvious mysteries in *Treats* and so it is easy to assume, as many of the first-night reviewers did, that it is no more than an ably written play about a woman choosing between two men. The fact that Hampton cannot suggest any sort of remedy to counteract the breakdown of his characters' lives is slightly unsatisfactory. Even though there are no solutions to the problems he raises in *The Philanthropist* at least we care more about the people he portrays. Philip especially, with his need for love and his awareness of death, manages to win our sympathy, and this gives the play depth and universal significance. Even so, in *Treats*, comedy is generated through the use of language. Hampton's acute ear for patterns of speech comes across when he shows us Patrick's nervous habit of adding qualifiers and disclaimers to everything he says, which is further emphasised when set against Dave's remorselessly coarse but shrewd irony.

Hampton resisted the temptation to turn *Treats* into another epigrammatic comedy like *The Philanthropist* and perhaps this is why so many reviewers were disappointed. But it scored a success with audiences and transferred from the Royal Court to the Mayfair Theatre. By Hampton's own exacting standards, though, it was a comparative flop. It was the first time a play of his failed to make it to Broadway, although it did tour the American provinces.

Treats reunited Hampton with Jane Asher—the original Celia in *The Philanthropist*—as Ann and also starred James Bolam as Dave, and Stephen Moore as Patrick. Hampton found the rehearsal period a difficult and unhappy time and he was not to write another stage play for five years.

Yorkshire Television broadcast a version of *Treats* in 1977, with Kate Nelligan as Ann, Tom Conti as Patrick and John Hurt as Dave. Conti switched roles to play Dave in 1989 for the revival at the Hampstead Theatre, alongside Peter Capaldi and Julia Ormond, directed by Geraldine McEwan.

Hampton was accused of deliberate perversity in giving a woman a stark choice between a bully and a wimp but he defends his position: "One does want, in a play, something that worries people and makes them question what they've seen. That seems to me more interesting for an audience than something that reinforces their convictions or hopes." *Treats* presents a bleak view of human relationships but many people respond to it. "Women who've been in that situation," he said, "understand the play best."

CHAPTER SIX

TALES FROM HOLLYWOOD (1982)

. . . it seemed, gentlemen, as if all my wishes had come true. Except for one: my eager, constant, burning desire to be of service to my community.

White Chameleon

Peggy Ramsay, Hampton's agent, used to say that a modern playwright's working life was often no longer than ten years. 1976 was Hampton's tenth year as a professionally performed dramatist and he began to fear that she was right. That year's production of *Treats* had been fraught with difficulty: the rehearsals had been gloomy (as, in fact, they had been for *The Philanthropist*) and the play was coolly received by the critics. Hampton said later that at that time he felt "a terrible urge never to write for the theatre again". All of his plays to date had been commercial successes, all transferring to the West End and, in the case of *Total Eclipse, The Philanthropist* and *Savages*, playing on Broadway as well. *Treats* marked the end of a ten-year association with the Royal Court Theatre after which he entered what he later came to recognise as a five-year dry period.

During the years that elapsed between *Treats* and *Tales from Hollywood* Hampton lost his connection with the theatre that had served him so well and, more painfully for him, his close friend and regular director, Robert Kidd, died. Hampton wrote of him, in an obituary published in the *Guardian* on 19 July 1980: "Bob was a marvellously controlled, unshowy director whose commitment to the text was absolute. If he drove his actors hard, he drove himself harder. His enthusiasm and energy were unparalleled and he worked with more dedication than anyone I have ever known. I scarcely know how to begin to go back to the theatre without him."

Hampton has not found a regular director since. He felt that the Royal Court was a theatre for new writers, a description that no longer applied to him. Many of the emerging dramatists showed a hard-edged, left-wing bias and he found himself increasingly out of step. "I felt very out of the mainstream," he said. "All my contemporaries were writing very political agit-prop plays." The 1970s saw the formation of a wealth of alternative theatre companies, such as Joint Stock founded by Max Stafford-Clark and 7:84 formed by John McGrath. It was a time of 'quick response' theatre that reacted swiftly to the issues of the day.

Although he was broadly in sympathy with their political views, Hampton was at odds with those writers and directors who saw theatre primarily as a tool for social change. He felt that form and structure were being sacrificed to platitudes. What he saw as the main trend was what was happening amongst his contemporaries at the Royal Court and the National Theatre. The real mainstream was, as ever, the West End diet of musicals, thrillers and bed-hopping farces.

Perhaps simply because he had something else to do, Hampton gave up playwriting for five years to concentrate on film work. He wrote the first draft of *Carrington* and completed screenplays based on Graham Greene's *The Honorary Consul,* Somerset Maugham's *The Moon and Sixpence*, David Storey's *A Temporary Life* and Lord Bethell's historical work *The Last Secret*. The only things that reached the screen during this period were his uncredited contribution to Michael Apted's film *Agatha* and his screenplay (co-written with Maximilian Schell) for *Geschichten aus dem Wienerwald* [*Tales from the Vienna Woods*], which was released in 1979 but not shown in Britain.

Hampton had not broken into Hollywood but his time was not wasted and it was America, paradoxically, that gave him the chance to return to the theatre. Kenneth Brecher, the Associate Director of the Mark Taper Forum Theatre in Los Angeles, had worked on the LA production of *Savages* in 1974 and he called Hampton to tell him that he was commissioning a series of plays about aspects of Los Angeles life. One of the topics he suggested was the fate of the writers who had fled from Nazi Germany in the 1930s and had ended up on the fringes of the Hollywood film industry.

To a film buff like Hampton this idea was an inspiration and he embarked on the research straight away. One of the challenges that faced him was how to draw together a lot of people who in real life had never met each other. He got round this difficulty by using the Austro-Hungarian dramatist Ödön von Horváth as his central character. He had translated Horváth's best-known play, *Tales from the Vienna Woods*, for the National Theatre in 1977 and knew a great deal about his work. The real Horváth never went to Hollywood, having died in a freak accident in Paris in 1938, but after his death some notes for a novel were found in his room, one of which read: "Ein Poet emigriert nach Amerika . . . "

Having a narrator who was technically speaking dead gave Hampton the freedom to put him wherever he liked within the action of the play. In the opening scene of Act One he rewrites history by showing Horváth avoiding the falling branch that killed him in reality. We see him sheltering under a tree on the Champs Élysées during a thunderstorm. Standing next to him is a man in a chauffeur's uniform and it is he who dies when the branch falls. In the final scene in Act Two the young man returns to witness Horváth's death.

Once again he is dressed in a chauffeur's uniform. Horváth tells the audience that he is reminded of "that new Cocteau picture". He is referring to *Orphée*, where death appears in a chauffeur-driven black limousine. This figure is a reference to Charon in Greek mythology, who ferried departed souls across the poisonous river Styx to the underworld.

Horváth acts as our guide to the lives of the exiled artists he meets. His first encounter with the madness of the Hollywood is played out in a fantasy sequence in the opening scene of Act One where Tarzan swings across the lawn and introduces himself—"Me Johnny Weissmuller, you Thomas Mann"—and Chico and Harpo Marx act out a routine where Harpo explains, with his usual mixture of frantic mime and extravagant props, that he has played tennis with Arnold Schoenberg. "You gotta be careful with him," Chico says, "he gotta very sneaky rhythm."

We are told that Weissmuller did indeed know Thomas Mann, and Harpo Marx did play tennis with Schoenberg, though, as Horváth warns us, "the reality was very different". This is true, of course, but in Hollywood reality is the last thing that matters and the fantasy that the stars behaved in real life as they did on screen is potent. Literature, as Horváth says, has to do more than be right, and this served for Hollywood also.

As a central character Horváth is rather a wraith-like figure—just as we start to get to know him he seems to vanish (which is what the women in his life used to say as well). He is polite, detached and non-committal, taking no sides and making no judgements. He acts like a more benign version of the Master of Ceremonies in *La Ronde*: he observes people making a mess of their lives but does not intervene. He is never off stage and in between the scenes where he talks to the other characters he speaks directly to the audience. When he is involved in the action his English is broken and he has a heavy accent but when he addresses the audience his speech is grammatical and he has no accent. This was the first time that Hampton had used a narrator (although in the 1981 rewrite of *Total Eclipse* he gives Verlaine a voice-over soliloquy at the beginning of each act) and it was a device that he re-used in 1991 in *White Chameleon*. The fact that Horváth was a real writer gives his status as narrator a historical resonance that a fictional character would have lacked.

Tales from Hollywood has a broader scope than any of Hampton's other plays. There are twenty-two scenes and twenty-three featured roles and the time scale stretches over twelve years, from Horváth's emigration in 1938 to his death in 1950. The first act covers three years, leading up to the Japanese bombing of Pearl Harbor, and the second act covers the nine years between the entry of the US into the war and the beginning of the House Un-American Activities Committee anti-Communist hearings.

The main characters in the play are Bertolt Brecht, Thomas and Heinrich Mann, and Heinrich's wife, Nelly. Hampton invents a Jewish girlfriend for Horváth called Helen Schwarz and he creates two fictional movie moguls—Charles Money and Art Nicely—who, like the characters in a Restoration comedy, have personalities to match their names.

Charles Money is a writer-producer who hires Horváth to ghost-write for him. This was a common practice in both Hollywood and Europe—Billy Wilder, for example, often supplied scripts for busy writer-producers in Germany—and while Horváth is rather more than a mere hack he accepts the commissions. "Anyway, at least he paid me . . . " he remarks drily, "which is more than I can say for some later employers, however amiable their manner." Hampton himself had been ripped off by Harry Saltzman in 1970 over an outline for a film based on the life of Nijinsky and, in the late 1970s a "fly-by-night New York company" had reneged on a promise to pay him for a film dramatisation of *The Moon and Sixpence*.

Money asks Horváth to write a screenplay based on the life of Edward II. The script is delivered within a week and although Money doesn't realise that it is largely plagiarised from Marlowe's play he rejects it because it portrays the King of England as a "faggot". (This too is straight from Hampton's own experience. He had been asked to script a film version of the play after Ian McKellen took the role of Edward II in 1969, first in Edinburgh and then in London. This idea lasted just as long as it took the producer to discover the truth about the King's sexuality.)

The commission that Art Nicely offers Horváth is less ambitious: it is a sequel to *Bedtime for Bonzo*, a surprisingly successful comedy starring Ronald Reagan and a chimpanzee.

Brecht gives Horváth his opinion on working for the movies. "You have to write badly, you have to write very, very badly," he tells him, "*but you also have to write as well as you possibly can.*"

In a play so full of writers it is not surprising that Hampton returns to one of his favourite themes: the nature of writing and the political role of the artist. Helen joins the Communist Party but Horváth refuses to do the same, claiming that a writer cannot function if he is too committed to a single point of view. Party membership ultimately costs Helen her job with the film studio.

Horváth and Brecht differ fundamentally in their concept of what theatre is for.

> BRECHT: You people don't understand that in the theatre it's not enough just to interpret the world any more: you have to change it.

> HORVÁTH: I really think you underestimate people's intelligence. They don't want blueprints, they don't want instructions. They're being told what to do all day: they don't want to come into a theatre and be told what to do all over again. They want to be told what they are.

Brecht's confidence in himself as an artist is entertainingly displayed by the manner of his entrances. When he comes on stage he draws attention to the fact that he is in a theatre by rattling the scenery, having the lights turned up full or hauling up placards and banners to explain the action. When he is in a scene it has to be played in a Brechtian way; he will not trifle with what he sees as bourgeois naturalism.

Hampton allows himself some dramatic licence by making Brecht and Horváth rather more opposed in their views than they probably were in real life. Brecht never referred to Horváth in his own essays but he was on the panel of judges, along with Carl Zuckmayer and Robert Musil, that awarded him the Kleist prize for playwriting in 1931.

Brecht, the Marxist radical, and Horváth, the traditional Western liberal bring to mind the characters of Carlos and West in *Savages*. Hampton sympathises with Carlos even though he is a less talented writer than West but in *Tales from Hollywood* the bias is towards Horváth. Brecht is portrayed as didactic and sceptical while Horváth is tolerant and forgiving of human weakness. "The Left attack always: they say easy pessimism," says Horváth, referring to his own work. "But they love the people without knowing any people. I know the people, how terrible they are, and still I like them."

Towards the end of the play, however, Horváth admits that he had probably taken this laissez-faire attitude too far. Tolerance becomes a fault if it means not speaking out against injustice. We learn that he had once joined the Nazi Writers' Union. He tries to explain to Helen why he had remained a member for two and a half years.

> HELEN: I don't understand how you could want to do that.
> HORVÁTH: Did you read *Death in Venice*?
> HELEN: Yes, of course.
> HORVÁTH: It was a little like this, I could not leave the plague-infested city. But it was not beauty and innocence which kept me . . . enthralled, it was the grotesque, the triumph of stupidity, the ugliness.
> (*Silence.*)
> But no, there are no excuses.

He tries to redeem himself by saying that during that time he wrote nothing that "was worth shit" and so had come to Hollywood where, even though producers regard writers as no more important than the studio hairdressers, he would at least be paid for producing rubbish. Brecht of course has declared all along that writing in Hollywood is shit. This is not the first time that Hampton has equated writing with shit. Rimbaud calls Aicard's dreadful poem "authentic shit"; Wordsworth, declares Jack Boot in *The Philanthropist*, is "self-indulgent shit"; and Thomas Able has decided that all writers are dishonest shit-merchants. T.S. Eliot and A.E. Housman both likened the writing of poetry to the act of defecation—an accumulation of poisons followed by a degrading expulsion.

With the character of Thomas Mann Hampton creates another example of the self-obsessed writer. "There's nothing wrong with Thomas Mann. Except that he believes his reviews," says Horváth, who had earlier observed that some people felt the Nobel Prize for Literature awarded to Thomas in 1929 had gone to the wrong brother. Hampton has been accused of caricaturing Thomas Mann but nowhere in the play does he ridicule the work (except perhaps when Horváth falls asleep while Mann reads to him from *Lotte in Weimar*). "Even if *The Genesis of a Novel* is one of the most sublimely pompous books ever written," said Hampton in an interview in the *Sunday Times* in 1983, "I still think Thomas is a wonderful writer, probably in the end better than Heinrich. But he *was* that kind of man."

Thomas is acclaimed and successful whereas Heinrich is unknown in America and struggles for the recognition that he had enjoyed in Germany. In Hollywood Heinrich is associated only with Josef von Sternberg's film *The Blue Angel*, loosely based on his novel *Professor Unrat*. "My entire American reputation stands on the legs of Marlene Dietrich," he says stoically.

Thomas regularly gives Heinrich and Nelly money as they are living in poverty. Nelly is also going mad. Cut off from her home country and without any friends of her own age, she starts drinking heavily and having affairs with unpleasant young men. She takes to driving around recklessly in a car they can ill afford and, like F. Scott Fitzgerald's hack Hollywood writer Pat Hobby and Joe Gillis in *Sunset Boulevard*, she is always on the run from the repo-man.

Nelly is the embodiment of the sense of displacement and hopelessness that hangs over all the exiles. She is intelligent enough to recognise the cause of her misery but she has no mental reserves to draw on. As the play progresses she becomes more outrageous in her behaviour. At Horváth's fortieth birthday party she walks into a crowded room naked, carrying his birthday cake, saying: "Well, I've had to sell all my jewellery, every last piece, so I thought, what the hell, why wear anything?"

Heinrich tells Horváth that his daughter and his first wife are still in Europe. "I know what you're thinking, my boy," he says. "How is it we've managed to be so lucky?" But he is not that lucky. Once the war is over the exiles will have to go back and face those who stayed and fought.

Nelly also feels guilty when she thinks about those who have been left behind in Europe, but she has an added burden: she is Jewish but has kept her identity secret, not only in Germany but also in America where she pretends that she is from an old German family called Kröger.

But Heinrich and Nelly never return to their homeland. The police track Nelly down after she has run into another car on the road while she was drunk. Fearing that she will be sent to prison, she takes an overdose. Heinrich discovers her, lying unconscious, and takes her in a taxi to the nearest hospital. But they refuse to help because he doesn't have enough money on him and they will not accept his cheque. A second hospital also turns them away and by the time they reach a third Nelly is dead. Horváth contrasts the manner of her treatment with his memory of Thomas Mann at an official luncheon a few weeks earlier. "And from then on, whenever I thought about America, the two images, one seen and one imagined, rose before me: Thomas, on that white podium in that manicured garden; and Heinrich, weeping and covered with vomit, pleading with the admissions clerk in some casualty department, trying to get some attention paid to his dying wife."

After Nelly dies Heinrich tells Horváth how he had first met her in a bar. They had had a brief affair and then parted. Then, on her own initiative, she had travelled halfway across Europe to see him again. They got married and walked across the Pyrenees so that they could reach Lisbon and escape on a ship to America. But in America she had no money, no friends, no role. She had survived the terrors of Europe but was unable to conquer the banality of her new life.

The story of a barmaid's love for a distinguished novelist seems to echo that of Heinrich's Professor Rat (disrespectfully nicknamed by his pupils Professor Unrat, which translates as 'Professor Turd') for the showgirl Lola Montez. Hampton underlines this similarity by having the main song from *The Blue Angel*, 'Und Sonst Gar Nichts' ['Falling in Love Again'] playing in the background when Heinrich explains how he and Nelly got married. But Lola was a tougher and more determined woman altogether.

The last image we have of Heinrich is of a lonely, broken old man, pressing his cheek against the red blouse that his wife used to wear. Horváth tells us that Heinrich died just a couple of weeks later, after an evening of listening to "divine Puccini". Once again Hampton links music and death.

Heinrich Mann had little cause to feel guilty. In books such as *Man of Straw*, published as early as 1918, he had recognised the dangers of militarism, commercialism and anti-Semitism. But Thomas Mann, Brecht claims contemptuously, waited until Hitler had been in power for three years before speaking out. Brecht's statement is not true, however. Mann had criticised the Nazis in his 1929 Nobel acceptance speech and in 1930 he satirised Italian fascism in his story 'Mario and the Magician'. He tells Horváth that his books had been ceremonially burned by the Nazi Party and that Goebbels had said on that occasion: "Tonight, the intellect awakes."

It is as a public figure that he could have done more. Hampton includes a scene where Mann and some of the other leading émigré writers sign an open letter to President Roosevelt arguing that Hitler should not be identified with the German people as a whole. Mann waters the statement down until it is almost meaningless and then withdraws his signature. This incident is reminiscent of the scene in *The Honorary Consul* where the author Dr Saavedra refuses to sign a letter pleading with the world's governments to take action to help Charley Fortnum. Saavedra says that he couldn't possibly endorse anything that was so badly written. (This scene was cut from the original draft of Hampton's screenplay.) Mann's prevarication is political rather than aesthetic: he doesn't want to be seen to be criticising America after it has offered him protection. There is also a hint of self-interest in his caution; he believes that after the war Roosevelt might help make him President of Germany.

In spite of its deft humour, *Tales from Hollywood* paints a bleak picture of life in the States. Hampton, like so many of America's own writers, is seduced by the glamour of the country even though he is aware of its rottenness. At times Horváth sounds like a Fitzgerald hero himself: "Also, I still loved America. Despite everything, I was still devoted to its tragic innocence."

Fitzgerald chronicled the 'tragic innocence' of America and Hampton makes several allusions to *The Great Gatsby* in his play. (He had worked as a rewrite man on Jack Clayton's 1974 film version of the novel.) Brecht says of Thomas Mann at one point that "his mouth is full of money", echoing Gatsby's remark that his lover Daisy has a voice that is full of money. Horváth, like Fitzgerald's narrator, Carraway, is an observer rather than a participant in the action. Even when Gatsby is revealed as nothing more than a bootlegger Carraway is still enthralled by the mythical aura that the man has created for himself. He sees the truth but prefers to go on believing in the illusion. This is a common theme in American writing—the inability to let go of the trappings of glamour even when the underlying corruption has been exposed. Biff Loman sees through his father's self-deceptions in *Death of a Salesman* but remains moved by his enduring capacity for feeling. Blanche DuBois in *A Streetcar Named Desire* is revealed as a nymphomaniac but her desire for beauty still sets her apart from Stanley Kowalski's ignorant brutality. And Norma Desmond in *Sunset Boulevard* still clings to the glamour of her past while everything around her is sinking into decay.

Hampton pays his own tribute to *Sunset Boulevard* by having Horváth drown in a swimming pool, which is where Joe Gillis also meets his end, and he underlines the connection by specifying that Horváth dies in 1950, the year that Wilder's film was released.

A thesis could be written on 'The American Swimming Pool as a Symbol of Corruption'—it has become such a potent metaphor. Jay Gatsby's body is found drifting in a swimming pool after he is murdered and in Nathanael West's *The Day of the Locust* the lunacy of the Hollywood system is summed up by the inflated rubber horse at the bottom of the movie mogul's pool. The poolside interview has become one of the most clichéd images of Hollywood.

Thomas Mann feels that American authors are "drowned in success" for such praise is heaped on them that they lose all sense of values. The phrase is a gruesome foreshadowing of what will happen to Horváth and yet it could hardly be said that he had succeeded in Hollywood. His death contrasts ironically with what happens to Gillis. Gillis is destroyed by a gun fired out of jealousy but Horváth dies accidentally. Art Nicely invites him to swim in the pool and then leaves. Horváth bangs his head on the marble steps and drowns. This is a powerful moment in the play. Lighting effects suggest rippling water and Horváth is isolated in a spotlight as he narrates the circumstances of his own death. The chauffeur appears downstage and stands silently looking on while Horváth describes the sensations he feels as he drowns. It is a ridiculous end in what he had always perceived to be an absurd universe.

This ending was inspired by a real encounter Hampton once had with a Hollywood swimming pool and the chauffeur of a studio limousine. In 1980 he had an appointment with the producer Ray Stark. For nineteen minutes of their twenty-minute meeting Stark was on the phone to New York. He then said he had to go but told Hampton to make himself at home and to use the pool if he wished. Hampton cut his head quite badly while swimming and struggled out of the water, blood dripping everywhere. He asked the chauffeur who had been sent to fetch him to take him back to his hotel on Sunset Boulevard (where else?) but was told that it was too far and so was dumped, blood-encrusted, at the nearest taxi-rank.

The most shocking thing about Hollywood is the squandering of the prodigious amount of talent that came its way. One only has to look at how Irving Thalberg mistreated Erich von Stroheim in the 1920s to understand that. America's inability to maintain its talent, and its capacity for consigning experience and maturity to the scrapheap is one of its main drawbacks. Oscar Wilde summed it up: "The youth of America is their oldest tradition. It has been going on now for three hundred years." F. Scott Fitzgerald once wrote that "there are no second acts in American lives" and more recently John Updike, in one of his Henry Bech stories, spoke of "the senility that comes early to American authors". In *Tales from Hollywood* Thomas Mann complains that American writers "have no conception of a developing life-work", although Helen objects to this view, citing Fitzgerald, Hemingway, Faulkner, Dos Passos, Steinbeck and West.

The talents of actors were often wasted in Hollywood too. Peter Lorre, for example, had appeared in the original production of *Tales from the Vienna Woods* and was a member of Brecht's Berliner Ensemble. His first film role was the child-murderer in Fritz Lang's *M.* Then he went to America. He had distinguished roles in *The Maltese Falcon* (1941) and *Casablanca* (1942) but mostly he played caricatured eye-popping Germans (when he wasn't appearing in the Mr Moto films). Hampton refers to this in *Tales from Hollywood:*

> HORVÁTH: Peter Lorre works all the time.
> BRECHT: Yes, sinking slowly into the quicksand, grinning from ear to ear.

Horváth reminds Brecht that he liked America once, and Brecht replies that that was before he arrived there. In the 1930s, with Roosevelt's New Deal and popular left-wing writers such as Odets and Steinbeck, it may have seemed a promising place from a distance but the reality proved very different. In fact the only artists working in America that Brecht admits to liking are Erle Stanley Gardner, the creator of Perry Mason, and Charlie Chaplin. Unlike Carlos in *Savages*, Brecht is not seduced by America. In fact it brings on moments of severe depression: "I can't believe there is such a place and I don't know what the hell I'm doing here," he says. "I used to read Shelley sometimes and think the poor bastard's been dead a hundred years and all those injustices are still as bad, if not worse, and then I'd think, will they be reading us in another hundred years and feeling the same, and then I'd get depressed for a while. But here I feel like that all the time." His view is the opposite of Patrick's in *Treats*, who assumes that everything will be better in a hundred years, when he and everyone he knows is dead and gone.

Hampton does not deride the films Hollywood made nor the many talented people who worked there; he only criticises the studio bosses for treating film-making as an industry rather than an art-form.

After its debut in Los Angeles, where the critics failed to appreciate that Hampton had intended the play as an affectionate tribute to Hollywood, it was taken on by the National Theatre (where David Hare was the Resident Dramatist) in May 1983. Although Hampton's translations of Horváth's *Tales from the Vienna Woods* and *Don Juan Comes Back from the War* had appeared at the National in 1977 and 1978, *Tales from Hollywood* was his first original play to be produced there. He dedicated the text to David Mercer, a playwright whom he greatly admired. (He had been responsible for selecting extracts from Mercer's plays when the National Theatre put on a special tribute at the Cottesloe when Mercer died in 1980.)

Peter Gill directed the National Theatre production of *Tales from Hollywood* and the cast included Michael Gambon as Horváth, Billie Whitelaw as Nelly, Michael Bryant as Thomas Mann, Philip Locke as Heinrich Mann, Ian McDiarmid as Brecht and Barbara Flynn as Helen. In November 1992 it was televised for BBC2 as part of the 'Theatre Night' season of plays, directed by Howard Davies, with Jeremy Irons as Horváth, Sinead Cusack as Nelly, Sir Alec Guinness as Heinrich Mann, Robin Bailey as Thomas Mann, Jack Shepherd as Brecht and Elizabeth McGovern as Helen.

As a play about the clash of cultures between Europe and America it is full of wit and acute observation, enough so to win it the Evening Standard Best Comedy Award, but there is something slightly insubstantial about the characters. Irving Wardle wrote in *The Times* that "Philip Locke extracts every particle of irony and intelligence from the character, but the lines impel him inescapably into playing a sweet, simple old man bravely enduring his last days".

Sheridan Morley wrote in his review in *Punch*: "... as a dramatist [Hampton's] main problem here is threading some totally diverse strands of social, political and literary history into a play that says something coherent about the nature of exile. In this, at the last, I have to say that I think he has failed; but along the way he has created such wonderful confrontations ... that the evening is still a constant delight."

We don't learn a great deal about the writers either as artists or as people in *Tales from Hollywood*. Horváth is too reticent to be a leading character. We are told very little about him, and his relationship with Helen, which might have offered an opportunity to develop him more fully, is merely sketched in. In *Total Eclipse* Rimbaud refuses to come to terms with a world that deceives him so painfully and his spiritual crises give the drama a backbone that *Tales from Hollywood* lacks. Horváth himself is a just a link-man for a series of set pieces, and although some of them are very amusing—the scene where Thomas Mann's speeches at his 70th birthday party go on for so long that the dinner is burnt, for example—they fail to bring the play into focus.

While Hampton does not succeed in presenting a coherent view of the role of the artist he does create some memorable moments. All the scenes with Brecht and the politely overbearing Thomas Mann are written with urbanity, invention and wit and are highly enjoyable. Michael Billington wrote in the *Guardian*: "I felt as if I was seeing a play that took a fascinating slice of cultural history and transmuted it into the complexity of art."

At this point in his career Hampton may have shared with Horváth a certain lack of success within the Hollywood film industry but at least he was able to return to the theatre and survive.

CHAPTER SEVEN

THE PORTAGE TO SAN CRISTOBAL OF A.H. (1982)

For who seeing his own image his own skin
Could destroy his own kind?

Savages

Shortly after Hampton had finished *Tales from Hollywood* and was waiting for it to reach London he was commissioned by Sir Bernard Miles to dramatise George Steiner's 1981 novel *The Portage to San Cristobal of A.H.* for production at the Mermaid Theatre. Steiner, author of books such as *In Bluebeard's Castle* and *The Death of Tragedy*, is best known as a cultural critic but Miles had often pressed him to write a play. Steiner had always declined but he did send Miles two copies of *The Portage to San Cristobal of A.H.*, asking him to find someone else to adapt it for the stage.

Hampton respected the author's wish that the play should stay close to his original both in purpose and structure, and Steiner, who attended rehearsals, pronounced himself pleased with the result: "For a writer and scholar to watch his most personal allegories and metaphors spring into physical shape and blaze into tremendous life is just immensely moving and stimulating. It has been a marvellous privilege."

The main action of the play is concerned with a group of five Jews who are members of an organisation dedicated to tracking down Nazi war criminals. Set in May 1979, it begins with the search party's discovery of a shack in an almost impenetrable swamp somewhere in South America. Here they find the 90-year-old Hitler, who had escaped from his bunker in Berlin and has been living in hiding since 1945. Their problem is to bring Hitler out of the jungle alive so that he can be tried for his crimes. San Cristobal in Venezuela, near the Colombian border, is the nearest city that they can reach.

Simeon, the leader of the group, is the least developed character; we learn nothing of his past history and are never told his other name. The four men under his command come from different backgrounds. Elie Barach is a rabbi and is there, so to speak, as the group's spiritual adviser. Unlike the others, he is unarmed. The calm and enigmatic John Asher was raised in England and avoided the Holocaust. Strictly speaking, he is not Jewish at all—his mother is a Gentile—but he has joined the expedition for the challenge. He sees the task of tracking Hitler down as a complex mathematical problem that has to be solved. The youngest member of the group is Isaac Amsel. Too young to remember the war himself, he is there because his father was a secret agent who had been killed in the hunt for escaped Nazis. Amsel is immature and panics easily. He dreams of being a film-maker. In the novel Steiner presents Amsel's ideas more fully and makes it clear that he lacks the talent and vision to be successful but Hampton, being perhaps more kindly disposed towards film directors, presents him rather more sympathetically.

The most complex member of the search party is Gideon Benasseraf. Before the war he had lived a quiet, ordered life as a scholar but, having seen his wife and children murdered by the Nazis, he wants to see justice done, even though he knows that such crimes can never be truly avenged. When Amsel tells Gideon of his fantasies of having Hitler publicly tortured Gideon explains that that would give people the false impression that the suffering had somehow been expiated and could therefore be forgotten. This view echoes that of the writer Gershom Scholem (quoted in the programme notes to the play), who wrote, regarding Eichmann's execution: "Such an illusion [that justice had been done] is most dangerous because it may engender the feeling that something has been done to atone for the unatoneable."

Gideon's idea of punishment is much subtler. He would let Hitler walk free as a beggar in the state of Israel. Whenever he asked for food or shelter he would have to identify himself. Gideon doesn't want to kill Hitler as it would tidy him away; people would then feel that the Jews had had their revenge and so the rest of the world need no longer be concerned. He would prefer to leave Hitler at the first hotel they come to and allow the Gentile authorities to decide his fate. "He's *theirs*," Gideon says. Isaac asks him what he will do once they get out of the jungle. "Afterwards? I'll go look for Adolf Hitler," he replies. For him there can be no return to normal life.

The man who has organised the search party is Emmanuel Lieber. He doesn't go into the jungle with the others but maintains radio contact with them. He is a mysterious figure and we only see him, isolated on stage by a spotlight, when he talks to the group over the radio. We don't even know where he is calling from. He is not working for a government—we hear from Elie that 'the Ministry' (presumably Israeli) does not take Lieber seriously. He is in the grip of an obsession and when he speaks in Scene Five of the people who had suffered at the hands of the Nazis he starts the litany by saying "I want you to remember". Sometimes Lieber's speeches come across on the radio and we just hear his voice. In Scene Nine he intones a catalogue of those who died in the concentration camps but he cannot complete the descriptions. In *The Death of Tragedy* Steiner describes this kind of incident as one "under which language breaks".

> LIEBER: Four hundred and eleven thousand three hundred and eighty-one in section three at Belsen
> The one being Belin the tanner whose face they sprinkled with acid and who was dragged through the streets of Kershon behind a dung cart but sang
> The one being Georges Walter who when they called him from supper in the rue Marot spoke to his family of an administrative error and refused to pack more than one shirt and still asked why why through his smashed teeth when the shower door closed and the whisper began in the ceiling
> The one being all because unnumbered hence unrememberable

Because the number of deaths is so high, no one can count them and so, in a sense, they are unremembered. Lieber says that only if all the names of the victims were remembered and spoken they would spell the name of God; in other words, the only way to regain a belief in God is to make sure that the victims are not forgotten.

Lieber's voice is heard for the last time just before the makeshift trial of Hitler begins, reminding the audience of some of the atrocities he had previously described. At this point the radio is not switched on but Lieber's disembodied voice represents the search party's memories of what he has told them before.

Inadvertently Lieber glamorises Hitler. Even in his hatred he mythologises him: "It was he. None of the others could have done it. Not the fat bully, not the adder. He took garbage and made it into wolves." The making of Hitler into an other, a being from beyond, makes him seem as if he was possessed of some awesome power. But this is not true. The shocking thing about him is not his inhumanity, but his humanity.

The search for Hitler is like the search for Kurtz in Conrad's story 'Heart of Darkness', and Hitler, like Kurtz, exercises a terrifying power over the natives. But we cannot raise Hitler to the status of a mythic being and it is ducking the issue to console ourselves with the belief that he wasn't human. He *was* human, and so were all the people who helped him, or did nothing to stop him. It lets us off the hook to pretend otherwise.

The real fault of the play lies, as playwright Arnold Wesker said in an article in *The Times* on 20 March, in the attempt, whether conscious or not, to invest the Holocaust with a sense of inevitability. In Scene Three Gideon suggests carrying the frail Hitler back to civilisation on a hammock tied between two poles. "And dance before it?" Asher suggests, referring to the Ark of the Covenant in the Old Testament. The Ark of the Covenant was carried on two poles through the desert, and it represented the presence of God to the Jewish people. When entering into Jerusalem, King David danced before it as a symbol of triumph. At the end of Act One Gideon, ill with fever, shivers convulsively as if in an involuntary dance. But just as Hitler is a perverted travesty of God, so Gideon's helpless twitchings are a parody of a joyful dance.

While he is dying Gideon confides to Elie his suspicion that Hitler may have been Jewish. Although this is unlikely to be historically true, it is known that Hitler feared that he had some Jewish blood. Gideon feels that Hitler's supposed Jewishness explains his ability to organise the concentration camps. "How else could he have understood us so perfectly? How else could he know we would walk so calm into the fire?" he asks. This speech is based on the false idea that the Jews were mysteriously passive victims of the Holocaust. But they were no more passive than the other five million victims of the death camps, nor indeed than most victims of political terror. It is true that some Jews cooperated with the authorities, but so did many Gentiles, and there were many Jewish resistance fighters.

Gideon wonders if Lieber and Hitler are the same person. He thinks that they need each other to fuel their raging obsessions—Hitler's with anti-Semitism and Lieber's with discovering Hitler. Gideon seems to be hinting that if there wasn't a Hitler, Lieber would have had to invent him. His name, after all, is derived from the word 'love'—it is almost as if he loves Hitler. But there is no real comparison between the two men, not even superficially. Gideon's remarks might have passed muster as something Hitler said, but not something that an intelligent Jew would say, even when dying.

It is possible that Lieber has neglected everything else in his life in his obsessive quest but this doesn't make him the same as Hitler. Lieber wants justice, that is all. Hitler was not a figure of wish-fulfilment for the Jews. There was no deep-seated masochistic desire for suffering on their part and they did not accept it with weary resignation; the work of people like Simon Wiesenthal in bringing murderers to justice clearly displays that.

The main plot of *The Portage to San Cristobal of A.H.* is intercut with scenes that deal with the various reactions around the world to the news that Hitler has been found. The British refuse to believe that the man is really Hitler; the Russians once more interrogate a witness from the Berlin bunker; a German lawyer, Dr Röthling, says that trying Adolf Hitler now would be impossible and thinks that there has been too much fuss about the Holocaust; and the Americans and the French decide separately to ambush and murder the search party in order to avoid the re-opening of old wartime issues.

The setting for Scene Two is a familiar one for Hampton: the room of an Oxford don. Professor Sir Evelyn Ryder entertains two British intelligence men to sherry while dismissing the possibility that Hitler escaped from Germany at the end of the war. It is in this scene that we discover that the British having been listening in to the search party's radio signals. They have a man in Orosso ready to seize Hitler and his captors when they emerge from the jungle. Ryder speculates on the possibility that the man is a double whom Hitler had employed to impersonate him as the war progressed. However, this idea is not discussed by any of the other characters in the play, and later events show it to be an unlikely explanation.

The man working for the English in Orosso, Rodriguez Kulken, has to deal with Marvin Crownbacker, an American agent posing as a radio ham. The Americans have also picked up the search party's radio messages and have sent Crownbacker to deal with the situation. He eventually agrees with Kulken to kill the members of the search party and rescue Hitler. Kulken is keen to have Hitler to himself because he thinks that he can make a lot of money out of the media interest in him.

Hampton remained remarkably faithful to Steiner's original text. He dropped Dr Röthling's meditation on the timeless nature of music but managed to work in his own obsession with music and death by having Röthling playing Mahler. Scene Eleven begins with the passage from the last movement of Mahler's Second Symphony—the dialogue between the Last Trump and the Bird of Death—and ends with the Resurrection Ode from the same movement.

After Gideon dies of a fever the others realise that they may not make it out of the jungle so in the final scene they decide to hold their own trial of Hitler. Simeon is the judge, Elie reads the law, Amsel and an Indian who has been following the search party are the witnesses, and John is the reluctant counsel for the defence. But Hitler decides that he doesn't need a defender. Although he has barely spoken before, he now embarks on a twenty-five-minute speech that explains why he instigated the Holocaust.

This long monologue right at the end of the play has enormous dramatic impact, particularly when contrasted with Hitler's virtual silence up to this point. He launches into an articulate and passionate defence of himself. The power of his evil is obviously undimmed and we can now witness this directly for ourselves.

Hitler claims that he learned his apocalyptic approach from the Jews. He tells how he met a man named Jahn Grill in a dosshouse shortly before the first world war, who gave him the idea of a *Herrenvolk* by explaining the Jewish doctrine of the chosen people. The concept of *Lebensraum* was derived from Moses, who conquered heathen countries to create the Promised Land. And his cry of "ein Volk, ein Reich, ein Führer" echoed the Jewish demand for one religion under one God. Hitler's theory is that it was the harsh, uncompromising nature of their theology that made the Jews unpopular: "The Jew emptied the world by setting his God apart, immeasurably apart from man's senses. No image. No imagining even. A blank emptier than the desert. Yet with a terrible nearness. Spying on our every misdeed, searching out the heart of our heart for motive. A God of vengeance unto the thirtieth generation (these are the Jews' words, not mine)." His point is that, three times in history, the Jew has been responsible for "the call to perfection" which makes life insupportable. There was Moses' demand to end idolatry and worship the true God in the Old Testament; there was Jesus's call to endure persecution for righteousness' sake in the New Testament; and there was Karl Marx's demand for a secular apocalypse and a secular paradise to be built on earth. Hitler asserts that their high moral standards made the Jews unpopular and argues that non-Jews were relieved to think of them being permanently removed. This seems to echo the cynical Dr Relling in *The Wild Duck*, with his demand that mankind should be allowed to be peacefully mediocre and not have to live up to high ideals.

Steiner returned to this point in his book *In Bluebeard's Castle*. He describes the "nostalgia for barbarism" that often overtakes highly civilised societies: "In his exasperating 'strangeness', in his acceptance of suffering as part of a covenant with the absolute, the Jew became, as it were, the 'bad conscience' of Western history."

Hitler also offers as justification for his actions his opinion that Stalin committed worse crimes than he did, and claims that it was thanks to the Holocaust that the state of Israel was founded: the world wanted to do something to compensate the Jews after the end of the war.

At the end of the speech the Indian who has been brought in as a witness kneels before Hitler. He cannot understand the language but the power of oratory has transfixed him. We then hear the sound of helicopters: the search party has been located. The play ends here and although we don't know which of the world's powers is responsible for discovering them it is highly likely that they are all about to be murdered. It seems that even now Hitler's words can bring about destruction.

The Portage to San Cristobal of A.H. opened on 17 February 1982 at the Mermaid Theatre, starring Alec McCowen as Hitler. This role had originally been offered to Laurence Olivier but ill health had forced him to retire from the stage by this time. McCowen was supported by Benjamin Whitrow as Ryder, Sebastian Shaw as Lieber, Morgan Sheppard as Simeon, Bernard Kay as Gideon Benasseraf and Harry Landis as Elie Barach. The director was Peter Shaffer's regular collaborator, John Dexter.

The play met with some of the most angry notices of Hampton's career. In his article in *The Times* Wesker defended the Jews from the charge that they created what the play called the "bacillus of perfection". With Jesus, he countered, the Jews had created the "bacillus of mercy". Jesus's message of forgiveness and redemption had, he said, made the harsh demands of the Old Testament bearable. He also deplored the fact that the play seemed to offer such a fatalistic view of the Holocaust, as if it could not have been avoided.

Steiner's idea about the demand for perfection being at the heart of Jewish culture is not new. Neither is the call to perfection something to be ashamed of. As Nietzsche says in *Beyond Good and Evil*: "What Europe owes to the Jews?—Many things, good and bad, and above all one thing that is at once of the best and the worst: the grand style in morality, the dreadfulness and majesty of infinite demands, infinite significances, the whole romanticism and subliminity of moral questionabilities—and consequently precisely the most attractive, insidious and choicest part of those iridescences and seductions to life with whose afterglow the sky of our European culture, its evening sky, is now aflame—and perhaps burning itself up. We artists among the spectators and philosophers are—grateful to the Jews for this."

The historian and biographer of Winston Churchill, Martin Gilbert, was commissioned by David Nathan, then Drama Critic of the *Jewish Chronicle*, to write a riposte to the play. In his article (republished in *The Times* on 6 March) he complained that the piece made no mention of the millions of people who risked their lives sheltering Jews. He protested that when Hitler launched into his defence speech at the end of the drama the search party seemed to be "meek, mawkish schoolboys, caught out by the legacy of their own wrong-doing, and forced to listen to an unexpected but deserved rebuke". He also felt that Steiner's view of Churchill was unfair. The character Sir Evelyn Ryder claims that telling "the old man" about the gas-chambers wouldn't have done any good, and Bennett, a fellow-spy, agrees, saying that it was "not his kind of war". In fact Churchill was about the only world leader who did see the horror of what was happening and behaved honourably. Gilbert explained that Churchill demanded of Eden "Get anything out of the Air Force you can and invoke me if necessary." (Despite this order the camps were never bombed.) Gilbert's article was turned into a pamphlet and sold at the Mermaid Theatre during the play's run.

The critics had many reservations about the character of Hitler. In any drama, to give a charismatic villain centre-stage is to run the risk of inviting too much sympathy for the character, especially when the part is played with conviction by an actor as accomplished as Alec McCowen. The closing speech became something of a *tour de force* for McCowen, who would nightly receive cries of 'Bravo' from the audience. This led some reviewers to believe that it was not just the brilliant acting that was being applauded. It was as if the play, albeit inadvertently, had tapped into some undercurrent of popular anti-Semitism which, through the medium of drama, had gained the courage to express itself. Victoria Radin in the *Observer* said: "I think they [the cheers] were in some measure for Hitler as much as for McCowen. Steiner had brought Adolf Hitler back to life and crowned him again." And the point was perhaps further reinforced when McCowen went on to win the Evening Standard Award for Best Performance in a West End Play. Yet it is difficult to imagine a more obvious set of inverted commas to put around a speech than to put it in the mouth of Hitler. The play reminds us of what Hitler had done. When he claims to have been responsible for fewer deaths than Stalin the point is not contradicted because it is not relevant. Despite Radin's doubts there was no danger of arousing a wave of popular anti-Semitism. But Hitler's arguments are so obviously specious that little is achieved by allowing them to be heard for twenty-five minutes.

The Portage to San Cristobal of A.H. did get some good reviews: Milton Shulman, writing in the *Evening Standard*, found Hitler's monologue "a fascinating climax to a disturbing analysis of the nature of language, terror and revenge" and Michael Billington wrote in the *Guardian* that "in the end it is the ideas that make this an unmissable theatrical event". But it is more of a formal debate than a full-blooded drama and although the characters are sketched in deftly they don't come across as unique individuals. Hampton uses his dramatic skill to keep the play's momentum going but doesn't inject any of his own more personal concerns into the work, perhaps fearing to impose a pattern onto other people's suffering.

CHAPTER EIGHT

LES LIAISONS DANGEREUSES (1985)

> I've split up with enough people in the past, but it's always been a kind of ritual disembowelling. Never the guillotine.
>
> *Treats*

Hampton first told Peggy Ramsay that he was thinking of dramatising Choderlos de Laclos' epistolary novel *Les Liaisons Dangereuses* in 1975. She asked him so often when he was going to get on with it that it is said she finally grew to believe she had originally suggested the idea herself. Even though she hadn't, it is quite likely that it was her persistent bullying that made him finally get started. After a decade of mentally gearing himself up, he wrote the first draft in seven weeks. During this time Ramsay often gave him a nine o'clock alarm call to make sure he got out of bed and got on with it.

Hampton gave the Royal Shakespeare Company director Howard Davies a copy of the novel to read. " . . . sometime during my work on it he rang me up and pleaded: 'Are you sure you want to do this?'" Hampton said in an interview in *Time Out* in 1986. "I persuaded him that I did, so he said, 'OK, but do I really have to finish it!'" Whether he ever did get right to the end of the book or not, Davies managed to convince the RSC to take a gamble and to stage it at The Other Place in Stratford. One reason for the RSC's initial reluctance was that John Barton had directed his own adaptation of the novel as a rehearsed reading called *The Art of Seduction* in the 1960s, with Keith Michell and Diana Rigg, which had not been a great success.

For Hampton *Les Liaisons Dangereuses* was the "supreme example" of its genre. In an article published in the *Guardian* he wrote: "In a sense, Laclos' novel inaugurated that period of literature which has always meant the most to me, the period of Balzac, Stendhal and Flaubert with its ideals of objectivity and lucidity, characterised as a mirror travelling along a road (Stendhal) when the author's personality is missing (Flaubert)." He admired the work's "vigorously classical" qualities and wanted to recreate its remarkable blend of passion and detachment. Despite its frank depiction of sexual immorality the writing has, as he pointed out in an interview in the magazine *City Limits*, "an astringency so dry it anaesthetises any hint of pornography". He also added: "On the other hand it would be disingenuous to deny that the reason I went to see Roger Vadim's film *Les Liaisons Dangereuses* when I was 14 was because

I had heard it was extremely scandalous. I think it was rather disappointing in that respect."

The novel was a *succès de scandale* when it was first published in France in 1782. Laclos writes about people who are detached from love but without the work becoming cold, and he writes about passion without being sentimental. The main themes are those that often emerge in Hampton's work too. Both he and Laclos are interested in those who judge their lives by aesthetic rather than moral standards. Laclos' protagonists, the Vicomte de Valmont and the Marquise de Merteuil, are malicious charmers who take pleasure in causing harm to others. These are what Peter Quennell would call sexual snobs, the type of person he defines as "a power-addict disguised as a pleasure-lover".They manipulate the affairs of friends and rivals in order to humiliate them. To use Don's phrase in *The Philanthropist*, they enjoy "trying to make elegant patterns out of people's hopelessness".

Valmont and Merteuil emerge as two of the most accomplished conspirators in literature and the novel is almost a correspondence course in debauchery. Their schemes focus on two innocent victims. One is Cécile de Volanges, a fifteen-year-old convent-educated virgin, who is about to enter into an arranged marriage with Gercourt, an ex-lover of Merteuil's. The other is La Présidente de Tourvel, a young married woman of good character. Urged on by Merteuil, Valmont seduces both women and ultimately ruins their lives. Caught up in the plot are Valmont's servant, Azolan, who acts as a spy in the intrigues, and Cécile's true love, Le Chevalier Danceny, who is seduced and then betrayed by Merteuil. Cécile's mother, Mme de Volanges (who is also Merteuil's cousin), and Valmont's aunt, Mme de Rosemonde, are also unwittingly drawn into the conspiracies.

Laclos seemed to share Hampton's "fascination with consciencelessness", and the relationship between happiness and morality is a theme that interests them both. As Hampton has said, he often writes plays about people "who view life as a competition where they have to do other people down and emerge on top", and Laclos presented him with a perfect subject. We can even find a direct reference to the novel in the first version of *Total Eclipse*, where Verlaine compares his marriage to Mathilde with the relationship between Valmont and Cécile.

Hampton's main task was to make the novel work dramatically while preserving its essential character. Short of dramatising the *Tractatus Logico-Philosophicus* it is difficult to think of a work that presents a greater challenge, but he brought it off. He has always enjoyed solving elaborate technical problems and it appealed to him to adapt a book where the two main characters never meet. As Irving Wardle observed in his review for *The Times*,

" . . . just as Laclos shows his skill in devising ways of keeping people apart to write letters to each other, Hampton finds means of bringing them together".

The novel is structured with mathematical precision. It is divided into four sections: the first has fifty letters, the second and third both have thirty-seven and the fourth has fifty-one. Many dramatists would have been inhibited by such a rigid form but Hampton uses it as a support rather than a straitjacket. His play has two acts, each made up of three groups of three scenes, each trio of scenes covering a time-span of one month. Each group of three has two scenes taken from a variety of letters, plus what he described as "one interlude-like scene (always in second or third position) covering a single event, often in a bedroom, always featuring some form of single combat". He gives as an example the fourth and fifth scenes in the first act, which amalgamate twenty-five to thirty letters, while the rape of Cécile in Scene Six uses two.

The letters the characters write to each other still form an integral part of the plot and when they fall into the wrong hands they become weapons for blackmail and coercion.

Characteristically, Hampton imposes a mirror design on the play, which begins and ends with a card game between women. In the first scene Merteuil plays piquet with Mme de Volanges while Cécile looks on, and in the last scene Mme de Volanges and Merteuil play cards with Mme de Rosemonde. It is a powerful metaphor. Merteuil and Valmont see life as a game and they play to win and to be admired for winning.

In the first scene, Mme de Volanges and Cécile leave just after Valmont arrives and Merteuil proposes her scheme to take her revenge on her lover Gercourt, who has abandoned her. She wants Cécile deflowered and the deed made public after her marriage to Gercourt so that he will be humiliated as a cuckold. Valmont tells Merteuil that he has no interest in the plan as to take advantage of such an innocent young girl would present no challenge whatsoever. But he suggests that the pious Tourvel would be a different proposition altogether, saying, "To seduce a woman famous for strict morals, religious fervour and the happiness of her marriage: what could possibly be more prestigious?"

In this opening scene it is established that Merteuil and Valmont were once lovers and this creates a strong tension between them throughout the play. They are now co-conspirators but are not above deceiving one another and concealing the true motives for their actions. Their relationship is that of two grandmasters of sexual gamesmanship who like to compare notes and score points off one another. Merteuil carefully registers Valmont's reaction after she has made disparaging remarks about Tourvel:

VALMONT: Take care, now, you're speaking of the woman I . . .
MERTEUIL: Yes?
VALMONT: I've set my heart on.
(*Silence. He smiles at her.*)
I haven't felt so strongly about anything since you and I were together.

Merteuil is jealous and when she suspects that Valmont might be genuinely in love with Tourvel she fears that she will lose her hold over him. This realisation provides the driving force for most of her subsequent actions. For one of them to fall in love is against the rules and something she hadn't bargained on. As she reminds him, "Love is something you use, not something you fall into, like a quicksand, don't you remember? It's like medicine, you use it as a lubricant to nature." But she is able to turn the situation to her own advantage, at least to begin with. She sees that Valmont is determined to seduce Tourvel and so decides to offer herself as a reward if he can prove that he has succeeded. Her trump card is that she knows that Valmont is in love with Tourvel, while he doesn't yet realise it. She will see to it that he regards the seduction only as another of their elaborate games.

Laclos was familiar with the epistolary novels of Samuel Richardson (there is a reference in *Les Liaisons Dangereuses* to Tourvel's reading *Clarissa Harlowe*) and Valmont is the just the sort of unprincipled aristocrat that eighteenth-century readers would have met before. He is a remorseless philanderer for whom, like Don Juan, Casanova and Richardson's Robert Lovelace, the thrill is in the chase. He is more interested in his elaborate schemes for collecting lovers than in love itself.

Valmont, like Lovelace, is taken by surprise by love, but it is an emotion he feels compelled to destroy even though this means betraying the woman he loves. He first meets Tourvel while they are both staying at his aunt's house. Tourvel rejects his advances and tells him to leave, which he reluctantly does. He sends her many letters but she returns them all unopened. Mme de Volanges has written to Tourvel warning her of Valmont's reputation and when he sees this letter (stolen by his servant) he resolves to take his revenge by seducing Cécile after all.

On the pretext of offering to help Cécile continue her secret romance with Danceny he persuades her to give him the key to her bedroom so that he can get a copy made and act as a go-between for the couple without being suspected. But he uses the key to enter her room that very night. He warns her not to scream and threatens to tell her mother that she had given him her key. Hampton observed that at that point in the play "You can almost hear the audience change their minds."

Despite the fact that Cécile subsequently becomes Valmont's mistress, it is an act of rape because he has blackmailed her into submission. When she confides in Merteuil and tells her what has happened she is assured that Valmont's behaviour is normal and in her naivety she has no way of knowing this is not true. Valmont has aroused her sexuality but she is too inexperienced to suspect his motives. If Cécile were a saint she would have shouted for help and taken the consequences but, like most people, she is not heroic and so she keeps her experience a secret. And it is this secrecy that brings about her downfall.

In his introduction to the text of the play Hampton points out that Laclos believed in the education of women. If Cécile and Tourvel had not been so sheltered from the ways of the world they would have been better able to defend themselves. But although the novel as a whole can be seen as a feminist work Merteuil is not a feminist heroine. She is intelligent enough to see how women can fall victim to men's cunning and society's hypocrisies but, despite her claims to be avenging her sex, she is not above making other women suffer if it amuses her. She sees them either as rivals to be outwitted or as fools to be mocked. She acts in this way because her own character has been partially formed by the unjust treatment that men and society have meted out to her. "I often wonder how you managed to invent yourself," says Valmont, to which she replies, "I had no choice, did I, I'm a woman."

Valmont and Merteuil both pretend to be educators of the young; they refer to their malicious games with Cécile and Danceny as if they were lessons. When Cécile talks about how she was seduced Merteuil shows her no sympathy and says cruelly: "And am I to understand that what generally brings a girl to her senses has deprived you of yours?"

Valmont boasts to Merteuil that after he has finished with Cécile her future husband will have "a wife trained by me to perform quite naturally services you would hesitate to request from a professional". He treats Cécile as a pupil to be instructed in the art of sex. And he continues her tutelage when he dictates the love letters that she sends to Danceny.

If that part of Merteuil's plan is going well the other part is going very badly. Valmont has kept her informed of his campaign of seduction of Tourvel stage by stage but she remains singularly unimpressed by his slow rate of progress. He has returned to his aunt's house under the pretext of having urgent business in the area but Tourvel will not succumb to his advances. In the last scene of the first act she pleads with him to leave and then has a convulsive fit. Valmont places her on the chaise longue and begins to undress her but with the prize finally within his grasp he cannot bring himself to take advantage of her. Instead he calls his aunt, Mme de Rosemonde, for help, explaining that Tourvel has been taken ill. After he has left the room

Tourvel confesses her love to Mme de Rosemonde, who suggests that she should be grateful for this rare sign of mercy and return to Paris before Valmont has a chance to see her again.

Mme de Rosemonde has already guessed at what is happening between them. She is an old woman, full of experience, and her virtue has not blinded her to the ways of the world. She is unsurprised when Tourvel confesses that she loves Valmont, and says wisely: "The only thing which might surprise one is how little the world changes." Although she loves her nephew she is fully aware of his faults, and says "what is true of most men is doubly so of him". She explains to Tourvel that "those who are most worthy of love are never made happy by it". Tourvel is somebody who enjoys giving love, while men, says Mme de Rosemonde, only enjoy the love they feel. An unselfish nature like Tourvel's cannot hoard up pleasure but has to share it.

Ashamed that he has allowed Tourvel to escape, Valmont redoubles his efforts to conquer her. She has returned to her house in Paris but will not see him. He finally succeeds in gaining admittance by pretending that he wishes to be reconciled with her before entering into instruction with a priest. As soon as he is in her presence once more he makes the declaration that succeeds in melting her resolve: "I must have you or die." Like Don Juan he is able to seduce women by playing on their emotions and claiming to be willing to die rather than suffer rejection.

Tourvel may be high-minded but she is not a prig. She desperately fights her growing obsession with Valmont but finally gives in to him while her husband (never seen during the play) is away presiding over a court case in Burgundy. She blames herself for being tempted: "I know God is punishing me for my pride. I was so certain nothing like this could ever happen to me."

Valmont, hearing this, later echoes the sentiment: "What has happened is probably a just punishment for my presumption." Like Braham in *The Philanthropist* he is able to pick up other people's phrases and use them. But in playing the desperate lover he finally discovers that he is an actor who is playing himself.

Once Merteuil knows that Valmont has finally succeeded in seducing Tourvel she sets about destroying the relationship. She tells Valmont that the affair is making him a laughing stock and her remarks unerringly hit the target. As she explains to him towards the end of the play, after she has ended Valmont's affair, "You couldn't bear even the vague possibility of being laughed at. And this has proved something I've always suspected. That vanity and happiness are incompatible."

Valmont insists that his feeling for Tourvel is merely an infatuation that won't last, but he declares that for the moment "it's beyond my control". He doesn't yet realise that he has given Merteuil just the ammunition she needs.

Like him she also remembers other people's phrases and uses them later to her advantage. She tells him the story of a man she knew who felt that his infatuation with a woman was beyond his control. But finally, because he feared the ridicule of his friends, he broke with his mistress and answered all her questions with the phrase "It's beyond my control." Valmont later breaks with Tourvel in just this way, reducing her to a state of hysteria. In spite of her reaction his vanity gains the upper hand for although he is filled with regret for what he has done he is now able to boast to Merteuil that he has regained control of the situation. He tells her that he can win Tourvel back whenever he chooses. But Merteuil knows better.

> MERTEUIL: You see, I'm also inclined to see this as one of my greatest triumphs.
> VALMONT: There's nothing a woman enjoys as much as a victory over another woman.
> MERTEUIL: Except, you see, Vicomte, my victory wasn't over her.
> VALMONT: Of course it was, what do you mean?
> MERTEUIL: It was over you.

On the night that Merteuil tells him this she breaks her promise to sleep with him. And so she ends any chance of a relationship with him, having first ensured that he cannot have one with Tourvel. Valmont tells her that if she denies him his reward he will take it as a declaration of war. She concurs. The next scene shows Valmont preparing for a duel with Danceny. Merteuil has kept all the letters that Valmont had written to her in which he describes how he has used Cécile, and has shown the evidence to Danceny, knowing that he will demand his revenge. During the duel Valmont has a clear opportunity to kill Danceny but he draws back. Then, with apparent carelessness, he allows himself to be killed. It is thus suggested that Valmont's death is really suicide, or something very close to it.

In the final scene, as Merteuil is once again at the card table, we learn that Tourvel died of a fever after hearing of Valmont's death. Danceny has fled to Malta and Cécile, her reputation sullied, has returned to the convent to become a nun. Merteuil is left to face an uncertain future. She remains unpunished by society—she is still, on the surface, a respectable and pious woman—but she suffers inwardly. She is still intensely jealous of Valmont and Tourvel even though they are both now dead. She abruptly cuts off Mme de Volanges when she says that Tourvel was the only woman that Valmont ever loved, thus showing that she cannot bear the thought that she had been superseded in his heart. And, with the play's final speech, she suggests that they accept what the future may bring and continue with the game. But as she deals the cards, a silhouette of the guillotine briefly appears. This, it is implied, is what the future holds for her.

Hampton's main problem in writing the play was not the plotting but the style. In his *Guardian* article he explained how his first draft had become a pastiche of eighteenth-century dialogue while the second draft turned out to be too colourlessly modern. "Finally, at the third attempt, I hit a note which I then made every effort to sustain, a kind of language, artificial but tied to no period, elaborate but direct, the object of which was to mirror the novel's difficult combination of scientific detachment and perilous emotional extremes."

During a discussion on translation (printed in *Platform Papers*) at the Royal National Theatre in 1992 Hampton told the audience that when he was working on *Les Liaisons Dangereuses* he found it "much more liberating to adapt a French novel than it would have been to adapt an English novel of the period". He was able to take more liberties with the rhythms of Laclos' speech than he felt he would have been able to do with an English author although he made the characters in the play speak more formally than they do in the novel. His intention was to make them sound like people in eighteenth-century England. Their manners might be coarse and their morals questionable but their language is elaborate. He does occasionally allow the characters some bluntness. Merteuil questions Valmont after he has let Tourvel get away from him.

> MERTEUIL: Why did you let her escape?
> VALMONT: I was . . . moved.
> MERTEUIL: Oh, well, then, no wonder you bungled it.

This is hardly elegant and yet it works. Merteuil needs a vulgar-sounding word like 'bungled' to offend Valmont and deflate him.

The language Merteuil and Valmont use is riddled with innuendo. Just as they secretly corrupt people so they secretly corrupt language. The most sustained passage of double meaning occurs in Scene Three when Valmont writes a letter to Tourvel. He is in bed with a whore at the time and he uses her back to lean on for support while he is writing. He takes a malicious pleasure in stating only what is literally true—"I have just come to my desk" and "I hope one day you may feel the kind of disturbance afflicting me now"—confident that Tourvel won't guess his real meaning.

In Scene Eight when Valmont and Cécile are in bed for the second time he tells her: "As with every other science, the first principle is to make sure you call everything by its proper name." She must learn the "correct polite vocabulary", by which he means the language of sexual euphemism. "Now. I think we might begin with one or two Latin terms," he says.

Merteuil and Valmont also use terminology that combines military and sexual imagery, as when Merteuil talks of Tourvel's "defences being pierced". When she tells Valmont that she had to have him she says: "It's the only one of my notions has ever got the better of me. Single combat." This militaristic attitude leads to an inevitable conclusion: Merteuil's calm, emphatic declaration to Valmont—"War".

In his dramatisation Hampton pares down the roles of the innocent victims and concentrates on the plotters. It might be objected that in doing this the subsidiary characters are turned into puppets and that the villains are turned into heroes but the emphasis is on the conspirators as it is they who move the action along though we are never invited to condone the suffering they inflict on those around them.

One of Hampton's achievements is to subtly draw parallels between France in the 1780s and Britain in the 1980s and he offers us a clear comparison in Merteuil's closing speech, which ends the play: "A new year tomorrow and more than half-way through the eighties already. I used to be afraid of growing old, but now I trust in God and accept. I dare say we would not be wrong to look forward to whatever the nineties may bring."

Hampton departs from the novel somewhat at the very end. Laclos makes sure that Merteuil pays for her sins immediately and in the closing chapters we read of how she is forced to leave the country, having been exposed as a hypocrite. She is also penniless following the failure of a lawsuit, and her beautiful face has been disfigured by smallpox. By showing an image of the guillotine Hampton prepares a fate for Merteuil that takes account of developments in history. John Peter in the *Sunday Times* praised the changes, saying: "If anything, the ending flatters the novel by altering its starkly moralising conclusion." (When the play was performed in France, however, the director demanded that Hampton restore the original ending, complete with smallpox.)

Les Liaisons Dangereuses was first put on in 1985, when we were "half-way through the eighties". And apathy towards the poor, which will most probably soon destroy Merteuil, is a problem which is just as rife today. As in *The Philanthropist* and *Treats*, the characters are self-absorbed and scarcely notice the upheavals in the outside world, but this time we know that the outside world is going to catch up with them.

The play's epigraph emphasises the fact that the book is as relevant today as when it was written. It is from a 1969 essay by the French novelist and statesman André Malraux, which translates as: "As with many works of our own day—and not only literary works—the reader of *Liaisons* was in a position to say 'It can't go on like this'."

In the 1989 *City Limits* interview Hampton said: "These people are unchecked greed, that on the whole seems to be what's encouraged in this country over the last few years. People are familiar with the notion of people in power behaving badly—on the other hand the people in this country who behave badly have not got the excuse of charm. One of the things that the play and the film manage, which I had not foreseen, is that they seduce the audience into collusion; then they confront the audience with the implications of that collusion so that people start to feel bad."

Les Liaisons Dangereuses could be seen as the only genuine tragedy that Hampton has so far attempted. The deaths of West and Carlos in *Savages* are dwarfed by the mass slaughter of the Indians; the deaths of Heinrich and Nelly Mann in *Tales from Hollywood* exemplify how two people can be destroyed by a society to which they do not belong but neither of them has sufficient weight to be regarded as a tragic figure. And even though we see the self-destructive path that Rimbaud takes in *Total Eclipse*, in the end he is reconciled to God; his death is closer to martyrdom than tragedy. But Valmont and Merteuil are brought down by the flaws in their own characters. Their tragedy is a peculiarly modern one in that it is a tragedy of superficiality. They are afraid of true emotion and so cut themselves off from their deepest desires.

George Steiner, in his book *The Death of Tragedy*, says that to write tragedy one needs either to believe in God or to rage against his absence and by this criterion Hampton is not by and large a tragic writer. Greek tragedy tends to deal with men destroyed by a perverse and cruel universe and Elizabethan and Jacobean tragedy focuses on men who are destroyed by their own greed, lust and ambition. Many of Hampton's characters certainly have more than their fair share of these vices but, with the exception of Rimbaud, he does not see them in relation to God or fate. He finds, like Protagoras (as quoted by Plato in the *Theaetetus*) that man is the measure of all things. His main area of interest is how people relate to one another.

Hampton perhaps doesn't have the temperament to write tragedy. He has declared himself an optimist and even though many of his characters suffer terribly, the vigour of his dialogue seems to create at least the semblance of hope. Death (suicide, even) features in many of his plays but he doesn't often dwell on the nature of mortality. One obvious exception is in *The Philanthropist*, where Philip's awareness of death helps to give the play a universal quality that makes it his most successful comedy.

If Hampton is not much given to contemplating death neither does he spend much time analysing that other theme essential to tragedy: evil. The evil in *Savages* is generalised and belongs to a corrupt system rather than an individual, and his most evil character, the 90-year-old Hitler in *The Portage to San Cristobal of A.H.*, is reduced to a charismatic man with an unconvincing line in banal self-justification. *Les Liaisons Dangereuses* is the only play where Hampton successfully treats evil as a metaphysical reality rather than a manifestation of mere human selfishness or stupidity. Until then the most convincing portrayal he had created was in *Treats*. Dave's callous misogyny is unexplained yet entirely credible but as a study of true evil it comes nowhere near the controlled malevolence that Valmont and Merteuil display. Their evil becomes all the more shocking as we learn that because of vanity and pride they have trained themselves to destroy all vestige of feeling towards others. And Hampton doesn't soften or sentimentalise the damage that Valmont and Merteuil do. They live to cause pain, a point made in the first scene.

> VALMONT: I thought betrayal was your favourite word.
> MERTEUIL: No, no, cruelty, I always think that has a nobler ring to it.

Their intelligence is cut off from any useful or fulfilling purpose and so it turns in on itself, making them, under their calm facade, bitter and envious. Their cruelty has made their lives sterile. But Hampton never forces this point home, allowing it instead to emerge through the story and remorselesslessly showing the consequences of their determined pretence at indifference.

Hampton had originally planned a lot of scene changes in the play but was told by Howard Davies that at The Other Place in Stratford, where the play was first performed, it was not possible to move the chaise longue offstage as there was nowhere to store it except out of doors and he couldn't risk it getting soaked on a rainy night. Hampton overcame this problem by setting all his scenes indoors which meant that the designer could create a set that would, with some re-arrangement, suggest a number of different rooms. Davies assembled a brilliant cast. Alan Rickman as Valmont and Lindsay Duncan as Merteuil were both praised for their skill in balancing the cold-bloodedness and sensuality of their characters (Duncan won the Olivier Award for Best Actress), and they were ably supported by Juliet Stevenson as Tourvel, Fiona Shaw as Mme de Volanges, Lesley Manville as Cécile and Margery Mason as Mme de Rosemonde.

The critics were uniformly impressed. Michael Billington wrote in the *Guardian*: "Giraudoux described the book as 'the one French novel that gives us an impression of danger'. What Mr Hampton has done is turn it into an elegant comedy with the menace of a stiletto." David Coward in the *TLS* said: "His *Liaisons Dangereuses*, if inevitably underfleshed in its range of implications, is handsome and well-boned, and it captures the mood of the original novel quite brilliantly." In 1989 it was filmed as *Dangerous Liaisons.*

Hampton was bombarded with honours: the 1985 Plays and Players/ London Theatre Critics Best Play Award (shared with Howard Brenton and David Hare's *Pravda*), the 1986 Time Out Best Production Award, the 1986 Laurence Olivier Play of the Year Award, the 1986 Evening Standard Award for Best Play, and the 1987 New York Critics Circle Best Foreign Play Award all found their way onto his mantelpiece. They were well-deserved.

It has always been Hampton's belief that the theatre is "a strategy for dealing with the horrors of the world and that it should not pretend to console for things for which there is no consolation". The unsparing cruelty of *Les Liaisons Dangereuses* comes as a necessary antidote to the anodyne blandness of most modern drama and the play is a welcome reminder of an age that did not treat wickedness with fashionable admiration.

CHAPTER NINE

WHITE CHAMELEON (1991)

> I said: you mustn't cry because I'm leaving, I shall come back some time. Then one of them said: we are not sad for ourselves, that we shall be without you; we are sad for you, that you can bear to leave us. You see they look into your eyes and they know it all.
>
> *Savages*

Writers are often told to stick to what they know but, as Clive James once observed, that sort of advice is best reserved for people who shouldn't write at all. Hampton seems to have agreed with this sentiment for none of his plays had been remotely autobiographical until he produced *White Chameleon*. His childhood had been so extraordinary, however, that eventually he felt he had to make use of it. As a boy of ten, living in Alexandria at the time of the Suez crisis, he was, for the only time in his life, right at the heart of a major event in political history. As he said on the *South Bank Show* in 1989, Suez was "a subject which has lain in wait for me".

It was Richard Eyre, the Artistic Director of the Royal National Theatre, who finally prompted Hampton to write the play. Eyre had originally approached him and David Hare to develop separate plays dealing with the political situation in 1956. Hampton was to have written about the Suez crisis and Hare was asked to tackle the Hungarian uprising. But Hare pulled out, saying that he couldn't find anything to say about the situation. Similarly, Hampton couldn't find what he wanted in the Suez crisis itself—he thought that there was nothing to add to the already well-documented story of monumental British incompetence—but his own personal recollection of the events of the period made him think about writing something more personal.

Drawing directly from his own memories was a new and uncertain experience for him. "It made me feel very raw doing it," he said, "and I was sort of nursemaided along by Richard Eyre because I was very, very nervous and he kept looking at it when it was in progress and being encouraging." He found that "rehearsing it and seeing it put on was one of the most satisfying things I've ever done".

The play begins in 1956 aboard an ocean liner bound for England. The central character, Chris, aged ten, is teaching the Egyptian cross-Channel swimming team their new national anthem, known as the liberation hymn.

Hampton explained in an interview with Mark Lawson in the *Independent* Magazine that the liberation hymn was already three years old in 1956 and so the real team would almost certainly have known it. "But I'm hoping no one will notice," he said.

After the opening scene the action moves back to 1952 and deals with the events leading up to the boy's evacuation and the beginning of a new life in England. Chris and his family live in Alexandria, where his father, an affectionate and reassuring figure, is Chief Engineer for Cable and Wireless.

The story is narrated by the adult Chris, now called Christopher, and the actor playing him takes a double role. When he is wearing spectacles he is Christopher and when he takes them off he becomes his own father. (Hampton had earlier used this device in his television play *Able's Will*, where the same actress plays Able's wife, May, in flashback, as well as his daughter, Kate.)

The pivotal relationship in *White Chameleon* is in fact between Chris and Ibrahim, the family servant. Ibrahim is loyal to his British employers but as an Egyptian he has no more status or authority in the household than a child, and Chris treats him like an older brother who can explain the workings of the adult world to him. The characters of Chris's parents are deliberately rather shadowy figures and this has the effect of placing the boy at the centre of the action though he cannot fully understand what is going on. To emphasise that this is not entirely an autobiographical play, they are referred to in the playtext as Christopher's Father and Christopher's Mother instead of by their real names. But Hampton did dedicate the play to his father, who died in 1965 (a year before *When Did You Last See My Mother?* was staged).

The young boy Chris and the adult Christopher can only loosely be identified with Christopher Hampton the writer. One of the play's epigraphs is taken from Albert Camus' 1950 essay 'The Enigma'. It reminds us that "even if a writer does happen to put himself in the picture, it is only very exceptionally that he talks about what he is really like". Hampton has used his life as raw material and fashioned it into art and, as he explains in an afterword to the published text, the events in his play are not all strictly autobiographical.

The play's other epigraph is taken from 'The God Abandons Antony' by C.P. Cavafy, who wrote in Greek and spent his life in Alexandria. The poem is based on the myth that tells how the god Hercules abandons Mark Antony to his fate just before the Battle of Actium in 31 B.C., and ends:

> listen — your final pleasure — to the voices,
> to the exquisite music of that strange procession,
> and say goodbye to her, to the Alexandria you are losing.

This desertion is symbolised by the sound of beautiful music in the heavens. (There is also a scene depicting this in Shakespeare's *Antony and Cleopatra*.) Mark Antony loses the battle and kills himself shortly afterwards.

Cavafy alters the legend so that it is Alexandria herself who is leaving Antony. In these circumstances, the poet advises stoicism and gratitude, not cowardice, guilt or self-deception, because sooner or later all of us must lose our Alexandria.

In *White Chameleon* Christopher explains the poem and tells the audience that people with roots take them for granted while people without them feel the loss "like some phantom ache in an amputated limb". (Hampton's literary hero Horváth was also born into what he referred to as "the half life of exile".)

The rootlessness that Christopher feels is symbolised by the chameleon that lives in his family's garden in Alexandria. The chameleon, of course, can change its colour. Christopher says that it is probably a myth that it does this to blend in with its surroundings. But the image is a useful one. It sums up his status as someone who grew up without a fixed home, who had to adapt to whatever environment he found himself in.

It takes Chris some time to learn the art of camouflage. When he is in Egypt he is bullied by Egyptian classmates for being one of the "filthy British". In England, when there is a widespread rumour of imminent revolution in Egypt, he is taunted as a foreigner by the other children at his prep school. Whichever country he is in Chris is always an outsider. When the family returns to Egypt, thinking that the threat of war has passed, he settles into a school where he is happy. But he is evacuated to England again in 1956, this time permanently, and is unpopular at school for being a 'wog-lover'. He gradually learns to keep quiet about his love of Egypt and, like a chameleon, begins to blend into his background. Later, as an adult, he acknowledges just what a formative experience it was to have been bullied by both sides for being different: " . . . these symmetrical assaults made a valuable contribution to my political education," he says. "I've been wary of every known brand of confident certainty ever since."

This scepticism pervades all of Hampton's work: his belief is that anyone who puts forward a simple solution to any political problem is either "a knave or a fool".

Ibrahim too has problems with conflicting types of certainty. He has two wives (they don't appear on stage) who are divided over politics. One is fervently pro-British but the other is pro-Nasser. Ibrahim tells Chris that they have frequent arguments. His comments feed into the debate in the play about colonialism and its effects. Chris's father is a decent, liberal man but he is a still a representative of the ruling powers and looks upon the Egyptians with the degree of paternalism that was customary when Britain ruled the world. The ugly face of imperialism is portrayed through the character of Albert Etheridge, a brutal man who mistreats his half-Egyptian son Paul.

In both *Savages* and *Tales from Hollywood* Hampton presents a running discourse between a liberal (West or Horváth) and a radical (Carlos or Brecht). In *Savages* the argument is tilted slightly in favour of the radical and in *Tales from Hollywood* the bias is towards the liberal, but neither side is shown to have the monopoly on the truth. In *White Chameleon* there is no radical figure and Hampton is concerned to pay tribute to his family and friends in a more personal way. The collapse of imperialism does have a bearing on the action of the play but its effects are demonstrated rather than discussed.

The political events leading up to the Suez crisis are filtered through the eyes of Chris as a child. On Black Saturday, a day of anti-English rioting following the massacre of some auxiliary policemen in Ismalia by British troops, he is upset that his birthday party is spoiled because his guests have to go home early. While his parents discuss the possibility of their being evacuated he is more interested in imitating James Dean in *East of Eden*. (Hampton's love of the cinema obviously dates from an early age.)

One piece of writing about childhood that inspired Hampton was a short piece by Kafka called 'Up in the Gallery'. This story, only a couple of paragraphs long, describes a boy at a circus. He sees an acrobat riding a horse and feels that if only there were some physical sign of her or the animal being mistreated he could protest. But both seem perfectly content and the ringmaster seems to care for them; so the boy simply lays down his head and weeps. He is unable to articulate his instinct that some awful cruelty is being hidden from him. Chris, in the way children often do, senses that something terrible is going on but he cannot get anyone to explain it to him. When he asks Ibrahim what 'colonialism' means, the question is brushed aside. "Means you talking to the wrong people," he is told. Chris's father doesn't shed much more light on the matter: "Well . . . " he says, "it's to do with colonies. Some countries, like Britain, for various historical reasons, control other countries and colonialism is a . . . not particularly polite word to describe that position."

Colonialism is a subject that Hampton has returned to repeatedly. *Savages, The Honorary Consul, The Wolf at the Door* and his as yet unperformed television play, *The Price of Tea*, catalogue the various disasters that have befallen those countries unlucky enough to have been colonised by European powers.

Chris begins to find out for himself what colonialism means. The headmaster of his English boarding school warns him that he should not be criticising the fact that the RAF are bombing Alexandria. Chris is forced to watch his beloved tarboosh being burned. "This may seem harsh," the headmaster says, "but when you're older, I'm sure you'll understand that there are very good reasons behind what I've done." It is a painful lesson, for Ibrahim had given him the tarboosh as a going-away present and it had powerful and symbolic associations with his childhood identity and was his last link with Egypt. (Hampton took this incident from real life but it actually happened to his older brother, Robert, who does not feature in the play.)

By this time Chris has discovered the consolation to be found in writing. He is given a homework assignment to write a play entirely without words—an experiment that Hampton would probably not care to repeat in his professional life. Ibrahim helps him by thinking of a plot about three robbers who fall out. They all meet violent deaths, one of them being bitten by a snake. He makes Chris a pastry snake as a prop, but is not pleased to hear later that it was broken during the play's performance. Chris's next play is the first of many literary dramatisations, and his future interest in emotional extremes is hinted at in his choice of material. He takes Edgar Allan Poe's story 'The Telltale Heart' as his source material. He shows his efforts to Ibrahim, his first literary critic, who is not impressed by the plot but is struck by the image of the murder victim's heart beating under the floorboards. Ibrahim himself has a weak heart, which is not helped by his habit of helping himself to the household's drinks. "But one thing is always tempting me to be a Christian," he tells Chris, "the whisky."

Chris's introduction to live theatre is the school production of Ibsen's *An Enemy of the People*. He is shocked to see some boys heckling Stockmann during a scene set at a public meeting, not realising at first that they have been deliberately planted in the audience to add realism to the proceedings. It makes him aware of just how powerful the theatre can be. Ibsen remains one of Hampton's strongest influences.

Having discovered the excitement of theatre, Chris also develops his feeling for language. On the *South Bank Show* Hampton recalled his experience of Alexandria as a multilingual city. "You'd often be talking to someone who'd begin a sentence in English and they'd finish it in French," he said. Chris's own transformation into a polyglot is gradual. He explains to his friend Paul Etheridge that he had once mistranslated the French word 'blessure' as 'blessing', not knowing that it meant 'wound'. And so he had translated a sentence as "The soldier's blessing is bleeding slowly." Hampton develops this image later on in the play when Christopher talks about his father's attitude to writing: "Becoming a writer suggested to him some kind of an adventure, he envisaged such a vocation as a blessing; whereas my French lessons had alerted me to the idea that it was far more likely to be a wound."

Chris's French lessons will lead him ultimately to the darkness of Verlaine and Rimbaud, but it is with Paul that he suffers his first really horrifying experience. The two boys are left to play together and for want of anything better to do Chris starts to climb up the stairs on the outside of the bannisters, encouraging a reluctant Paul to join him. Halfway up Paul freezes in fear. Chris, who is ahead, cannot climb past him to get back to the ground, so they have to shout for help. It is Paul's father, Albert, who rescues them and he takes Paul into another room to beat him. Chris feels responsible for his friend's predicament yet cannot stop himself from looking on through the open door. He has already begun to learn that to be a writer means to be a witness, maybe even a parasite, on other people's pain.

Paradoxically, Hampton's innate distrust of the process of writing means that he is always writing about writers. Time and again—in *Total Eclipse*, *The Philanthropist*, *Savages*, *Able's Will*, *Tales from Hollywood*—he is drawn back to the problem of what art, and especially writing, can achieve. In *White Chameleon*, however, we see someone at the beginning of an artistic career rather than at the end. Christopher remembers with affection the help and encouragement he received when he was young. His father, although his taste is for Sir Arthur Conan Doyle and Robert Louis Stevenson rather than Flaubert or Laclos, startles him by approving of his ambition, though without realising just how much it means to him: "Out in the desert was a statue of Memnon that was sometimes heard to sing: but only as the sun went down," says Christopher. "I could tell that was how it would be. And when my father spoke of seeing the light, I knew that wasn't it. I saw the darkness."

This scene is one of the most elegiac that Hampton has written. It is reminiscent of the final scene in *Total Eclipse* where Verlaine dreams of the Rimbaud he once knew, as the sun goes down. In *White Chameleon* Christopher is thinking of the Alexandria that he has lost and it is the interior darkness now that makes him write.

As the political situation in Egypt worsens, Chris and his mother are evacuated back to England, this time for good. His father, having been held under house arrest by order of Nasser for some weeks, is suddenly given twenty-four hours to get out of the country. He warns Ibrahim that he should leave immediately as well, as anti-British feeling is running high. But Ibrahim stays on. While he is in the house he hears, like Mark Antony, "a strange sound, like a burst of exquisite music" as if he too is destined to lose his Alexandria. He stands in the fading light, ready to face the looters who are breaking into the house.

White Chameleon opened at the National Theatre on 14 Febuary 1991, right in the middle of the Gulf War. This gives an added resonance to the line in the play explaining that whenever Chris's father was about to receive a new posting he used to pray " . . . please God, don't make it the Persian Gulf." As Hampton pointed out in an interview with Mark Lawson in the *Independent* Magazine, it was "an odd sort of time to be discussing a pro-Arab play". Rehearsals, he added, had been grave affairs, as the cast included Jordanian, Kurdish and Egyptian actors. Tom Wilkinson doubled as Christopher and Christopher's Father, Saeed Jaffrey was Ibrahim, and David Birkin was Chris. Stephen Boxer, who had played Alfons in Hampton's translation of Horváth's *Faith, Hope and Charity*, was the repulsive Albert Etheridge.

The press response to the play was not very enthusiastic. Hampton was accused of wallowing in "personalised nostalgia" while the Middle East destroyed itself. He has always suspected all writers, including himself, of self-indulgence. But in the midst of crises it is essential to remember that people are not just part of the political scene but have their own lives. Hampton now accepts that self-indulgence is a writer's occupational hazard. When Chris rejects Ibraham's suggestion that he should go into politics, we feel that Hampton is speaking for himself, with his customary sense of irony:

> CHRIS: I'm not going to be Prime Minister, Ibrahim, I couldn't be Prime Minister, even supposing I wanted to be.
> IBRAHIM: No. You want to write stories.
> CHRIS: That's right.
> IBRAHIM: Yes. Is much better job than the buggering up everybody's life.

In spite of the cool critical reception, *White Chameleon* certainly struck a chord with many members of Hampton's audience. He has received more mail in connection with this play than with any other he has written, mostly from people who themselves have lived in the colonies. He was very touched by the stories they told: "One man wrote to me about how he'd been a child at the time of partition in India, and once came home from school to find his servant, who he'd been particularly fond of, had been beheaded and his head was in the front garden."

In his final speech Christopher pays tribute to to the family's loyal servant: "As for Ibrahim, I never found out what became of him, but all my life I've heard his faulty old heart, beating under the floorboards."

Hampton largely avoids the sentimentalism of many childhood reminiscences and the play, though slight, gives off an agreeable charm. But something of the dramatic tension is lost by having Christopher casually walking on stage and telling us what he learned from the events just seen. He becomes a sort of buffer between the action and the audience and this is too consoling. It takes away the immediacy of the young Chris's happiness or pain and so lowers the emotional temperature.

In *Tales from Hollywood* Hampton uses a narrator to try and make sense of what is going on as it is happening but in *White Chameleon* Christopher displays no uncertainty and so seems invulnerable. Yet the play lingers in the memory as a record of the end of childhood and the end of imperialism. Hampton shows that the decline of empires can be detected in small personal details as well as in national conflicts.

CHAPTER TEN

SUNSET BOULEVARD (1993)

Ah, Hollywood! The kitsch! The *désespoir*!

Tales from Hollywood

Hampton had long hoped to turn *Sunset Boulevard* into an opera and as the plot is about a star who doesn't know when to retire an operatic treatment seems singularly appropriate. As he wrote in an article in the *Daily Telegraph* in 1993: " . . . with its larger than life characters, its mood of hermetically sealed nostalgia and its emotional extravagance [it] was perfectly suited to musical adaptation."

The original film was directed in 1950 by Billy Wilder from a script that he wrote in collaboration with Charles Brackett and D.M. Marshman Jnr (who provided the scenario). It begins with the image of a man floating face-down in a swimming pool. He turns out to be a young writer called Joe Gillis. In one continuous flashback, Joe, played by William Holden, tells the story of the events that led up to his violent death.

A few months before, while on the run from the repo-men who were trying to repossess his car, he had pulled into the drive of a house on Sunset Boulevard. He discovers that the occupant is Norma Desmond, a once famous star of silent films who is now a recluse. The only other person living there is an elderly servant named Max.

In Wilder's film Norma is played by Gloria Swanson, then in her early fifties, who was herself a screen idol of the silent era. Norma dreams of making a comeback, and because he is short of money Joe agrees to look over the unfilmable script she has written for her return performance. He is drawn into a relationship with her. But she finds out that he is working on another screenplay with a young scriptwriter, Betty Schaefer. Too late, Joe tries to walk out on Norma. In a fit of jealous rage she shoots him. The plot is the stuff of melodrama but with Wilder's sure directorial touch and outstanding performances from Swanson and Holden, a cinematic masterpiece was created. It won an Academy Award for best script and a nomination for best picture.

Oddly enough, although she had never sung professionally, Swanson wanted to reprise her role in a stage musical but Paramount Pictures refused to release the rights. Although this seems curmudgeonly of them it is doubtful whether such a venture would have been successful, especially as Swanson believed that the musical would have to have a happy ending.

Through his friend Tim Rice (another alumnus of Lancing) Hampton first met Andrew Lloyd Webber in the early 1970s and was offered the chance to write the book for *Jesus Christ, Superstar*. He turned it down as he decided they didn't need a book, and the show went ahead without one. But in 1984 he and Lloyd Webber were having lunch together and discovered that both shared an ambition to turn *Sunset Boulevard* into a musical and agreed that they should work on the idea together. Lloyd Webber was working on his musical version of *Phantom of the Opera* at the time and Hampton told him that it would probably be a disaster at the box office.

Hampton had steered clear of musicals until then although he had had plenty of opportunities. There was a proposal for a show based on the life of Henry VIII, another adapted from a lesser known book by Nabokov, a musical version of Baroness Orczy's *The Scarlet Pimpernel*, and one about the life of a Venetian castrato. And he had already made one unsuccessful attempt to turn *Sunset Boulevard* into an opera. In the early 1980s he had met the composer David Pountney to discuss the possibility of writing a work based on the film for the English National Opera, but the project was abandoned when Paramount once again withheld permission to use the material. It was only when Lloyd Webber, a composer and producer with a sufficiently impressive track record, approached the studio that the rights were finally released.

So, in spite of several near misses, Hampton was new to musicals when he started work on the book and lyrics of *Sunset Boulevard*. His collaborator was Don Black, a man with a proven reputation, who had written lyrics for composers such as Jules Styne, Elmer Bernstein and John Barry, and who first worked with Lloyd Webber on the song cycle 'Tell Me on a Sunday'.

The book to *Sunset Boulevard* is devotedly faithful to the original screenplay, with an estimated 75% of the dialogue taken directly from the movie, though Hampton admits that it was impossible to recreate the somewhat unsettling feeling that the film evokes with its casting of genuine silent stars whose fame had faded. Lloyd Webber ideally wanted a former musical comedy star like Jessie Matthews for the role of Norma but found that there were none still around who were suitable.

Swanson, playing an actress who hadn't worked since the silent days, was an actress who had scarcely worked since the silent days. One scene in the movie shows her playing bridge with Buster Keaton, Anna Q. Nilsson (a silent star whose career had been cut short by a riding accident) and H.B. Warner (the man who had played Christ in Cecil B. De Mille's *King of Kings*).

De Mille also appears as himself. He had directed some of Swanson's greatest successes and in the film he explains that he had directed some of Norma's,

Erich von Stroheim, the man responsible for such films as *Greed* and *Foolish Wives*, played Max von Mayerling, Norma's ex-husband and former director, reduced now to working as her butler. When Norma watches one of her old movies, the extract we see is from *Queen Kelly*, the massively expensive unfinished project directed by Stroheim and starring Swanson. Stroheim's erratic directing career effectively ended when Swanson finally sacked him from that film in 1928 and shooting was abandoned.

Hampton and Black's book also follows the chronology of events in the film. It opens with Joe's body being discovered by the police. (As in *Tales from Hollywood* a lighting effect is used to suggest the rippling water of the swimming pool.) Joe then begins to narrate the story. The first act has fourteen scenes altogether and ends with the New Year's Eve party where Norma tries to commit suicide.

In the beginning we see how Joe is rejected by Hollywood. The song 'Let's Have Lunch' is sung by the chorus as they dash from place to place at the Paramount Studios looking busy and important. Joe is isolated in this crowd of successful film people and cannot get to have lunch with anyone. When he tries to interest a producer in his screenplay, Betty Schaefer is called in and she tells him that the script is weak and derivative.

Only the two men sent to repossess his car show any interest in him and when they catch up with him at the studio he drives off and they follow him. The chase, which plays such an important part in the movie, is projected onto a screen on stage, ending at the point where Joe manages to shake his pursuers off by pulling into the driveway of the house on Sunset Boulevard.

Joe is invited in because he is mistaken for the undertaker who has been called to bury Norma's pet monkey. She allows Joe to stay when she hears that he is a writer. A funeral is duly held for the monkey and during the service Joe hears the sound of the wind blowing through a disused organ somewhere in the house. The idea of the wind as a force for melancholy has occurred before in Hampton's work. In *Able's Will* Able finds sadness in the sound of the wind and in *White Chameleon* the wind that blows through the statue of Memnon creates strange music.

Norma's importance as a star is established with her solo 'With One Look', which refers to the famous line of dialogue from the movie: "We didn't need dialogue in my day—we had faces then." This is reinforced by Max's song in the next scene, 'The Greatest Star of All'. He sings this as he is showing Joe to the room he will be sleeping in. Norma has invited him to stay so that he can read the screenplay she has written for her comeback performance.

When Joe reads Norma's script he knows that it is unusable but he figures that he can string her along and make money out of her by offering to act as a rewrite man. As his stay at the mansion lengthens, however, he begins to feel trapped. Max has moved all his possessions from his apartment to the house and has allowed the repo-men to take his car.

In spite of his misgivings about the situation Joe decides to go along with it, though with increasing unease. His contradictory emotions are expressed in the duet 'The Lady's Paying', which they sing in the scene where Norma insists on buying him new clothes. He protests at first but then gives in to her. The chorus of salesmen echo his decision with lyrics that say that he might as well take all that he can get because, after all, the lady is paying.

The climax to Act One comes with two New Year's Eve parties that Joe attends. At the first one he is horrified to discover that Norma has hired an orchestra and ordered champagne but has invited no other guests. The duet that they sing at this point, 'The Perfect Year', expresses Norma's mistaken belief that Joe will stay with her for ever. He flees as soon as he can to the house of his friend Artie Green, an assistant director, who is holding a cheerful, crowded party for all the underemployed writers and actors he knows. In this scene everyone sings 'This Time Next Year', which expresses their hopes and dreams for the future. They may be deluding themselves but they are the normal delusions of people who cannot afford to stop hoping. Norma's delusions are far more absurd. She believes that she can still play a sixteen-year-old ingénue and that she can still have a young boyfriend.

Just as everyone is preparing to sing 'Auld Lang Syne' at Artie's, Max phones to say that Norma has slit her wrists so Joe returns to the house on Sunset Boulevard.

At the beginning of Act Two it is clear that Norma has succeeded, for the time being at least, in luring Joe back into her bizarre ménage. To begin with things seem more hopeful for them both. The house is cleaned up and the swimming pool is brought back into use. But Joe's solo at this point in the action, the title song of the musical, expresses his misgivings about his situation. He sings of having to "Kiss someone's wife / Kiss someone's ass" in order to get ahead in his career. (It is not unknown for composers to borrow material from their own work and for this song Lloyd Webber re-uses a tune from an instrumental piece that he had first composed for Stephen Frears' 1971 film *Gumshoe*. It is featured during the scene where Albert Finney, playing a bouncer turned private eye, is saying goodbye to Billie Whitelaw at a railway station.) Norma, on the other hand, sings a reprise of 'A Perfect Year' to show that her dreams are still intact.

When Paramount contact her and ask her to call in at the studio she thinks that they have accepted her script and want to talk to her about the movie. She meets Cecil B. De Mille, her old director, on the lot. He is glad to see her and treats her with respect but can't bring himself to tell her that he won't be using her screenplay. Norma sings 'As If We Never Said Goodbye', which expresses her belief in herself and her ability to recapture the audience that hasn't seen her on screen for over twenty years.

De Mille later discovers that the studio had called Norma not to discuss her script but because they wanted to borrow her car, a rare and expensive model from twenty years before, to use in another movie. Norma is unaware of this and she prepares for her comeback with a regime of diets, exercise and massage, and illustrated by the song 'Eternal Youth is Worth a Little Suffering' in Scene Four.

In the meantime Joe starts slipping out at night to meet Betty. She has found an earlier script of his that she thinks has possibilities and they begin to rewrite it together. And although Betty is engaged to Artie Green she and Joe become lovers. They know what they doing is deceitful but, as their song says, they are 'Too Much in Love to Care'.

Norma's suspicions are aroused when she finds a phone number in Joe's jacket and she calls Betty anonymously telling her to come to the house. Betty arrives to discover the true state of affairs and she and Joe sing a reprise of 'Sunset Boulevard', which reiterates the bitter view of life in Hollywood. Their relationship is at an end but it is Joe, with a desire for self-punishment, who finishes it. He guesses that it was Norma who had exposed him and in revenge he tells her that the studio had no intention of using her script, they just wanted to borrow her car. On top of that he tells her that he is leaving for good. Norma becomes hysterical and as he prepares to go she says 'Nobody ever leaves a star', points a pistol at him and shoots him three times. He staggers out of the house and falls. The rippling lights indicate that he has toppled into the swimming pool.

In the last scene the police arrive but Norma, by now quite mad, believes that the crowd of people in her living room are an enthusiastic film crew. In her mind the glorious comeback is about to begin. She makes a majestic entrance down her magnificent staircase and delivers the film's famous final line: "And now, Mr De Mille, I'm ready for my close-up." The show ends with a reprise of 'The Greatest Star of All', which Max and Norma sing as a duet.

The musical is fine as a West End or Broadway spectacular but it doesn't take on an independent life of its own: it works simply as a tribute to a classic movie. It is like a photograph of a great statue—although the contours and the proportions may be right it is still only a copy. When Norma says "I am big. It's the pictures that got small", there is a laugh of recognition from the audience but the statement has lost something of its original irony. What was once an indignant protest made by a proud woman has become a parody of itself and a sort of in-joke. Hampton's version of *Les Liaisons Dangereuses* doesn't refer back to its source in a such a knowing way. It works as a piece of theatre because while it takes its plot and its astringent tone from another medium it creates its own atmosphere and its own dynamic. *Sunset Boulevard* doesn't find any significant modern parallels for its story and so remains a pleasant excercise in nostalgia.

Lloyd Webber, who has often been accused of being crassly commercial, does show a genuine desire to take risks and explore new areas. Musicals about an Argentinian dictator's widow (*Evita*), or the work of the largely forgotten David Garnett (*Aspects of Love*), were hardly rock-solid certainties at the box office. He is often unfairly pilloried, but it remains true that his work is marred by a tendency to easy sentimentality. Songs like 'Don't Cry for Me Argentina' or 'Tell Me on a Sunday' are sung by innocent victims who are determined to let you know how noble they are.

In *Sunset Boulevard* this tendency is checked by the plot; Norma is a murderess and Joe a hustler. When, at the New Year's Eve party, Norma sings 'A Perfect Year', her love song to Joe, the piece gains resonance because we know that she is deceiving herself. There is more pathos in this scene than there is in the movie; Norma subsides into tears on stage as if realising for a moment how vain her illusions are, whereas in the film she simply runs away. The music is melodic but the spectre of self-indulgence still hovers behind Lloyd Webber's elaborate orchestrations.

As far as Hampton and Black's script is concerned, they have made small changes to the screenplay that put a new angle on a line. When Norma calls Betty to warn her of Joe's infidelity, the film version has her saying "You can bet that he doesn't live with his relatives". In the musical she says "I can guarantee you. He doesn't live with mother", which underlines the irony that he is living with a woman old enough to be his mother.

In the musical Joe's relationships with Norma and Betty are both more obviously sexual. Film censorship in America in the 1950s would have prohibited Wilder from showing Joe's role as a gigolo explicitly but he does give hints. Hampton's treatment of course means that Norma's reactions are wholly justified and are a straightforward matter of one woman feeling jealous because another has stolen her man. In the film her hysterical rage is seen as another symptom of her paranoia.

Hampton and Black, having the benefit of hindsight, add some jokes that indicate the way that Hollywood was to develop after 1950. As in the film, the producer Sheldrake explains that he had turned down *Gone with the Wind*, but a later phone call is added where he says: "Brando? Brando? Take it from me, nobody wants to see that Brando kid."

There are links too between the plot of *Sunset Boulevard* and Hampton's own preoccupations as a writer. Not only is Joe a dead writer, like Thomas Able, John in *The Philanthropist* and Horváth in *Tales from Hollywood*, he is also one who becomes "irredeemably bourgeois". Early on Betty criticises his clichéd screenplay but softens the blow by telling him that some of the magazine stories he had published were good. "This year I felt like eating," is his laconic response. He mocks her as "one of the message kids" because she thinks that a film should "say a little something". Betty is shocked when he announces that he won't be writing any more because he no longer needs the money. But his rejection of his own talent brings about his downfall. If he had acted with responsibility as an artist as Betty does, and had put up with the hardship that being a writer entailed, he wouldn't have been drawn into the situation that finally costs him his life.

The theme of the writer losing touch with his talent is a common one in American literature. The pressures to be successful are strong everywhere, but in the USA, as Horváth points out in *Tales from Hollywood*, "it is difficult to be poor with dignity".

American writers, reacting against the country's culture of success, often view wealth as a sort of seduction that destroys talent and integrity. That sort of story usually features an idealistic writer and a tempter, often in the shape of a studio head (Budd Schulberg's novel *The Disenchanted* is a case in point). But Joe is not seduced or deceived by Hollywood: he makes his choice with his eyes wide open. He allows Norma to go on thinking that he loves her but just as he tries to regain his self-respect, by telling her the truth, giving her back her presents and walking out on her, she kills him. He has left it too late and her fragile ego can't take the final rejection.

In the career of Joe Gillis there are echoes of the life and work of F. Scott Fitzgerald. Wilder was meticulous in his use of details in his films and it is surely no accident that Gillis's birthday is given as 21 December, the day (in 1940) that Fitzgerald died in Hollywood. Gillis has the same initials as Jay Gatsby and they share the same fate: both end up, bullet-ridden, in a swimming pool. But taken from a different perspective, it is Norma who is like Gatsby. Both have grand mansions, once the scene of fabulous parties in the 1920s, that fall into decay. Norma's tragedy, like Gatsby's, is that she won't accept that the past can't be recaptured. Gatsby believes that he can win back his first love, Daisy, and Norma believes that she can win back her audience. But at least Gatsby dies before he grows old. Norma, like Miss Havisham in *Great Expectations*, is compelled to pretend that time has not moved on. As the lyrics to the song 'Eternal Youth is Worth a Little Suffering' imply, she wants to be more than young, she wants to be timeless.

Wilder declared that he was delighted with the musical. He met the writers during the rehearsal period and they showed him a videotape they had made of the work in progress. Owing to a technical hitch the video played in black and white but he said, "Don't worry, I prefer it like that". (*The Apartment*, which he made in 1960, was the last black and white film to win the Acadamy Award for Best Picture.) Lloyd Webber tried to get Paramount Pictures to pay Wilder a percentage of the substantial copyright fees they had demanded but they refused. Wilder was sanguine about this, merely remarking that he was not surprised as most producers would wear rubber pockets to steal his soup.

In an article he wrote for the *Daily Telegraph* in April 1993 Hampton said that so far he had thoroughly enjoyed himself although he had been warned by Mel Brooks that writing a musical was hell. "My question is," he said, "When does the bad bit start?'." The answer came soon enough. The show opened in London at the Adelphi Theatre some three months later, on 12 July. It was directed by Trevor Nunn, with Patti Lupone as Norma and Kevin Anderson as Joe. Lloyd Webber was not happy with the previews of the work and demanded extensive rewrites to tighten the structure before it opened in LA.

The bad bits continued when Faye Dunaway sued Lloyd Webber for firing her from the LA production during rehearsals because he felt that her voice was not strong enough. (It seems somehow appropriate that in Roman Polanski's film *Chinatown* Dunaway tells Jack Nicholson: "I don't get tough, my lawyer does".) She was replaced by Glenn Close, already known to Hampton from *Dangerous Liaisons*. More trouble came when Patti Lupone sued Lloyd Webber, who, she claimed, had promised her the role of Norma on Broadway. Lupone and Dunaway both won undisclosed sums in out-of-court settlements. Glenn Close went on to star in the Broadway show when it moved from Los Angeles, while Betty Buckley and John Barrowman replaced Lupone and Anderson in London.

Critical response to the show has been varied. Clive Barnes, the main theatre critic on the *New York Post* and dubbed 'the butcher of Broadway', because of his power often to make or break a show, said of the LA opening of *Sunset Boulevard* that "the lyrics remain unutterably banal but utterly unmemorable". On this occasion, however, he was unable to make a dent in Lloyd Webber's reputation and the audiences flocked in.

Lloyd Webber's phenomenal capacity for success has not deserted him and *Sunset Boulevard* looks set to run for a long time in London and New York. And, in a unique step, his production company, the Really Useful Theatre Company, has persuaded a hotel group to fund the building of a £25 million theatre near Frankfurt for the sole purpose of presenting his own musicals. This theatre will be showing *Sunset Boulevard* for the foreseeable future. It will certainly be as if we never said goodbye.

CHAPTER ELEVEN

ALICE'S ADVENTURES UNDER GROUND (1994)

You never understand what I'm trying to say.
Maybe not, but I think I usually understand what you do say.

The Philanthropist

Alice's Adventures Under Ground started life when Diane Borger-Zampi, deputy head of the Royal National Theatre Workshop, went to New York and saw some of the work of the choreographer Martha Clarke. They discussed a proposal to devise a dramatised life of Lewis Carroll.

Clarke came to London in 1991 and during the course of her visit she met Hampton to discuss a film that she wanted to direct based on a story by Paul Gallico. Hampton told her that this idea didn't particularly appeal to him but was much more interested in her plans to do something with *Alice in Wonderland*. They decided to collaborate and met again at the end of 1992 for two weeks of workshops at the National. The piece was originally scheduled for production in the autumn of 1993 but it took them until early 1994 to produce a workable script. After a further series of workshops in England and America the play was presented at the Cottesloe Theatre in November of that year.

Hampton's original idea was, working exclusively from Carroll's own writings, to switch freely between *Alice's Adventures in Wonderland* and *Through the Looking Glass*. However, after trying this out he felt that the structure was getting too complicated and so he decided to work through the two books chronologically. The final script that emerged was divided into seventeen scenes, the first ten from the first book and the last six from the second, separated by material taken from a series of Carroll's letters, which became Scene 11.

In the course of the play we see many of the famous characters and set pieces from the books: in the first half, for example, the Mad Hatter's tea party, the Duchess playing croquet using flamingoes as mallets and hedgehogs as balls, and the Mock Turtle and the Gryphon's quadrille, and in the second half the Walrus and the Carpenter, Tweedledum and Tweedledee, and Humpty-Dumpty. Curiously there is no scene with the White Rabbit, the reason being that Hampton "never liked him".

As the director of the play Martha Clarke was responsible for blocking the actors' moves but even though she is best known as a choreographer *Alice's Adventures Under Ground* is very much a text-based piece. There is just one set dance, in Scene 10, where the Mock Turtle and the Gryphon dance the quadrille for Alice, and three songs, with music specially written by Richard Peaslee.

Altogether the piece runs for about 90 minutes and is intended to be played straight through without an interval and it uses a single set throughout —Lewis Carroll's room in Christ Church, Oxford. For the Cottesloe production designer Robert Israel created a space that was deliberately misshapen and looked like a surrealist painting, thus hinting at the strange mixture of reality and unreality of incidents in Carroll's life as well as in the stories he tells.

In the opening scene Carroll entertains Alice Liddell, the daughter of the Dean of Christ Church, to tea. A moment before she arrives at his door she appears as an image in his mirror. We are therefore prepared for the room to become a magic kingdom that can be reached by travelling 'through the looking glass'. And so Alice is both real and a figment of Carroll's imagination.

He starts to tell her part of the story of *Alice's Adventures in Wonderland*. We can assume that she hears the story in instalments each time she visits him. They have reached the point where Alice, on first arriving in Wonderland, drinks from a bottle marked 'Drink me'. Carroll gets the real Alice to describe the taste of a drink he pours out for her. "Cherry tart," she says and Carroll says, "Roast turkey". "Toffee," says Alice, reconsidering, and Carroll responds with "Hot buttered toast".

The play then fuses into a strange mixture of reality and fantasy as Alice meets the bizarre characters Carroll has invented. Most of these roles are played by a supporting cast of two actors and an actress but Hampton and Clarke reinforce the link between the author and his own creations by having the actor playing Carroll taking on also those parts that they considered were closest to the different facets of the writer's own personality. Thus we see him as the Caterpillar, the White Knight and Humpty-Dumpty, which show him as an isolated figure, as the enigmatic Cheshire Cat, and, above all, as the Dormouse and the Red King, which portray him as a dreamer.

In his review of the play for the *Independent* Paul Taylor pointed out that the portrayal of Carroll as the Red King indicates that he is a fantasist, and this is borne out by the text, in Scene 13, when Tweedledee, Tweedledum and Alice discover the Red King asleep.

> TWEEDLEDEE: He's dreaming about you. And if he left off, where do you suppose you'd be?
> ALICE: Where I am now.
> TWEEDLEDEE: No. You'd be nowhere. Because you're only a sort of thing in his dream.

Carroll appreciated that children are frequently baffled by the rules and rituals of conventional adult life so Hampton and Clarke emphasise the point by presenting his characters as humans dressed in Victorian costume. The various bullying couples, such as the March Hare and the Mad Hatter, the Mock Turtle and the Gryphon, Tweedledum and Tweedledee, are like substitute parents. They often recite poetry and ask Alice bizarre questions as if conducting a lesson in subjects that they haven't bothered to explain to her.

More than once in the play Hampton and Clarke portray Carroll as a threatening figure. In Scene 9 he plays one of the flamingoes that Alice is worried will bite her during the croquet match and he later appears as the crow that scares Tweedledum and Tweedledee sufficiently to stop them fighting. At this point in the action the stage is filled with a dark menacing shadow.

Sometimes Carroll is cruel to Alice. When he dozes off in his armchair she begins to sketch him but he wakes up and destroys her drawing in a fit of temper. Although he observes her all the time, he is uncomfortable with the idea that she is observing him. He prefers children not to grow up.

After Alice has drunk from the bottle labelled 'Drink me' he stands her on the mantelpiece and tells her that she has increased in size. She is frightened and starts to cry. "Of course, growing is always a terrible sadness," he says. He tells her about his friend Mr Gnome Emery, who gives lessons in forgetting, and promises to visit him "when it's time to forget you". He is dismayed by how fickle children can be and how quickly they seem to forget. He reiterates the point when, in the role of Humpty-Dumpty in Scene 15, he asks Alice how old she is and she tells him she is seven and a half.

> ALICE: One can't help growing older.
> HUMPTY: *One* can't, perhaps. But what about two? With proper assistance, you might have left off at seven.

At the end of this scene Carroll locks Alice in his room and in the next scene he taunts her as she tries to get out.

Throughout the play Carroll is often seen as a silent spectre in scenes of his own making. He looks on while the Mock Turtle and the Gryphon sing and dance and later on he disturbs the banquet that the Red and White Queen are holding by watching them through a window. Alice is trapped physically in his room and mentally in his own imagination and he is destined to be a disconsolate observer of his own fantasies.

Alice's Adventures Under Ground was Carroll's own first choice of title for *Alice's Adventures in Wonderland*, and one can see why he changed it to something less sinister. Hampton said that he had noticed "a perceptible darkening in tone" between the two books (published in 1865 and 1871 respectively), and he wanted the play to reflect this. He also wanted to explore the darker side of Carroll's personality, which emerges in his overall attitude towards children.

In Scene 1 Carroll explains to the audience: "I have always been fond of children: except boys" and his fascination with pre-pubescent girls is the main theme of the play. His photographs of nude and semi-nude girls have become the subject of intense speculation ever since their publication. Michael Billington pointed out in the *Guardian*: "... the Victorian cult of the idealised, naked, sexless child was very strong: Dodgson's only difference was that he was a photographer rather than a painter or illustrator."

It seems that Carroll wanted to prevent children from becoming sexually aware—he was in favour of censoring Shakespeare, for example, for fear that young minds might be corrupted by the work—but paradoxically he was unable to see why others might be suspicious of the motives behind the photographs.

In Scene 11 of the play, which represents the transition between the two books, we see him justifying his work as a photographer of children. The speech is drawn from a series of letters that Carroll wrote to a Mr and Mrs Mayhew, who had objected to his request to photograph their three daughters unchaperoned. The parents are seen on stage, standing silent and disapproving, while Carroll, whose tone at first is beseeching and conciliatory, works himself up into a fury. "It is not pleasant to know that one is not trusted," he says.

It is known, however, that Carroll would immediately abandon his plans if any girl showed the slightest reservation about being photographed nude, and he specified that on his death all the pictures were to be destroyed or returned to their models to protect them from embarrassment. In fact he seems more courteous and less exploitative than many modern photographers who sell similar images for public display.

There is no evidence that Carroll ever physically abused any child but his attitude towards them remains ambiguous and it is a topic that arouses a certain amount of prurient interest in the media every time he is discussed. In an interview with the *Sunday Times* in November 1994 Hampton gave his opinion: "My best guess is that he was sexually attracted to small girls but incapable of admitting this to himself. What was in his mind never crossed his mind. I don't suggest anything 'went on'. I don't believe he laid a finger on any of them."

In the spring of 1996 the writer Karoline Leach discovered a fragment of paper in the Dodgson family archive which she believed to be a summary of two missing pages from his diary, made by Violet Dodgson, Carroll's niece. It indicated that Carroll may have been courting Alice's older sister Ina, or her governess, Miss Prickett.

Sex with under-age girls is a recurring motif in Hampton's work: in *The Philanthropist* Araminta tells Philip that her uncle raped her when she was twelve; Colin sleeps with his twelve-year-old cousin Julie in *Able's Will*; Valmont rapes the fifteen-year-old Cécile in *Les Liaisons Dangereuses*; and Gauguin indulges his passion for fourteen-year-old Tahitian girls in *The Wolf at the Door*.

Scene 12 of *Alice's Adventures Under Ground* shows Carroll preparing Alice for what is perhaps the most famous of all his photographs. He poses her as a beggarmaid, with bare legs, and wearing a ragged dress. But he is overcome with emotion and cannot continue. Alice senses his distress and asks him to go on with the story as a way of bringing him round. He agrees and tells her a story about Bob the bat, using a mechanical bat that flies around the room.

Perhaps the saddest moment of all in the play is in the final scene, where Carroll, as the White Knight, recites the words of his song from *Through the Looking Glass*, and ends up describing how he rides off on his horse: ". . . all this she took in like a picture, as, with one hand shading her eyes, she leant against a tree, watching the strange pair and listening, in a half-dream, to the melancholy music of the song."

As the narrator, Carroll explains that Alice's strongest memory after many years was of a sad old man making his lonely yet dignified way through the sunset. Hampton's concept of the evening light as a metaphor for melancholy and loss as seen in *Total Eclipse*, *White Chameleon* and *Sunset Boulevard* re-emerges here.

After Alice has left Carroll has the final line: "But you didn't cry as much as I thought you would." The fleeting image of Alice in the looking glass is reprised and the play ends.

The critics were, on the whole, unenthusiastic about *Alice's Adventures Under Ground*, with the exception of John Peter in the *Sunday Times* who described it as "90 minutes of sheer uninterrupted magic". The main complaint was that Hampton had failed to illuminate Carroll's character. He was accused of concentrating too much on the source material and putting menacing twists on seemingly innocent lines. The effect, said some, was to debunk the work. Instead of being celebrated as a brilliant combination of logic and surrealism the text had been used as mere coded pornography. This is hardly what Hampton intended. In the introduction to the published text he says that he wanted to avoid looking at the books in a "reductively causal way" yet by choosing to concentrate exclusively on Carroll's own material he effectively blocks the path to finding an objective assessment of the man.

Dennis Potter's screenplay for *Dreamchild* (1985, directed by Gavin Millar), which takes up the story of what happened to Alice Liddell when she grew up, is perhaps more successful in delving into Carroll's complex personality.

Whatever the critics said about the play itself, there was almost universal praise for Michael Maloney's remarkably intense and sympathetic performance as Carroll, which did a great deal to lessen the impression that the aim of the piece was to traduce the man in some way. Sasha Hanau as Alice (also cast as Mary's childhood self in Hampton's film *Mary Reilly*) also drew appreciative reviews. Hampton and Clarke felt that it was very important to use a girl of the right age for the role. Most other dramatisations have featured an actress much older than the specified seven and a half years, thus making Alice seem disingenuous or backward. Hanau was seven when the workshops for the play started and although she was nine when it opened she was still young enough to be convincing. She was admirably supported by the versatile cast of John Carlisle, Gabrielle Lloyd and Joseph Mydell who doubled up to play Carroll's numerous imaginary creations.

In *Total Eclipse* the characters of Rimbaud and Verlaine are used to examine ideas about life and art. As Rimbaud had proclaimed his intention to pursue the experience of the total degeneration of the senses, it was a valid exercise for a playwright to investigate the outcome of such a destructive course. We will never know the true nature of Carroll's sexuality but even so, Hampton seems to hold back and his restrictive approach gives us only limited access to his subject.

CHAPTER TWELVE

TRANSLATIONS (1967–89)

I wish I could read your plays. Aren't any of them translated into English?

Tales from Hollywood

Hampton graduated from New College, Oxford with a First in Modern Languages and is fluent in French and German, though he once ruefully remarked that he speaks them "like Ted Heath". Having been steeped in the European literary canon from an early age it is hardly surprising that he should have done so many translations.

In a discussion at the Royal National Theatre in 1992 he summed up his approach to tackling the work of foreign dramatists: "When I translate a play, my real concern is to try to follow the author's intentions as closely as possible. First of all to understand the author's intentions, then to reproduce them, and to achieve the same effects that are achieved in the original, particularly with regard to working out where the author wants the audience to laugh, and trying to make them laugh in those places, which is one of the most difficult aspects of it."

ISAAC BABEL: MARYA (1967)

In 1967 the Royal Court Theatre marked the fiftieth anniversary of the October Revolution with a production of Isaac Babel's 1935 play, *Marya*. It had never been staged in the Soviet Union although it was twice accepted for performance in Moscow only to be withdrawn each time after Communist Party officials criticised the text. His only other play, *Sunset* (1928), has yet to be seen in Britain.

Marya was directed by Robert Kidd and it was with this play that Hampton made his debut as a translator. The original English translation was done by two academics, Harold Shukman and Michael Glenny, who had separately worked on different sections of the text. The actors were finding it difficult to bring the play to life in rehearsal so Hampton was drafted in at short notice for some emergency rewrites.

Glenny was a lecturer in Russian at Oxford at the time and that year was to see his translation of Bulgakov's novel *The Master and Margarita*, published by the Harvill Press. Hampton telephoned him and explained that the text of

Marya needed some further work and suggested a meeting. When Glenny asked him what job he did Hampton had to explain that he was still an undergraduate. "Whereupon," Hampton recalled, "he became slightly frostier." But Glenny agreed to collaborate and together they produced a more actable version. In the theatre programme and the published script Shukman and Glenny are credited with the literal translation while Hampton is billed as the adaptor.

Isaac Babel is better known as a short story writer than a playwright and his most popular work is probably *Red Cavalry*, a collection of tales loosely based on his experiences as a soldier in the Red Army. Like all talented writers in the Soviet regime, he suffered from censorship, both overt and self-imposed; he enjoyed a privileged lifestyle as an officially recognised spokesman for the government but it was an uneasy position for a writer to be in and it inevitably cramped his creativity. He felt that he would be not be able to write at all if he left his homeland and yet he was not free to tell the truth about his own society. By the end of the 1930s he had not written anything for some years. The authorities thought silence was in itself a form of dissent as they believed writers ought to be praising the Soviet peasants forever scything down fields of grain, their clear eyes fixed on the horizon.

In 1941 Stalin ordered Babel's arrest and he was sent to a labour camp where he died soon afterwards. The exact circumstances of his death were never clear but it is almost certain that he was murdered.

Marya is set in Petrograd during the early years of the Revolution. The heroine, Ludmilla, is the daughter of a retired general. She is hoping to marry Dymschitz, a rich Jew, who has acquired his wealth through some unspecified shady dealings. But he already has a wife and has no intention of leaving her. Ludmilla is then raped by Viskovsky, a syphilitic cavalry officer who works for Dymschitz. A gunfight ensues between Viskovsky and his friend Kravchenko, who has found out what has happened. We are never told if either combatant lives or dies but later we see that Ludmilla has been arrested by the police. Her father dies of a heart attack and in the final scene we see a peasant couple moving into the family's now vacant house. To them the old man and his daughters are nothing more than names.

The Marya of the title is Ludmilla's sister, who is away fighting with the Red Guard. The fact that she is never seen on stage, but is only talked about by the other characters, indicates that Babel's own sympathies lay more with the dispossessed victims of the Revolution than with those engaged in the struggle to establish a new order. On the surface the message is one of optimism but Babel subtly underscores the irony of one group of individuals being ousted to make way for another. He makes it clear that the suffering that Ludmilla and her family have endured will not be recorded or remembered.

Throughout the play Babel warns his audience what to expect from the Communist regime. Viskovsky says: "They'll stop you from choosing your own drinking partners, they'll make you read lousy books and sing lousy songs [. . . .] Two gentlemen will pay a call on you: 'Shall we go, Comrade Kravchenko?' [. . . .] Four kopecks it'll cost them to get rid of you, that's all, exactly four kopecks. The cost of one Colt bullet. It's been calculated."

In spite of the fact that this speech comes from the play's most unsympathetic character it does not lose any of its truth or power. In the event Babel's own death, and that of many of his fellow intellectuals, was in all probability not unlike the one that Viskovsky describes. Katya, the General's family servant, indirectly criticises the new order when she tells a friend about her lover in the Red Army: "He says that only the masses count today—the rule of the greater number. But I'm a number as well. One. Doesn't that count?" So when, in the play's final scene, Andrei, a workman repairing the house for its new owners, says, "If you ask me the babies being born today are going to have a wonderful life when they grow up. Well, I mean, they're bound to, aren't they?" this seems more ironic than optimistic. Even so, the ironies in the play come not from the free exploration of a complex situation but are the desperate expression of an artist who is not allowed to tell the audience what they all know to be the truth. It is like seeing a man with a gun in his back miming the word 'help' while loudly assuring you that everything is fine.

Marya is an interesting play but it is underdeveloped. Ludmilla is the main character but she hardly appears before she is arrested and whisked away to face an uncertain future. She doesn't reappear after this and so the drama loses focus.

In the Royal Court production Diane Cilento, who had just enjoyed a big success in the film *Hombre* with Paul Newman, took the role of Ludmilla and veteran actor Niall MacGinnis played her father. The play enjoyed a modest success: it ran for thirty-five performances, was broadcast on BBC Radio 3 and published in J.C. Trewin's 1969 anthology *Plays of the Year 35*. In 1979 Jack Gold directed it for television as part of the BBC series 'Play of the Month'.

During the 1970s and '80s almost every playwright was persuaded to translate (or more usually adapt from a literal translation) a play from the classic European repertoire. This trend included Osborne's versions of *The Father* and *Hedda Gabler*, Stoppard's reworking of Nestroy (*On the Razzle*) and

Schnitzler (*Undiscovered Country* and *Dalliance*), Howard Brenton's *Galileo*, versions of *Tartuffe* from Simon Gray and Liz Lochhead, Michael Frayn's translations of Chekhov (*Uncle Vanya, Wild Honey* and *The Wood Demon*) and his version of *The Exchange* by the modern Soviet dramatist Yuri Trofimov.

The fashion has continued with Timberlake Wertenbaker's reworking of Sophocles' Theban plays and Howard Brenton's refashioned *Faust*, both for the RSC in the 1990s. It seems that theatre producers are more confident about a play's chances if they can put the names of two famous writers on the bill instead of one. One wonders, if this fashion had started earlier, how Coward's *Miss Julie* or Rattigan's *Mother Courage* might have turned out.

Pam Gems, whose version of *Uncle Vanya* was published in 1979, says in an afterword to the text that plays "must constantly be reborn". A new translation can keep up to date with modern speech patterns and a writer like Chekhov, who used a great deal of colloquial speech in his plays, needs language that doesn't sound stilted to English ears. Translations that aren't specifically tailored for performance are often more concerned with accuracy than with speakability, though this is not always the case. Michael Meyer's translations of Ibsen in the Penguin Classics editions, for example, are often performed. A 'literary' version of a play that is designed to be studied in depth, and has the advantage of explanatory notes, tends not to date so quickly and can allow itself to be more diffuse than one that is to be seen on stage. Many directors, on the other hand, are looking for a text that has parallels with their own times; they may update the action, switch the location or make other changes in order to make their point.

CHEKHOV: UNCLE VANYA (1970)

In February 1970 the Royal Court Theatre revived *Uncle Vanya*, directed by Anthony Page, in a new version by Hampton from a literal translation by Nina Froud. During his work on the play he also referred to the standard English text by Constance Garnett. The production reacted against the tendency to play Chekhov as if he were plagued by a winsome and sentimental nostalgia and Hampton's language was praised for being "natural and unobtrusive". Irving Wardle in *The Times* said of his approach that it "strips the literary flourishes down to the bone so that the people seem blunter, sexier, more direct and more desperate than they have been in the past".

Paul Scofield was Vanya and Colin Blakely played Dr Astrov. The play was broadcast on Radio 4 that October and was selected for publication by J.C. Trewin for his *Plays of the Year 39*.

Uncle Vanya has some interesting links with Hampton's own work. Astrov's complaint about the pointless destruction of the forests, with its potential harmful effects on the countryside, is echoed in the depiction in *Savages* of the devastation of the Indians' homeland. In *Uncle Vanya* the damage to the environment is not done by greedy industrialists but by ignorant landowners and lazy peasants who burn wood fires when they could use peat, and build wooden outhouses when they could make them from brick. Hampton was to show just how much worse the situation has become in the last hundred years.

Another recurring theme is the loss of idealism. Vanya, who dreams that he could have been another Schopenhauer or Dostoevsky (we don't know whether he has any real talent or is just deluding himself), is disillusioned with the life of the mind and has sunk into apathy. Even the energetic Astrov begins to lose his zeal for social reform and turns to drink. The sense of wasted life that hangs over Vanya's estate is a tangible force.

In Hampton's original work the apathy is in a way more pervasive because it is less noticed. Don in *The Philanthropist* has also drifted easefully into sloth but he is not concerned about it. The characters in *Treats* are so far gone in flaccid self-concern that they scarcely even recognise that they should care about other people.

Our duty towards one another, even towards the generations to come, is one of the major themes in *Uncle Vanya.* In Act One Astrov puts this point:

> ASTROV: I wondered if in a hundred or two hundred years' time the people we're trying to prepare the way for will remember us and think well of us. They won't, Nanny.
> MARINA: People may not remember, but God will.
> ASTROV: Thank you, that's very well said.

Astrov returns to this theme in Act Four: "In a hundred or two hundred years' time, people will despise us for having led such stupid, ugly lives, and perhaps they'll even find a way of being happy—but as for us . . . there's only one hope for you and me. The hope that as we lie there, in our graves, we might see visions—perhaps even pleasant visions."

Patrick, the least selfish character in *Treats*, and Brecht in *Tales from Hollywood*, also wonder what future generations might have done about the world's problems.

Hampton is more faithful to the original text of *Uncle Vanya* than Michael Frayn, who cut some of the more obscure literary references in the play in his version for the National Theatre. For instance Astrov, while looking for his cap, mumbles to himself a phrase that Elisaveta Fen, in the Penguin Classics series, translates as: "How could I anyway? . . . How could I?" which is meaningless unless one happens to know, as Frayn explains in his introduction to his published text, that this is a reference to a line in a play by Ostrovsky called *Wolves and Sheep*, where a timid aunt is reduced to talking incoherently by a bullying matriarch. This would probably be an obscure reference for most modern Russian audiences too and Frayn cuts it out altogether. Hampton has Astrov say: "Really I'd better not. Where's er . . . ?" thus making him repeat his refusal of a glass of vodka, and mumbling to himself while looking for his hat.

Uncle Vanya has become one of the most frequently revived classics of the 1990s. Julian Mitchell relocated the characters in rural North Wales with his version (retitled *August*). This was directed in 1994 by its star, Anthony Hopkins, who followed it up with a film version, released in 1996. 1995 saw three very different treatments of the play: Frank McGuinness presented a text in Irish dialect (although director Peter Gill retained a Russian setting), starring Stephen Rea—the production toured Ireland before opening in London at the Tricycle Theatre; *Country Life*, a film by Michael Blakemore, resets the action in Australia; and Louis Malle's *Vanya on 42nd Street*, with Wallace Shawn and Julianne Moore, is a filmed record of a performance of the play by a group of actors who had met every Sunday for several years to rehearse it, using an English translation by David Mamet, who had already tackled *The Cherry Orchard*. In Howard Barker's 1996 rewrite of the play, called *'Uncle' Vanya*, Vanya shoots the Professor and kills him, Sonya strangles Astrov, and Chekhov himself makes an appearance, to die in the midst of his characters. Although Hampton admires Chekhov he has not done any more of his plays. He explained in a *Time Out* interview in 1986 that he had spent a year studying Russian and had come out "no wiser".

IBSEN

"I've always had a special feeling about Ibsen," Hampton explained in an interview on the *South Bank Show* in 1989. "For one thing *Enemy of the People* is the first play I ever saw in my life." (He portrays the effect that this event had on him in *White Chameleon*.) Ibsen is the writer whose work he has adapted most and he feels that the man has been "wrongly characterised as this gloomy Scandinavian" when in fact he was "very subversive and very funny".

HEDDA GABLER (1970)

In 1970 the director Peter Gill was preparing to do *Hedda Gabler* and commissioned Heathcote Williams to write a new English text. When the script didn't arrive Gill asked Hampton to provide a version at short notice, which he duly did, using a literal translation by Hélène Grégoire, as well as referring to the William Archer version.

With *Hedda Gabler* Hampton realised that this was the first time he had worked on a play with a woman as the central character. And it is easy to see how the theme of a female sexual manipulator and her effect on a predominately male academic community would have appealed to him.

Gill put the play on at the Stratford Festival Theatre in Ontario with Irene Worth as Hedda Gabler, Gordon Jackson as her husband, George Tesman, Donald Davis as Judge Brack and Leo Ciceri as Eilert Lövborg. It was revived in 1984 by director Tim Albery at the Almeida Theatre in London, with Deborah Findlay, Paul Jesson, Donald Sumpter and Mike Bradwell. Reviews were mixed, but some critics liked the pared-down spareness of the production that did away with the crowded naturalistic sets. Nicholas de Jongh, writing in the *Guardian* said: "This is a production which makes you see the play anew." However, there were complaints that some of the double meanings Ibsen had used in the original had been lost. Martin Hoyle in the *Financial Times* pointed out, for instance, that Judge Brack's desire to dominate Hedda sexually is referred to as his wish to be "the only bull in the ring" when it is usually translated as "cock of the walk"

Hampton, perhaps feeling that he had not had enough time to tackle the job originally, returned to the play in 1989, working this time from a literal translation by Karin and Ann Bamborough. It was staged at the Royal National Theatre where Hampton was reunited with his director from *Les Liaisons Dangereuses*, Howard Davies. Juliet Stevenson, who had played Tourvel in that production, was Hedda.

Davies's operatic touches were too much for some reviewers. He added a thunderstorm to the beginning of Act Three and at the end directed Hedda to fire a shot into the air so that everyone looks at her before she kills herself, splattering blood onto her father's portrait (just as John in *The Philanthropist* splatters blood onto Philip's Picasso reproduction). In the *Listener* Jim Hiley declared that it was "a production whose boldness matches Ibsen's line for line".

In John Osborne's version of the play Hedda asks Eilert to wear roses in his hair. Hampton retains the vine leaves, a suitably Dionysian image, and a much less wispily romantic one. As always with his translations he aims for colloquial ease of expression. "It's easier for an audience to feel the characters are real if they are speaking a language they can identify as current."

A DOLL'S HOUSE (1971)

Claire Bloom saw Hampton's original version of *Hedda Gabler* in Ontario and she asked him to translate *A Doll's House* for her. His version, again from a literal translation by Hélène Grégoire, was staged in New York in 1971 and London in 1973. The director was Patrick Garland, and Torvald Helmer was played by Donald Madden, Dr Rank by Roy Shuman and the blackmailing Nils Krogstad by Robert Gerringer.

In Washington Hampton was excluded from a White House reception given for everyone involved in the production because, as he explained, President Nixon "couldn't cope with the flower shirt and velvet suit". Nixon might also have been upset by the applause that greeted one particular line in the play: "It was impossible to get on by honest means." Instead, Hampton got drunk with some Native Americans in the bar of the Watergate hotel. He could not have wished for an evening of more resonant irony.

In 1973 Hampton provided the screenplay for a film version of the play, again directed by Garland and with Bloom once more as Nora. Anthony Hopkins was Torvald, Denholm Elliott was Krogstad and Ralph Richardson was Dr Rank. All these actors were to work with Hampton again.

The production caught the crest of the women's liberation movement, and this fashionable endorsement of a once challenging play worried Hampton enough to write *Treats*, which he conceived as an attack on the complacent idea that *A Doll's House* was somehow a period piece about how women used to be exploited.

THE WILD DUCK (1979)

Hampton's version of *The Wild Duck* was produced at the National Theatre in 1979. It was directed by Christopher Morahan, with Ralph Richardson as Old Ekdal, supported by Stephen Moore as the sentimentalist, Hjalmar Ekdal, Michael Bryant as the idealistic Gregers Werle, Yvonne Bryceland as Hjalmar's wife, Gina, and Eva Griffith as Hedvig.

Ibsen knew that the character of Hjalmar could become ridiculous and Gregers merely spiteful if not treated carefully and he always feared that *The Wild Duck* would be played as broad comedy, which would mean that Hedvig's suicide would make no sense. With such a high-calibre cast Morahan was able to avoid this pitfall.

"The Duck has proved by far the most difficult of the four and I think it will be the last play by Ibsen I will tackle. It's my favourite among his plays, but it's exceedingly difficult to hit the exact tone, that mixture of the realistic and the symbolic," Hampton explained in an interview in *The Times*. "My starting point was to find the exact English equivalent of a number of key words, almost thematic words, that occur throughout the play." He adapted the text directly from the original, although he did have an English text and a Norwegian speaker to help him.

Hampton's text of *The Wild Duck* gives the full translation, but cuts were made for the performance. Michael Meyer, on the other hand, made some cuts in the published version of his translation. This is understandable. Ibsen's prose can become prolix, and, perhaps because naturalistic dialogue was such an innovation in his day he hadn't refined the technique; characters often take three or four lines to tell each other to sit down. And yet Hampton's decision to publish the whole thing without the director's cuts is useful; it is good to be given the opportunity to read the whole play, even if it is too long for performance.

The Wild Duck is an attack on the uncompromising desire for truth that Ibsen himself had espoused in his earlier plays. His character Dr Relling argues that life is unendurable unless one has a life-lie to sustain one and that no one should take this away. Events seem to prove him right. This idea was echoed by Don in *The Philanthropist*. Relling, like Hitler in *The Portage to San Cristobal of A.H.*, objects to the call to perfection, personified in *The Wild Duck* by the character of Gregers Werle.

Sheridan Morley pointed out in his review of the production in *Punch* that one almost feels more sympathy for the idealistic characters. "It's hard to believe," he added, "for all the evidence of his letters, that Ibsen didn't want something of that to happen in production." Relling, far from being portrayed as a compassionate man who protects people out of affection for them, is seen as a cynic who despises the people that he protects from self-knowledge. Hjalmar he sees (rightly, it must be said) as a fool who is so wrong-minded as to be convinced of his own genius without any external evidence for it. Relling mocks the petty illusions that the other characters have while encouraging them to go on believing them, as he thinks that they have to be protected from the truth. But his uncharitable assessments of everyone around him make it difficult to sympathise with him. And one can hardly imagine an audience eagerly agreeing with Relling and deciding that, in future, they too will live by a lie.

Ibsen's message seems to be that honesty is good if one can take it, but it should not be forced on one from outside. Certainly Gregers Werle is an unappealing and tactless figure who interferes with other people's lives without understanding their situation. Ibsen realised that the desire to improve one's life should come from within.

The press notices for the production were almost uniformly good and Sheridan Morley called Hampton's translation "beautiful". Yet it was more direct than previous translations. In the third line of the play, he has the servant Pettersen say "buggered if I know", which is more usually translated as something like "I wouldn't know". This is the wording that Michael Meyer gives and he explains in his introduction to the text of his version that Pettersen was a butler who was imitative of the gentry. This makes it unlikely that he would be so coarse. Also Pettersen is answering a question, asked by a servant hired for the evening, about his master's love-life. Having him saying "buggered if I know" implies either genuine ignorance or total indifference. But if he replies "I wouldn't know" it gives the line an extra resonance that is missing in Hampton's rendition; it could be that Pettersen is reminding the hired servant that it is not his, or anyone else's, business to know.

The final line of the play, where Relling curses Gregers Werle, is perhaps the most difficult one to convey in English. The literal translation from the Norwegian is "the devil knows if you're right", which indicates both scepticism and doubt. It seems to be saying, "Well you could be right, but damn you anyway". Una-Ellis Fermor, in the Penguin Classics translation, has Relling say "I wonder", which is ambiguous. It sounds as though he might be coming round to Werle's way of thinking, which under the circumstances is extremely unlikely. In Michael Meyer's version Relling says nothing but merely laughs and spits. Even if one takes this as a gesture of disgust it seems rather a yobbish thing for him to do. It doesn't have the passionate utter hatred of Hampton's "God damn you to hell".

Hampton explained in an interview with John Higgins in *The Times* that although the Norwegian language is not overendowed with swear words there are various carefully graded references to God and the Devil. He offers just about the strongest curse he could find in this context and one imagines that Relling really would like to see Werle burn in a lake of fire. It might seem to be a melodramatic renunciation but if played with the right degree of controlled anger it could be very powerful indeed. It is no more accurate than other versions of the line but it seems to make most dramatic sense.

In his interview in *The Times* Hampton said that he was unlikely to translate any more Ibsen. (He had completed a new translation of *Ghosts* for the Actors Company, who took it on tour to various regional theatres around Britain. The cast included Terence Alexander and Ken Jones, and Phyllida Law, the actress who had appeared as Phyllis in *Able's Will* the previous year. Hampton's hopes that Vanessa Redgrave would make a film of *Ghosts* came to nothing.)

It seems that he is less drawn to the early plays or the later symbolic dramas. This is perhaps because he is more interested in writing about complex people caught in realistic situations —the sort of thing that Ibsen wrote in his middle period. For Ibsen and Hampton the most profound emotional changes and moral crises can take place in the most ordinary suburban drawing rooms.

ÖDÖN VON HORVÁTH

Ibsen and Chekhov have never been short of translators willing to take a fresh look at them but in the case of Ödön von Horváth Hampton has helped to restore the reputation of a talented writer whose work had been neglected outside the German-speaking world for half a century. It was familiarity with Horváth that led Hampton to use him as a fictionalised character in *Tales from Hollywood*.

Born in 1901 in Fiume (now Rijeka), a seaport on the Adriatic coast in what was to become Yugoslavia, Horváth, the son of a diplomat, spent his childhood going from one European city to another. He was fourteen before he spoke a word of German. He was at the University of Munich at the same time as Brecht although it is not known whether they met each other there.

Horváth was only 37 when he died, by which time he had completed seventeen plays and three novels. Before Hampton came on the scene only one of these plays, *Sladek, The Black Militia Man*, had been performed in Britain. This is a play about a society in decay because of rising inflation. It was broadcast on Radio 3 in 1970, in a translation by Victor Price, with Alan Howard as Sladek. More recently a few of his plays have been put on in small venues in London. Martin Esslin's translation of *Judgement Day* was staged at the Old Red Lion in May 1989, and Ian Huish's version of *Figaro Gets Divorced* was put on at the Gate Theatre in 1990.

It is regrettable that so little of Horváth's work is available in English. Esslin has translated three other plays—*Kasimir and Karoline*, *Faith, Hope and Charity* and *Figaro Gets a Divorce*. Ian Huish, a teacher of German at Westminster School, is Britain's leading Horváth scholar, and he is the editor of two of Horváth's novels—*Jugend Ohne Gott* [*Youth Without God*] and *Jungste Tag* [*A Child of our Time*]—published in German.

The work of both Horváth and Hampton shows the influence of French drama. Horváth conceived his play *Figaro Gets Divorced* as a sort of sequel to Beaumarchais' *The Marriage of Figaro*, propelling the familiar characters of Count Almaviva, the Countess, Figaro and Susanne into a world of darkness and chaos like that of Europe in the 1930s.

Hampton was a student in Germany when he first heard about Horváth. His work, which had been suppressed by the Nazis and largely ignored in the postwar years, underwent a large-scale revival in the 1960s. Hampton revealed in an interview in the *Independent* in 1989 that he first read a Horváth play in 1970 and although he was initially confused by its unusual style he was also "astonished by its immediacy" and found that "its *tone* was so extra-ordinarily modern; more like Fassbinder than a writer of the Thirties". The play was *Glaube, Liebe, Hoffnung*.

One of the things that attracted Hampton to Horváth was his sense of the bizarre. Horváth once told friends that he was walking along a woodland path when he found a skeleton dressed in mountain gear, complete with knapsack. Inside the knapsack was a postcard which said: "Having a wonderful time". When Horváth's friends asked him what he did next, he replied: "Posted it". Another time he saw a prostitute in tears at a health fair. He asked her what was wrong and she said that she hadn't had a single customer. She was illiterate and hadn't realised that she was standing next to a platform promoting the latest advances in the cure of venereal disease.

Whether or not these stories are true they reflect Horváth's macabre sense of humour. And even some thirty years after his unusual death in Paris he was involved in an incident that is pure black comedy. In the 1960s the Austrians decided that they wanted to reclaim Horváth as their own and rebury him on Austrian soil. They arranged the exhumation and got Horváth's French translator to bring the body over. He discovered that the coffin had rotted away and so he removed Horváth's remains and put them in a plastic bag. When he arrived at his hotel in Vienna he found that a room had been booked for Horváth but not for him. He fled, leaving the bag behind. The next day the authorities collected the remains and duly gave them a dignified state funeral.

TALES FROM THE VIENNA WOODS (1977)

Horváth's most famous play is probably *Tales from the Vienna Woods*, a title he borrowed from Johann Strauss. At intervals throughout the drama we hear a pianist in a house on the town square playing a random selection of waltzes from Strauss's 1868 operetta. The music always ends abruptly in mid-phrase. This is appropriate as the characters' dreams are always interrupted by reality.

The plot is similar to most other Horváth plots: a good-natured but helpless person is destroyed by a corrupt society and the cruelties of fate. The innocent protagonist, Marianne, lives in Vienna, and is engaged to the pious local butcher, Oskar. But she is seduced at a bathing party by a wastrel called Alfred, who does nothing but gamble. Marianne has a baby, which Alfred leaves with his grandmother while he goes to France. Marianne is left without any money and she finds work as a nude singer in a cabaret.

One night a party from her street arrives. Her pompous father, the Zauberkönig, (literally the 'magic king'—a sort of local official) is disgusted when he finds out what she is doing and will not help her in any way. She is then falsely accused by a tourist of stealing a wallet and sentenced to a month in prison. When she is released she goes to Alfred's grandmother and finds that her baby has died of a chill—effectively murdered when a window was deliberately left open during a cold night. She is distraught. Oskar, who has accompanied her to the grandmother's house, tells her that he still wants her. After cursing God, she agrees to marry him, more in despair than love.

Marianne doesn't dominate the play even though it is her story we are following most of the time. In the scenes where she is offstage we are introduced to various subsidiary characters, such as Valerie, the widow with a taste for men, and Erich, the ridiculous law-student who is a card-carrying Nazi. (Nazis could still be portrayed as comic figures in 1931.)

Horváth wrote about ordinary people—mainly the *Lumpenproletariat* and the lower bourgeoisie. He presents life as a series of fleeting, impressionistic episodes rather than building up dramatic momentum through elaborately structured plots. In short scenes he shows not only the lives of his protagonists but the way of life of a whole community. A more recent equivalent of this approach might be Edgar Reisz's *Heimat*, a sixteen-hour film that chronicles events over sixty-odd years in one village in the Hunsrück area of Germany.

Like most of Horváth's plays, *Tales from the Vienna Woods* belongs in the tradition of the *Volksstück* (literally a 'folk-play'), a genre that has no exact counterpart in the English theatre. *Volksstücke* are tragi-comic plays rooted in a specific culture and location and are usually written in a form of local dialect. They originated with a group of nineteenth-century Austrian dramatists that includes Nestroy and Raimund, whose work is largely unknown outside their own country.

One play that has travelled well, however, is *Einen Jux will er sich machen*, written in 1842 by Nestroy, who took the basic plot from A *Day Well Spent; or Three Adventures* by the English playwright John Oxenforde. This story of young men on a spree in the big city was used by Thornton Wilder in his 1938 play *The Merchant of Yonkers*. Wilder added a new character, Dolly Levi, rewrote the play as *The Matchmaker* and presented it at the Edinburgh Festival in 1954. Ten years later the play was adapted yet again; with a score by Jerry Herman and a book by Michael Stewart, the successful musical *Hello Dolly!* was launched. In 1981 the National Theatre presented a new version of Nestroy's original stage play, translated by Tom Stoppard, who renamed it *On the Razzle*.

Stoppard's attitude to translation tends to be more freewheeling than Hampton's. With *On the Razzle* he made less effort to render the *Plattdeutsch* into an equivalent form of English and one can appreciate why. Horváth's distinctive dialogue gave Hampton a fair amount of trouble. *Tales from the Vienna Woods* was written for an Austrian audience and uses the familiar form of German (rather than *Hochdeutsch*) spoken by the Viennese in the 1930s. Dialect is not so strongly associated with class in Austria and Germany as it is in Britain (although it may identify a certain lack of education in a speaker), so Hampton felt it would be wrong to specify any particular regional accent. He succeeds in creating a form of language that is idiomatic without exactly being specific to any one particular class or region.

Horváth wrote an essay entitled 'Instructions for Actors' where he explained that the actors "should all play characters who normally speak dialect but are trying to improve themselves. It is a complicated concept. It means that everyone is trying to sound like a doctor". (In *Tales from Hollywood* Horváth says that he gave up English lessons as he decided that he "sounded like a head waiter".) Hampton manages to convey this remarkably well. Many of the speeches have a stilted, incongruous formality, often peppered with *non sequiturs*, and the characters often sound as if they are trying to appear educated. Marianne's father uses Latin phrases that he has picked up. At one point he asks where his suspenders are.

> MARIANNE: They're in your chest of drawers, top left-hand drawer, right-hand side at the back.
> ZAUBERKÖNIG: Top left-hand drawer, right-hand side at the back. Difficile est, satiram non scribere.

The Latin tag, from the poet Juvenal, means "It is difficult not to write satire" and has little bearing on where the suspenders are.

The structure of the play presented further difficulties. "He's the most difficult author I've translated," Hampton said in his interview in the *Independent*. " . . . there are so many traps; and one of the difficulties is where are the laughs? They're hardly anywhere you expect them. Often good plays don't read very well, and Horváth is an extreme case of that; the first time you *hear* what he's written, it's a revelation. The most difficult thing of all is to respect the musical structure: it's almost like a musical score."

Tales from the Vienna Woods was put on at the National Theatre in 1977. Maximilian Schell, with his experience of the lavish productions of German theatre, was asked to direct. In an interview for *Time Out* Hampton related how "my dear mad German friend" set about his task. "That was so funny because the actors took against poor old Max's Teutonic style. He would go up to Stephen Rea and say that he had not removed his hat on the preordained word. I said you can't talk to British actors like that."

Rea was playing the scrounging Alfred and Kate Nelligan was Marianne. They were admirably supported by Elizabeth Spriggs as Valerie and Warren Clarke as Oskar. Also appearing, as Emma, one of the young women of the area, was Toyah Wilcox, soon to become famous as a punk rock singer.

The production was the first one on the newly opened Olivier stage and had been delayed because building work had fallen behind schedule. But the audience could appreciate a revolving set and spectacular crowd scenes. Hampton remembers how Schell had "a great way of stretching the National's resources. If he wanted to hire an extra at huge cost because he liked their face, he would beam: 'I vill pay, I vill pay'. But when it came to asking him for the money nobody had the nerve to do it, so he got everything he wanted and paid nothing . . . "

The critics were greatly impressed by the production, although some had doubts about the play itself. Sheridan Morley in *Punch* said: " . . . a marvellous production of a marvellous play would have been nice, but a marvellous production of an occasionally all right play is still a theatrical treat." Michael Billington in the *Guardian* was more enthusiastic and declared that *Tales from the Vienna Woods* was "exactly the kind of play the National ought to be doing: a standard part of the European repertory never before seen in Britain". But Billington also had his reservations: "The action of the play leaves you feeling that Marianne and Alfred are the victims of their character rather than the political movement of society." But this, surely, is one of the play's strengths. Hampton has pointed out that Horváth is "not a didactic writer. If you look at the earlier drafts and scenes eventually not included in 'Tales' it is clear that Horváth drew back from anything that might seem too crudely simplified."

Schell was already planning to make a film version of the piece when he was asked to direct it for the National Theatre. He and Hampton collaborated on the screenplay and went on to make the film, which won a prize at the Oxford International Film Festival in 1979.

DON JUAN COMES BACK FROM THE WAR (1978)

The next play of Horváth's that Hampton translated was *Don Juan Comes Back from the War*, also for the National Theatre although this time on the more intimate stage of the Cottesloe. The National originally intended to present it alongside Molière's *Don Juan* as a companion piece. But plans for the Molière revival were abandoned when the Greenwich Theatre staged a production.

Horváth's play had not been staged in Germany until 1952 where it was retitled *Don Juan Comes Back* because, as Hampton explains in his preface to the published text "at that date it was thought that any reference to the war in the title of a play might be tactless". He called Horváth's play "perhaps the strongest and most despairing play he wrote".

Don Juan is portrayed as a weary soldier returning from the first world war to a Germany beset by spiralling inflation. He is looking for his fiancée who, it is revealed to the audience in Act One, has been dead for two years. Her grandmother, like the grandmother in *Tales from the Vienna Woods*, is an evil character, and she curses the memory of Don Juan.

The play is made up of three acts of short, fast-moving scenes and the cast consists of Don Juan plus thirty-five female roles (played by nine actresses). There are a further seven bit parts, again all female. None of the women has names but are identified by their role, eg 'Mother' or 'Lady from Berne', which implies a high level of depersonalisation in the society. Act One is entitled 'The War is Over' and Act Two 'The Chaos of Inflation', a theme that Horváth had touched on before in *Sladek*. Act Three, the final act, is called 'The Snowman', which signifies the transience of Don Juan's life.

Don Juan drifts from place to place and falls in and out of relationships. He is falsely accused of rape but his reputation is so bad that nobody will believe him when he denies it. As one woman puts it: "Even if he is innocent, he deserves everything he gets." Finally he reaches the grandmother's house and hears the news that his fiancée is dead. He goes to her grave and dies there alone, in the snow.

Don Juan's justification for his behaviour is that since women have always exploited him he is only taking his revenge. But his arguments ring false. Like Alfred in *Tales from the Vienna Woods*, only on a far bigger scale, he is a leech, a user of women.

With Horváth it is usually the women who are exploited and abused but in *Don Juan Comes Back from the War* it is the man who suffers and dies. But unlike Molière's or Mozart's seducer, he doesn't face the dramatic punishment of eternal damnation: he dies a miserable but unspectacular death. John Barber wrote in the *Daily Telegraph*: "hell [was] for him the birth of his conscience".

The original Don Juan was a nobleman, scornfully aware of what he had done and refusing to repent. Horváth's Don Juan ends his life as he had lived it, in a state of incomprehension, with no insight into himself or the harm he has caused other people. There is a scene in Act Two where Don Juan, now working as an art dealer, meets one of his clients at a performance of *Don Giovanni* just as 'Là ci darem la mano' ['There we'll take hands'] is being sung. Hampton used this same duet, during which Don Giovanni tries to persuade Zerlina to betray her husband on her wedding day, in his dramatisation of *The History Man* as Howard Kirk goes to seduce Annie Callendar.

Horváth says in his preface to the play that Don Juan is a mythical figure and so he can always be renewed. His hero returns from the war imagining that he is a changed man. "Nevertheless he remains who he is. He has no choice. He is not going to escape the ladies. [. . .] He is the great seducer, seduced again and again by women. They all succumb to him, but—and this may be the essential point—he is never really loved by any of them. (This is why the play does not have a single love scene.)" Don Juan, he explains further, secretly yearns for death but does not realise it. But the women understand this and so they leave him. He is a lonely wanderer with no title, no Sganarelle or Leporello to deplore or admire his deeds, and no quickfire wit to win over an audience.

Like Hampton, Horváth explores the link between apathy and cruelty but he comes across as more pessimistic in his outlook. His characters seem incapable of self-knowledge and have no idea how to deal with their problems. Hampton's creations are generally more articulate and they use their wit and verbal skills to try and get what they want (though not always successfully), whereas the humour in Horváth's plays tends to arise from the incongruity of what the characters say when set against the situation they are in. But both Hampton and Horváth appreciate how apathy and cruelty are strangely intertwined. Those who stop making an effort have given up caring about anything and this brings about a cruelty born of indifference.

Hampton's version of *Don Juan Comes Back from the War* was directed by Stewart Trotter, starring Daniel Massey. The women in the cast included Susan Fleetwood, Edna Doré, Elspeth March and Janet Whiteside (who was to appear the following year as Mrs Sörby in Hampton's translation of *The Wild Duck*).

As with *Tales from the Vienna Woods*, the critics were divided. Hampton admired Horváth's ability to pare away any topical or specific historical references in his work so that he could achieve a certain timelessness. Yet is it this very lack of local colour that troubled some of the reviewers. Michael Billington in the *Guardian* wanted more social context and found the play "almost perversely denuded of detail". On the other hand, Irving Wardle in *The Times* decided that: "Christopher Hampton's translation makes out a far more compelling case for Horváth than his earlier version of *Tales from the Vienna Woods*." Ian Stewart in *Country Life* said of Don Juan that "One is affected by his plight without ever really knowing who he is. He is a nameless spectre in a desolate world." Robert Cushman in the *Observer* remarked that although Horváth was still young when he wrote it he was already producing "the type of stripped and allusive play playwrights traditionally produce in their last years".

FAITH, HOPE AND CHARITY (1989)

Having been acquainted with Horváth's work for almost twenty years, Hampton possessed more background knowledge than most. However, *Faith, Hope and Charity* was the most difficult play for him to translate as it was incomplete and no definitive draft existed. He had to search through a mass of private papers in order to reconstruct the play from the many notes that were left behind.

Horváth was inspired to write *Faith, Hope and Charity* by a true story told to him by a friend, a journalist and writer called Lucas Kristl. The play's heroine, Elisabeth, is similar to Marianne in *Tales from the Vienna Woods*. They are both hapless victims: both are unfairly sent to jail and both put their faith in men who reject them. Once again the setting is Germany in the early 1930s. Elisabeth has no money so she tries to sell her body to the Dissecting Office, hoping that they will give her a cash advance against her eventual death. Her plan fails but she manages to persuade the Assistant Dissector to lend her 150 Marks so that she can buy a permit to sell ladies' underwear. But he finds out that she intends to use the money to pay a fine for selling goods without a licence and he reports her to the police for fraud.

When she comes out of jail after serving fourteen days she goes on the streets. She is picked up by a policeman called Alfons and becomes his mistress, but he abandons her after they are raided by the Vice Squad who suspect Elisabeth of being a kept woman. In despair she tries to drown herself in the river. She is pulled out only half-alive and is taken to the police station where Alfons works. In the ensuing chaos she quietly dies. The policemen and other spectators wander away, while Alfons sneaks a final look at his former lover.

Once again Horváth demonstrates his ear for the incongruities of everyday conversation:

> ELISABETH: I am not a criminal!
> MAGISTRATE'S WIFE: That's not what matters, miss, your opinion. Whether there's material evidence of fraud, that's what matters. Otherwise justice would grind to a halt.

The dialogue could almost have come from Joe Orton's *Loot*. But although Horváth's characters are more humanely drawn than Orton's they haven't got the same resilient spirit. Elisabeth is so passive and helpless that her death is pathetic rather than tragic.

In common with other plays by Horváth, *Faith, Hope and Charity* deals with what he refers to in the preface to the text as "the gigantic struggle between the individual and society, this eternal battle with no peaceful outcome—during which the individual can at best enjoy for a few moments the illusion of a ceasefire". He saw his characters as defenceless in the face of society, although, as Michael Billington pointed out in his review of *Tales from the Vienna Woods*, these small-time losers would fail in any society. Horváth never suggests what might give his characters hope; he did not see it as his role to suggest solutions to human problems but tried simply to portray people in a sympathetic light and without moral comment.

Hampton's Horváth in *Tales From Hollywood* says that he was accused by the left of "easy pessimism", and it is perhaps a valid criticism. Even accepting, along with Hampton, that Horváth had no wish to be a didactic writer, one can't help wishing that his heroes, and even more especially his heroines, didn't appear so weak in the face of wickedness. It is not that he is unmoved by evil and acts of cruelty, but he does seem to think that there is little one can do to change things. His heroines either end up dead or in such total despair that they might as well be. He seems to write with a resigned shrug, as if to say happiness and justice are both impossible. However much this may seem to be the case, and Germany in the 1930s would certainly give one plenty of reasons to think so, there is a difference between pessimism and defeatism. Pessimism says that men rarely have the right answer but defeatism says that they don't even understand the question. Horváth, it seems, was a defeatist.

Faith, Hope and Charity was directed at the Lyric Theatre in Hammersmith by Heribert Sasse, Artistic Director of the Preussische Staats Theater, who earlier that year had directed a German production of the play at the Renaissance Theater in Berlin. Julia Ormond played Elisabeth, and Stephen Boxer was Alfons. In the supporting cast was Pamela Cundell (best known as Walmington-on-Sea's *femme fatale* Mrs Fox in the BBC TV series *Dad's Army*) as Irene Prantl, the owner of the underwear business. Caroline Quentin (later to star in the popular TV series *Men Behaving Badly*) played the prostitute, Maria.

Press reaction was mixed; the reviewers agreed that Julia Ormond was a success but most found Sasse's production heavy-handed, as when, for example, he relied on the unsubtle device of filling the stage with Nazi flags in Act Five. Martin Hoyle in the *Financial Times* complained of the play's "general comic strip flatness, unenlivened by variety, depth or contrast" but Michael Billington was more impressed. He praised the play as "a lethally observed anatomical tragedy". Michael Ratcliffe in the *Observer* found it "a profoundly disturbing and timeless little play" and said that "Hampton isolates Horváth's scrupulous use of cliché into English very precisely and, as in earlier translations, has found a nice match for his spare and laconic style."

Hampton has plans to translate at least two more Horváth plays: *Italienische Nacht*, written just before *Tales from the Vienna Woods* and *Kasimir und Karoline*, which came just after it. Both are in the *Volksstück* tradition.

In 1990 Hampton wrote a piece for the regular feature 'Heroes and Villains' in the *Independent* Magazine and he chose Horváth as his hero. He quoted from a letter Horváth wrote to his best friend, Franz Theodore Csokor, who was also a writer: "As long as we stay afloat, we'll always have friends and we'll always have a home, because we carry it with us—our home is the imagination."

Hampton spoke about the influence Horváth had had on his own work in an interview with the *Observer*: "I've learned from him not to be too judgemental, too rigid." He also learned that it was a good thing for a writer to avoid being too easily categorised. "I think you ought to be something of an escape artist if you're going to carry on."

MOLIÈRE

With Horváth's work Hampton more or less had the field to himself but with Molière he had three hundred years of tradition to reckon with.

In England, Molière became popular in the latter half of the seventeenth and the first half of the eighteenth century. In 1667 Dryden adapted *L'Étourdi* as *Sir Martin Marall* and reworked *Amphitryon* for a production for which Henry Purcell wrote the music. David Garrick later turned *Amphitryon* into *The Two Sosias*. Kleist and Giraudoux have since based plays on the same Greek legend. Wycherley's *The Country Wife* (1675) was influenced by *L'École des femmes* and his *The Plain Dealer* was an English version of *Le Misanthrope*. Vanbrugh turned *Le Dépit amoureux* into *The Amorous Mistake* (1705) and he and Congreve collaborated to adapt *Monsieur Pourceaugnac* as *Squire Trelooby* (1704). Colley Cibber's 1717 hit *The Non Juror* is *Tartuffe* reworked to suit the English prejudice against Roman Catholics. In 1732 Henry Fielding translated *Le Médecin malgré lui* as *The Mock Doctor* and *L'Avare* as *The Miser*.

Molière fell out of favour in England with the advent of Romanticism. He was hardly performed at all on the Victorian stage but it was the scholars of that period who started to produce literary translations that were intended for reading rather than acting. He made something of a comeback in the early 1900s, with new versions of plays by dramatists such as Augusta, Lady Gregory, who presented several of the works under the umbrella title of *The Kiltartan Molière* for the newly opened Abbey Theatre in Dublin. In the 1950s

Miles Malleson translated several of the more popular pieces, including *The Miser*, *Tartuffe* and *The Imaginary Invalid*. Malleson was an experienced Shakespearean stage actor (though he is perhaps better known to modern audiences as the poeticising hangman in Robert Hamer's film *Kind Hearts and Coronets*) and his highly actable editions became the standard texts for repertory companies for the next twenty-five years or so.

John Wood published his two-volume collection of ten of Molière's plays in the Penguin Classics series in 1953 and although the publishers commended them to actors and producers as well as to the general reader, the translations are more scholarly in their approach than other versions undertaken by professionals working in the theatre.

More recently the poets Tony Harrison and Richard Wilbur have both applied their talents to the always difficult task of rendering French dramatic verse into English with versions of *The Misanthrope*, and Wilbur has tackled *Tartuffe* as well. And although writer and director Ranjit Bolt is not primarily a poet, he produced a witty verse translation of *Tartuffe* that was well received when it was staged at the Playhouse Theatre in London in 1991.

DON JUAN (1972)

When he was at Oxford Hampton made a special study of Molière. He produced a workable text of *Don Juan* without the aid of a literal translation and for that reason he regarded it as the first legitimate translation he had done. The BBC broadcast the play on Radio 3 in January 1972. Directed by John Tydeman, it starred Kenneth Haigh as Don Juan, with Bill Fraser as his servant, Sganarelle. It was later staged at the Bristol Old Vic in May 1974 under the direction of David Phethean, with Tom Baker as the Don and John Nettles as Sganarelle.

The very first performance of *Don Juan* was in 1665 at the Palais-Royal in Paris, with Molière playing Sganarelle. Probably because of political pressure, he made certain changes after the first night. Much of the scene where Don Juan promises to give a pious beggar a gold coin if he blasphemes was cut, for example, and Sganarelle's last speech was reduced to its final phrase, "My wages! My wages!" When Molière's complete works first appeared in print in France in 1682 these revisions were kept in although the original version was preserved in official files. However, an unexpurgated edition was published in Amersterdam a year later.

Don Juan was originally presented for just fifteen performances altogether and Molière never saw it performed again. The work fell into obscurity and it is quite possible, therefore, that Mozart and his librettist da Ponte were not aware of the play when they began working on the opera *Don Giovanni* over a hundred years later. Like Molière himself, they were almost certainly drawing on the material of the Spanish dramatist Tirso de Molina, who wrote the first play about the legendary Don Juan in 1632.

Molière's version is written in prose and its full title is *Dom Juan ou Le Festin de Pierre*. The subtitle is a pun on the name Peter, which is also the word for 'stone'. John Wood renders this as 'The Statue at the Feast'. Pedro is the name that de Molina gives to the Commander in his drama but Molière calls his character simply the 'Statue of the Commander' and so part of the joke is lost.

Hampton's translation was faithful to the original but, unusually for him, he made some small cuts to the text. He explains in a note on the translation that he had made the omissions "wherever I felt the weighty hand of the Spanish original, with its baroque concepts of honour and florid moralising, lying too heavily across Molière's sprightly prose." An example of this is the speech he cuts in Act Three where Don Carlos explains that a gentleman can be ruined through no fault of his own by being forced into a duel by his sense of honour. In Act Five he also shortens the scene where Don Louis tells his son how disgusted he is with him, as well as the scene where Elvira pleads with Don Juan to repent before it is too late. The speech that Don Juan makes to Don Louis, pretending to have turned over a new leaf when in fact he is merely adopting the disguise of respectability, is also omitted

Like Valmont in *Les Liaisons Dangereuses*, Don Juan is an unprincipled sensualist who abuses his rank as an aristocrat in order to seduce as many women as possible. In Act One, Scene Two he talks of his sexual conquests in military terms, as do Valmont and Merteuil: "I'm as ambitious as a general who advances continually from victory to victory, because he can't bear to limit his desires—nothing matches the sense of achievement I have when I make a beautiful woman give way, and nothing will stop me pursuing that achievement. I know I could make love to the whole world; and like Alexander the Great, I wish there were other worlds, so I could visit them and make new conquests."

Don Juan is the embodiment of consciencelessness, a vice shared by many of Hampton's own characters, and he is quite capable of feigning fidelity when it suits him. His impassioned cry to Charlotte—"I'd kill myself on my sword rather than think of betraying you"—is echoed in Valmont's plea to Tourvel: "I must have you or die". However, despite Don Juan's reputation as a philanderer, Hampton notes that he doesn't manage to seduce a single woman throughout the action of the play, which concentrates on showing the consequences of his immorality.

Hampton may well have been drawn to the play because of Molière's subtle handling of Don Juan's character, which is to make him attractive without glossing over his evil nature. As Hampton acknowledges, it is Sganarelle who is the spokesman for decent values, though Don Juan can always make him look ridiculous in debate. Sganarelle tells his master that he should remember his obligations to God and his family but also that he should believe in ghosts and the remedies sold by quack doctors. Sganarelle teases and criticises him but only when he knows he can get away with it. At the first hint of a threat he reverts to pretending to agree with him. Hampton says that the "harsh moral" of this "rigorous fable" is that those who allow it will be exploited. Sganarelle allows himself to be used more than any of Don Juan's women and consequently he is bullied and deprived of his wages. "This is not a comforting play," says Hampton, and his admiration for Molière's refusal to compromise is like his admiration for the "merciless intelligence" of Laclos' analysis of seduction in *Les Liaisons Dangereuses*.

Don Juan is himself merciless, both in his conquests and in his cynical attitude towards life. Hampton draws our attention to the fact that his first eight lines of dialogue are questions. Don Juan is, in a sense, a man of his time (the seventeenth century saw the beginnings of scepticism and scientific enquiry) and he rejects religion and morality, choosing to believe only in what he can understand.

> DON JUAN: I believe that two and two are four, Sganarelle, and that four and four are eight.
> SGANARELLE: Oh, that's very good. You believe in arithmetic. I must say, people have some funny ideas.

Sganarelle rejects Don Juan's cynicism but is forced to adopt a flexible approach to morality himself in order to keep his job.

We can admire Don Juan's courage when he fights off three robbers to save a man he doesn't know, and even his generosity when he offers money to a beggar if he will blaspheme only to give him a coin anyway "for the love of humanity" after the man has refused to offend God. But although he is dashing and attractive, he is morally empty and his behaviour is contemptible. He ignores all entreaties to repent and it is in fact his ultimate decision to become a hypocrite that seems finally to bring about his long-delayed damnation. When he says that from now on he will play at being virtuous Sganarelle says despairingly, "God's put up with you up to now, but He's not going to put up with this latest outrage."

La Rochefoucauld once defined hypocrisy as the tribute vice pays to virtue but Molière disagrees. His point is that vice's usurpation of the appearance of goodness is the final insult. If there are enough hypocrites in the world it breeds cynicism and mistrustfulness towards goodness, and this may destroy more faith than open wrongdoing. Molière's condemnation of Don Juan can be seen by the way he treats his damnation and descent into Hell as comic.

We are not invited to feel the pity for him that we might for Marlowe's Dr Faustus, the victim of an equally famous on-stage damnation. Certainly Sganarelle feels no pity for his master when he sees him being dragged down to eternal torture. As far as he is concerned, justice has been done, except for the fact that he still has not been paid.

Hampton's translation, as always, was designed to be fluent and easily actable, and he admits in his note on the translation that he had "occasionally sacrificed accuracy for grace". We can see an example of this if we compare one of his speeches with its counterpart in the John Wood version. In Act Three, Scene Five Don Juan and Sganarelle visit the tomb of the Commander. Hampton renders Don Juan's speech as: "What amazes me is that a man who spent his life in a relatively simple house should want such magnificent surroundings to rot in" whereas Wood translates it as "What is most remarkable to me is that a man who in his lifetime was content with quite a modest dwelling should want to have such a magnificent one for the time when he could no longer have any use for it."

Hampton uses shorter words, such as "house" instead of "dwelling" and "life" instead of "lifetime" and the whole speech is phrased more economically. And the word "rot" emphasises the physical side of existence (or death), as comedy often does, and it punctures the grandeur implied by the phrase "magnificent surroundings". This is not to say that either text is inferior; it is merely that they have different aims. Wood's more accurate translation is better for people who want to get as near as possible to what Molière wrote, while Hampton's version is for actors who want a clear and easily performable text.

TARTUFFE (1983)

Hampton returned to Molière some ten years later with his version of *Tartuffe* for the Royal Shakespeare Company. It was a more difficult challenge than *Don Juan* because it is one of the plays written in rhyming alexandrine couplets.

Hampton explains in his introduction to the text that while the rigid phonetic structure, regular participal formations and silent plurals in French make rhyming in that language comparatively easy, he feared that with an English translation the individual ingenuity of some of the rhymes used might turn out to be a distraction from the play as a whole. Molière didn't want his rhymes to draw attention to themselves and Hampton wanted to avoid this danger as well. But he did feel that it would have been "something of an evasion" to ignore the verse form, thus making the style indistinguishable from the plays Molière himself wrote in prose. His solution was to translate *Tartuffe* into unrhymed blank verse, which was the form used by Molière's English contemporaries and one that Hampton had not tried before. He didn't adhere strictly to the metre at all times, having observed that Molière himself didn't always count the syllables in his alexandrines. The result is a crisp and fast-moving text. Some cuts were made in performance though they were put back in the published version.

Tartuffe is one of Molière's most popular plays, especially at the Comédie Française, where it has had more productions than any other work. It has also enjoyed wide popularity in England. Over the last fifteen years or so there have been versions by Simon Gray (in prose), Ranjit Bolt (in verse) and Liz Lochhead (in rhyming Scots dialect).

Molière and his company of actors, La Troupe du roi, enjoyed the patronage of Louis XIV and the first version of the play, entitled *Tartuffe ou L'Hypocrite*, was staged privately at Versailles in 1664. But the King bowed to pressure from the church and denied the work a licence for public performance on the grounds that it was blasphemous. The careful reader will see that Molière was in fact attacking religious hypocrisy (as the play's original title implies) rather than religion itself. The work resurfaced briefly in 1667 under the name *L'Imposteur*; and in 1669 a licence was finally granted to a third version, which has the original title.

The first two versions of *Tartuffe* have not survived but Moliere clearly had to make revisions in order to stage the play at all in public. The fact that the King supported him would account for the glowing description of the King's virtues made by the King's Officer at the end of the play. Although not actually identified by name in the play, Louis XIV no doubt recognised the compliment.

Tartuffe does not appear in the first two of the play's five acts but by the descriptions given by the other characters in advance of his first entrance it is clear that he is a rogue and a hypocrite. Everyone can see this except for the bullying Mme Pernelle and her son Orgon, who has invited him to stay at his home. He believes Tartuffe to be utterly virtuous and wants his daughter Mariane to marry him instead of Valère, the man she loves. But Tartuffe abuses the family's hospitality and propositions Orgon's young wife, Elmire. When Orgon's son by his first marriage, Damis, tells his father this he is promptly disinherited in favour of the usurper. In order to convince Orgon of the truth Elmire tells him to hide under the table while she sets a trap. She pretends to make advances towards Tartuffe and when he responds his motives are revealed. Orgon is mortified to realise how he has been duped. Tartuffe threatens to turn them all out onto the streets now that Orgon has given him the house by a deed of gift but a King's Officer arrives and has him arrested. All ends happily. Orgon allows Mariane to marry Valère and puts his son back in his will. He is a chastened, but hardly a wiser, man.

The name of Tartuffe has become synonymous with hypocrisy in the same way that a tightfisted person is often called a Scrooge. Tartuffe pretends to all the virtues in public when in private his behaviour is despicable. He gives the maid Dorine a handkerchief to cover her cleavage for fear that the sight of her bosom will excite him when all the time he is plotting to seduce Elmire. When Damis accuses him of lechery he says that he deserves to be humiliated even though he is innocent, knowing that such seeming humility will make Orgon more angry on his behalf.

One of the reasons for the play's lasting popularity is that the role of Tartuffe provides such a superb opportunity for an actor to give a comic *tour de force*. In recent years Leonard Rossiter has played him as a shifty and sardonic creep and John Sessions has portrayed him as someone who puts on the air of a humble innocent. In Hampton's version Anthony Sher presented him as a wild-eyed visionary, an almost demonic figure of sensual malevolence, who slavers and drools his way through Orgon's sedate household.

Tartuffe is a farce and can be seen simply as a romp but the best productions appreciate that it is not a kind of 'No Sex Please, We're Parisian'. Molière is not just indulging in ridicule. With Orgon he is satirising the sort of man who seems reasonable but is prey to all sorts of hysterical impulses. It might be objected that *Tartuffe* is a snobbish play because the villain is a character who was born in the slums and tries to better himself, but the play's true comic figure is Orgon, who is meant to be a respectable pillar of bourgeois society. Tartuffe at least is clever and cunning, whereas Orgon is a fool. When Orgon hides under the kitchen table in order to find out whether Tartuffe will try to seduce his wife, the audience laughs at him because he takes so long to realise that he is in danger of being cuckolded. The maid Dorine is also intelligent and she is the one who comes up with this plan to expose Tartuffe's wiles. If the bourgeoisie is to survive, Molière implies, it is only through the good sense of its subordinates.

Orgon's stupidity is far from innocuous. It makes him cruel. Not only does he disinherit his son and try to make his daughter to marry a man she doesn't love, he also grows indifferent to the welfare of his whole family. In Act One he tells his brother-in-law, Cléante, how Tartuffe has influenced him.

> ORGON: Oh, yes, I've quite changed under his instruction:
> he teaches me to cast aside affection
> and clear my mind of any trace of love;
> now I could watch my mother or my brother,
> my wife and children die, and not give that.
> CLÉANTE: I see, he's a humanitarian.

Hampton emphasises Cléante's astute wit, which helps to establish him as the play's conscience. It is he who verbally demolishes Orgon's vices and argues for sane religion rather than hysterical show. And he expresses the wish that Tartuffe will repent of his sinful past and stops Orgon from hurling abuse at the man when his treachery is exposed.

The play's twin themes of gullibility and hypocrisy are ones that are often explored today. The modern mistrust of anyone who projects a virtuous image (which is in itself a justified mistrust for genuinely virtuous people are not too concerned with the image they create) is memorably expressed in *Tartuffe*. It is not as astringent as *Don Juan* nor as complex as *Le Misanthrope*, where the main character's irascibility is both good and bad, but it is probably the finest of Molière's farces.

There is one interesting inconsistency in the play, which probably arose because of the amount of rewriting that Molière was forced to do. One character, Laurent, is not mentioned in the original list of *dramatis personae*, and he has no lines to say, but in Act Three, Scene Two Tartuffe issues some instructions to him. Hampton and the director, Bill Alexander, agreed that they would put Laurent into several scenes in their version of the play, though still as a non-speaking character. As Tartuffe's manservant, after all, it is likely that he would be on stage a great deal.

Laurent came in useful in the scene at the end of the play where the King's Officer arrests Tartuffe. This is the point where Molière had put in the speech that lavishly praises the King. The King's Officer explains that when Tartuffe went to the King to denounce Orgon as a traitor (an incident that occurs offstage) the King had recognised Tartuffe as a wanted man and the perpetrator of many unnamed crimes. Hampton and Alexander agreed that the King's Officer should indicate Laurent when saying the line "he let slip something which allowed the King/to identify him as a wanted man", thus making it Laurent who betrays Tartuffe. This not only explains how the King sees through Tartuffe, it is also more appropriate that he should be punished because his servant had learned his master's treachery. Simon Gray's version, premiered in Washington the year before Hampton's, goes even further and makes Laurent a police agent.

The reviews for Hampton's *Tartuffe* were generally good and the critics praised the speed and fluency of the cast, although Sheridan Morley in *Punch* added that Nigel Hawthorne made Orgon too subtle and intelligent to be taken in so easily. The production was broadcast on BBC2 in November 1985 with the same director and cast.

In a discussion at the Royal National Theatre in 1992 Hampton explained why he had stuck to a small core of classic dramatists for most of his translations: " . . . there are a certain number of playwrights who are in your area, somehow. You can recognise what they're doing, and they come to mean a great deal to you. They come to be sort of dead friends, and it's probably unwise to embark on translating someone outside that field, to try and take over somebody that you couldn't instantly communicate with."

Until 1996, when his translation of the play *Art* by the French dramatist Yasmina Reza was produced in London, not one of the writers Hampton has adapted for the stage was alive when he was born. He has never updated the setting of a play but his modern vigorous language emphasises the fact that the past is not so different from the present. And his translation work gives him inspiration for his own plays. To see, for instance, how Molière portrays the character of a rake in *Don Juan* helped him to create his own in *Les Liaisons Dangereuses*. "I generally have a translation on the go and it feeds into my own work in a quite nourishing way," he said on the *South Bank Show*. "It never does anyone any harm to work closely on a masterpiece."

CHAPTER THIRTEEN

TELEVISION PLAYS (1977–89)

"What's on the telly?"
When Did You Last See My Mother?

Although Hampton had to wait so long to see any of his work reach the cinema, he had more luck with television. He said in an interview in the magazine *AIP and Co*: "TV work is a kind of half-way house between stage and film. There's more concentration on dialogue, it's more of an intimate medium—like stage writing. But you're working with an unknown quantity there too. Like films, the final product is the work of a team."

Many people, including Peggy Ramsay, have suggested that Hampton has spent too much time reshaping other people's material and has lost his own voice, but as he has explained, life in the theatre is not that simple: "My own projects have proceeded at such a snail-like pace that I've simply had to do other things. A play takes me about three years on average, and I've been at it for twenty-six years and I've written nine plays. They keep popping out at those three-year intervals." He adds, "As long as the thing connects with an audience I don't really mind whose name is on the bill."

So far *Able's Will* is the only original play for television that Hampton has had produced. Of his stage plays, *Total Eclipse, The Philanthropist, Savages, Treats* and *Tales from Hollywood* have all been televised. There is one project, *The Price of Tea*, that has not yet been made. It is an original screenplay set in Sri Lanka and tells the story of a journalist who investigates the case of a murdered doctor. But in order to help publicise the Tamils' cause she files a story that she knows isn't true. This raises the question of whether lying can ever be justified. *The Price of Tea* was originally commissioned by Granada Television in 1983 and, due to various contractual wranglings, has been optioned three times by the BBC.

ABLE'S WILL (1977)

> "You know in the Fu Manchu movies, when he says, I can promise you a beautifully painful and slow, slow death? For me this is called marriage."
>
> *Tales from Hollywood*

Hampton wrote *Able's Will* during what he regards as his dry period: the five years between *Treats* (his last play for the Royal Court Theatre) and his comeback play, *Tales from Hollywood*.

Able's Will opens in the mid-1970s as Thomas Able, a once successful novelist who mysteriously gave up writing shortly after the second world war, lies dying. His family gather round him to witness his death and to find out what he has left them in his will. Able has been rendered mute by hemiplegia and we hear his thoughts in voice-over. His older son, Stephen, is an emotionally frigid man, who arrives with his wife, Phyllis, and their eighteen-year-old son, Colin. Able's younger son, Charles, is less financially successful than Stephen and has borrowed a large amount of money from his father over the years. He brings his wife, Ada, and Julie, their oldest daughter, who is twelve. But Able's favourite child, his daughter Kate, stays away, despite his sister Sarah's desperate phone calls imploring her to come before it is too late.

Stephen and Phyllis speculate on the contents of the will. They are worried that Able will leave his large Georgian house to Sarah, who has spent the last thirty-odd years housekeeping for him, and they are already trying to think of ways to get her out. Charles is hoping to inherit enough money to solve his financial difficulties and hopes to find a painting that will turn out to be valuable.

Between the scenes set in the present there are flashbacks that show Able as a young man, and moments from his life with Sarah, who moved into the house to look after him after the death of his wife, May, in the 1940s. The action of the play builds up to his own death and cremation, followed by the reading of his will.

After this there is only one flashback, which shows Able explaining to Sarah that he could no longer write because of his relationship with May: "The joke of it was, you see, I loved her. I was lost without her. All that time I'd thought I was a writer, and I didn't even have the elementary self-knowledge to understand my own most basic emotions. It makes me heave to think of it. I'd spent years of my life waiting for a woman I loved to die, and then she did die and then I knew I was fucked."

Sarah promises never to tell anyone. Like Isabelle in *Total Eclipse* she becomes the keeper of the flame and is determined to preserve the public image of her brother. The very last scene of the play shows her lying on Able's bed, whispering "My love".

Able is like Verlaine: both are failed radicals who feel they have been tamed by marriage. Able feels resentful that his wife had refused to let him go and fight in the Spanish Civil War. He feels that he has become "irredeemably bourgeois" and has sold out by accepting the role of dutiful husband and father. This is one of Hampton's favourite themes: the artist's relation to society. Rimbaud and Verlaine both despise convention but only Rimbaud has the courage to break away.

With the possible exception of Kate, Able's children have all turned out to be "irredeemably bourgeois" too. His grandson Colin, however, has ambitions to be a writer and he is the only member of the family to show an interest in Able's past. When he asks Sarah about him she replies: "He thought writers should be like criminals, have their irresponsibility, I mean, and their guilts and their loyalties. Under certain circumstances, for example, nothing could be more criminal than to tell the truth, wouldn't you think?" But she refuses to be drawn further on the real reasons for Able's failure to go on writing after May's death.

Colin, it is implied, is heading the same way as Able, who sees something of his younger self in the boy: "When I was at Oxford, he reminds me of; myself at Oxford. I thought I was a bohemian anarchist." But later on in the same scene he reflects: "But perhaps he's more ruthless than I was. So at least when he feels guilty, it'll be about the things he's done, not about the things he never managed."

And Colin does indeed have something to feel guilty about for while they are all staying at Able's house he is drawn into an affair with his underaged cousin Julie, who uses his fear of exposure to blackmail him into continuing the relationship. She is reminiscent of Araminta in *The Philanthropist*, who was also a twelve-year-old victim of sexual abuse by a relative. Julie encourages Colin to seduce her, but even so it is he, as the older of the two, who has to bear the burden of guilt.

Occasions such as funerals are ideal vehicles for the exploration of the embarrassments and tensions of family life and Hampton uses the scene at the crematorium to demonstrate the awful banality of public grief. Everyone is waiting for Kate and her husband, John, to arrive. The frustration mounts and the vicar decides to proceed instead with the funeral of another man, who has no mourners at all. When Ada spontaneously bursts into tears Charles goes to her, ostensibly to comfort her. But he hisses "Don't!" between his teeth. He feels that her display of emotion is unseemly.

Kate is also in tears when she and John finally arrive. She seems to acknowledge the family's coldness by kissing only Sarah. She refuses to follow them into the service and locks herself in the toilet. John tries to coax her out but even in his fury he can't break the taboo forbidding him to enter a ladies' lavatory. Kate stays there until the formalities are over but she does join the gathering for the reading of the will.

As most of the family had feared, it turns out that Able has left the house and its contents to Sarah, plus £5,000 in cash. The residue is bequeathed to the three children. Then comes the bombshell. John, who is reading the will, reveals that there is no residue so they will receive nothing except for the royalties on their father's books, which amount to about £1 a week each. At this point Kate storms out the room, shouting "You really are a bastard" at her husband. This unexplained outburst is her only line of dialogue in the entire play.

The same actress plays the part of Kate in the present and May in the flashback scenes, which underlines the suggestion that Able has somehow linked the two women in his mind, pouring out the love he was unable to express to his wife onto his daughter. And maybe Kate, like her father, can't acknowledge her love until it is too late.

In the days following the funeral we see Stephen and Phyllis trying to think of ways to persuade Sarah to leave the house and move into a flat so that they can sell the property and take the proceeds. Charles is disappointed that he still has no way to resolve his financial worries and he tries, unsuccessfully, to borrow money from Stephen. Only Ada, whom Able had recognised as being less grasping than the others, shows any disapproval at their plotting, pointing out that Able had every right to do what he wanted with his own house.

One of Hampton's recurring themes is the descent into total apathy, as seen with Ian in *When Did You Last See My Mother?* and Don and Jack Boot in *The Philanthropist*, who all give up trying to achieve anything with their lives. Able, like Boot, comes to the conclusion that art has no point because it cannot affect how the world is run, and both men end up unable to move, Boot through catatonia and Able through physical paralysis. Unlike Rimbaud, Able doesn't give up writing in order to do something else but just vegetates. He maintains an artistic silence for thirty years and in the end he is literally mute as well. Ashes seem to be all that he has left behind—both the physical ashes after his cremation and the ashes of his talent. "Well, then," he says, "This time next week I shall be ashes on the wind. No. No, no, that's terrible. Let's see now. This time next week I shall be dead. That's better. That's more like it. Yes."

Colin uses this metaphor too in an article he is writing about his grandfather: "As for the man himself, he is ashes on the wind." He is pleased with the phrase that Able had rejected as hackneyed, which suggests that he has less talent. The image of ashes is also used when the family is playing a game of Scrabble. Colin spells out the word 'ashes', which his mother changes to 'cashes', saying: "That's all I can think of".

Hampton often makes the ending of a play mirror its beginning to show how a situation has developed. But in *Able's Will* the symmetries point to the future as well and bring to mind Santayana's belief that those who do not understand the past are doomed to relive it. Colin, it seems, has not understood his grandfather and so is destined to fail just like him. This suggests the futility of independent action and is an exceptionally bleak view for Hampton to take. His characters, however much they suffer, are usually allowed a small amount of personal freedom. Even if their lives are destroyed, they generally have enough insight to understand why.

Ultimately, the real problem for Able is his lack of self-knowledge. Hampton explains that one reason that Able gave up was because he didn't believe that he had the right to be a writer "since he was so bad at working out that his wife was the most important thing in his life".

"Self-obsession, that's all it was." Able's words on writing reflect Braham's in *The Philanthropist*. Maybe Able had nothing to say to begin with and this is what Colin begins to suspect. "Perhaps he never had it after all," he says. After all, the title of the play is a pun. The man is called Able, but he is unable; he leaves a will but has no real will of his own.

Hampton's obsession with classical music and its links with death are much in evidence. This provides another bond between Able and Colin. When Colin complains about the music on the car radio his father says: "I suppose you'd prefer Beethoven". When we first see Able Sarah has just put on Mozart's Requiem for him. He finds the gesture "tactless, but thoughtful." The Requiem is the last work that Mozart wrote before his own death. Don in *The Philanthropist* describes his idle habit of listening to baroque music all day while emptying his mind of any thought but Able has perfected the art of idleness even more fully.

Mozart's *Sinfonia Concertante*, Haydn's *Creation* (which also featured in *The Philanthropist*) and a Bach harpsichord concerto are all used as background music while Able sits and does nothing with his life. His last moments are spent trying to identify Telemann's *Concerto for Three Oboes and Three Violins*, and he dies as he had lived, in a state of uncertainty.

Able's Will was broadcast by the BBC in October 1977. Daniel Massey played Able with just the right degree of weary sensitivity, and Elizabeth Spriggs brought a tragic dignity to the enigmatic role of Sarah. The strong supporting cast, including Di Trevis as May and Kate, Benjamin Whitrow as Stephen, Anthony Jackson as Charles, Phyllida Law as Phyllis, Sharon Duce as Ada, Dominic Guard as Colin and Penelope Wilton as a journalist who tries to interview Able, were skilfully directed by Stephen Frears. Hampton was impressed by Frears, who had directed one cinema film, *Gumshoe*, and many television plays, including work by Alan Bennett and Peter Prince (author of *The Good Father*, which Hampton was later to adapt). He was Hampton's first choice for *Dangerous Liaisons*, a film that proved that he had no difficulty handling big-budget projects.

In many ways *Able's Will* resembles John Osborne's 1971 play *West Of Suez* and David Mercer's 1968 television play *On the Eve of Publication*. All three works deal with acclaimed writers who are uneasy with their reputations. This seems to be a twentieth-century obsession that perhaps emerges from the fact that while modern writers are more and more feted and publicised (without perhaps being more read) than in previous generations, art itself is less valued than before, with critics of both the far left and far right demanding that artists come out of their supposed ivory towers and tackle the problems of the real world. In all three plays the writer meets his death. Osborne's Wyatt Gilman is shot in a native uprising while Able and Mercer's Robert Kelvin die of natural causes, but in each case the artist seems to be out of tune with his time. Osborne is writing about the erosion of British influence in the world while Mercer's hero is disillusioned with communism. Like Able, Kelvin also has ambivalent feelings about his wife. "I love her. I need her." he says. "And I can't stand the sight of her."

Able's Will is also reminiscent of Simon Gray's *Close of Play*, which also has a central character, Jasper Rees, who cannot speak, except for a hysterical monologue at the end. This hero is also surrounded by a family that is driven by guilt.

Able joins the gallery of writers who have given up, a course of action that Hampton himself has never taken, despite all his doubts. If the artist can't do much to solve human misery, then the one who gives art up manages even less.

THE HISTORY MAN (1980)

In 1975 a play called *The After Dinner Game*, directed by Robert Knights and written by Malcolm Bradbury and Christopher Bigsby, was broadcast on BBC2's 'Play for Today' slot. One of the characters is a social psychologist called Flora Beniform, who also features prominently in Bradbury's novel *The History Man*, published in the same year. At the time Knights was filming *The Glittering Prizes*, Frederic Raphael's television series about a group of Cambridge graduates working in the media and he was very keen to see *The History Man* brought to the screen. Before this was achieved he directed *Love on a Gunboat*, another of Bradbury's contributions to 'Play for Today', and seen in 1977. They were to collaborate again on two more dramatisations: a short story by John Fowles, *The Enigma*, which went out on BBC2 in 1980, and Tom Sharpe's novel set in a fictional Cambridge college, *Porterhouse Blue*, for Channel 4 in 1987.

Bradbury had spent seven years writing *The History Man* and by the time it was published he knew that the political scene had changed. He had been satirising the spurious radicalism of the 1960s and early 1970s but the liberal-humanist values that he wanted to defend now seemed to be coming under attack from the right rather than from the far left. He had doubts about dramatising the novel himself as he felt that the emergent monetarist right would only use the play as ammunition to prove that all radicalism was outdated and ridiculous. In an interview that appeared in the *Observer* on 4 January 1981, the day the first episode of the four-part serial was transmitted on BBC2, he said that he disliked the "radical irrationalism and anti-humanism" that he had observed developing throughout the 1970s. Despite these reservations he allowed Knights to go ahead and ask Hampton to do the dramatisation.

In an article in the *Listener* in 1988 Bradbury praised Hampton's "brilliant script, which managed to turn the irony of the book into conflict and sharp observation". He pointed out in the same article that many series set in universities went out in the 1980s—Andrew Davies's *A Very Peculiar Practice*, David Lodge's *Small World* and his own dramatisation of *Porterhouse Blue* had all proved popular—and suggested that an UCCA handbook would perhaps be a more accurate guide to the schedules than the *Radio Times*.

Hampton had already satirised university life in *The Philanthropist* and Bradbury's academic world of promiscuity, backbiting and rampant ambition is one that he could identify with. But the leading character, Howard Kirk, is nothing like either Philip or Don; he is energetic, charismatic and sexy and an expert but heartless manipulator of both people and systems. As such he represents a much more modern, and ultimately more dangerous, phenomenon: the academic as revolutionary.

Howard, a sociology lecturer, is the 'history man' of the title. He sees history as a process of struggle leading to the liberation of the people. Once this goal is achieved, he believes, there will be no further need for a historical perspective or for personal responsibility. He proclaims that society is poised on the brink of revolution and so all the old traditions and conventions can be disregarded. Not only does Howard regard himself as sexually liberated, he behaves as though he is liberated from history as well.

The story is set in the autumn term of 1972 at the fictional University of Watermouth. The novel is written in the third person and the narrative is, unusually, given almost entirely in the present tense. The purpose of this is to reflect the way that Howard thinks and operates: in the present, with no regard for history and no thought for future consequences.

There are just two chapters in the novel written in the past tense and these deal with the time when Howard and his wife, Barbara, were hard-working and decidedly untrendy provincial students. Knights decided that he didn't want a flashback scene or any "do you remember?" dialogue between them and so most of the details about their past were dropped, though one character, Myra Beamish, hints darkly that she remembers them before they were trendy.

Howard epitomises all that was wrong with the sexual and political revolutionary movements of the late 1960s and early 1970s. He takes advantage of the prevailing changes in sexual morality and insists that his marriage should be an open one, meaning that he can have as many affairs as he likes. Barbara sees through this, as does his academic colleague and lover, the coolly amused Flora Beniform. One of his students, Felicity Phee, also sleeps with him and only later realises how exploitative he is. When a new English lecturer, Annie Callendar, arrives on campus, he sets his sights on seducing her too.

As well as pursuing women, Howard is very active politically and he is anxious to consolidate his position as a radical leader within the university. In Episode One he starts a rumour that Professor Mangel, a scientist whose blameless research into genetics has nevertheless been condemned by the radical press, is coming to give a lecture. In Episode Two he sneaks into the office of the principal, Professor Marvin, and leaves a memo on the dictaphone telling the departmental secretary to send an invitation to Mangel. This is the starting point for a complicated chain of events that will end up affecting everyone on campus.

During the first episode we begin to see that Howard's marriage is under strain. Barbara doesn't think much of his latest book, which argues that the concept of privacy and the private individual has no place in a truly open society. She argues that his work is empty but always manages to be on the right side. As we soon learn, Howard thrives on intrigue and the last thing he wants is for the details of his private life, either past or present, to be made public. Barbara links him to the past and now he has moved up in the world he finds her an embarrassment.

The episode ends with a beginning-of-term party at Howard's house. One of the guests is Annie, who is to be his most formidable opponent. Describing herself as "a nineteenth-century liberal", she represents the humane, bourgeois culture that he is dedicated to overthrowing. The fact that she is called Callendar indicates that, unlike Howard, she doesn't fool herself that she can escape history.

Howard, as always, is the centre of attention at the party, but he later slips down to the basement to have sex with Felicity. Meanwhile, in the bathroom, Henry Beamish, an accident-prone lecturer and the author of a book on charisma, puts his arm through the window and cuts his wrist, a suicidal action that he immediately regrets.

Episode Two starts in the early hours of the following morning with Henry being bandaged up by a couple of ambulancemen in Howard's bathroom while his wife, Myra, stands by and pours scorn on him.

At breakfast Howard antagonises Barbara by ignoring the unruly behaviour of their two children and then sets off for the university. He stops to give Annie a lift when he sees her waiting for a bus and in the van they discuss their different views of life. Just before Howard drops her off he quotes William Blake: "Sooner murder an infant in its cradle than nurse unacted desires." He takes this to mean that one should indulge every craving but Annie says that he has got it wrong. Howard later checks the reference and rings Annie to tell her that he was right. She replies that she meant that he had misinterpreted Blake's meaning, which is that it is better to kill desire at the outset rather than torment oneself over something that is unattainable. Howard has put his own interpretation on the saying to justify his chronically selfish promiscuity.

After the first tutorial of the term Howard comes into conflict with one of his students, George Carmody, who is upset about the low grades he has been getting for his sociology essays. George, an ex-public schoolboy (he insists on calling Howard "Sir"), is humourless and pedantic, which makes him an ideal scapegoat and a target for Howard's class antagonism. He accuses Howard of bias in his marking and tells him he intends to report the matter to Professor Marvin, adding: "I know more about you than you think," referring to the fact that he knows about Howard and Felicity.

Howard's marking is indeed biased and he believes that objective assessment is impossible but he won't concede that George has a legitimate cause for complaint. He accuses him of blackmail, reduces him to tears and orders him out of his office.

Later that morning Flora visits Howard in his office. She appreciates his cunning and his dedication to a life of deceit. When he tells her that Barbara had accused him of pushing Henry through the bathroom window she says: "Barbara really ought to know by now that if you wanted someone pushed out of the window you'd have hired someone else to do it, or persuaded him it was in his own best interests to do it himself."

Like Valmont in *Les Liaisons Dangereuses* or Dave in *Treats*, Howard clearly doesn't believe in friendship. When Flora talks to him about Henry she shows that she realises this:

FLORA: I'd have guessed you were friends.
HOWARD: Why?
FLORA: Your hostility towards him.

At the end of the episode Howard has a meeting with Professor Marvin to discuss George Carmody's allegations of unfair treatment. For his final line he comes up with another quote from Blake: "Opposition is true friendship." In his case, of course, it is anything but.

The third episode of *The History Man* continues with events on the same day as Episode Two. One major scene, and one of the funniest, satirises a typical academic departmental meeting. Professor Marvin's secretary tells him about the memo inviting Professor Mangel to speak but as he knows nothing about it he tries to dismiss the matter as an error. But the radicals in the department demand to know whether the college would be prepared to give the man they regard as a fascist a platform for his ideas. This accusation enrages another faculty member, Professor Zachary, who, like Mangel, had fled Nazi persecution of the Jews and so knows what real fascism looks like. He proposes that the invitation should be issued after all. As one of the radicals, Howard should be voting against the motion but he abstains when he realises that the result will be a fifty-fifty split, which could lead to the invitation being cancelled. Only Flora suspects that the whole thing might be one of his elaborate schemes and murmurs to him: "Oh, Howard, Howard, is this your doing?"

That evening, while Barbara is on her way to London to meet her lover, Howard visits Flora at her flat and when she asks him whether he feels that he is a fraud he replies: "I don't think so. Not more than anyone else." The implication here is that although he is aware of how he manipulates other people he thinks that everyone else behaves in the same way. He can't conceive of anyone being genuinely honest.

Although she is not a conspirator, Flora is quite similar to Merteuil in *Les Liaisons Dangereuses* and enjoys observing people from a distance though she is capable of showing some affection. She takes pity on Henry after Myra leaves him briefly, and becomes his mistress for a while.

The time span of the fourth and final episode is more spread out and covers the rest of the academic term. George has started stalking Howard and secretly filming him and Felicity together. He has also complained to Annie and Howard visits her in order to put his side of the case to her. Annie tells him that his version of events is very different from George's. "It just goes to show what happens when you change the *point d'appui*," she says, explaining that this is a literary term meaning 'angle of vision'. Annie judges things from a literary standpoint, though she is far more humane and sympathetic than most of Hampton's characters who do this.

But Howard is not impressed by her talk; he dashes a tea tray from her hand and shouts at her, telling her that she had made her home a hiding place, "somewhere where you'll hate and dry up and wither and grudge". He offers sex as a way of releasing her from herself, and she consents. It might be objected that by doing this Annie is agreeing to Howard's assessment of women, namely that their problems are all caused by not having enough sex. But Hampton and Bradbury are perhaps implying that Annie's nineteenth-century liberalism is not sufficient to fulfil her. Perhaps her situation is comparable to Ann's in *Treats*. Both of these women's lives are so sterile that they put up with relationships with appalling men simply in order to feel something.

On the two occasions that we see Howard approaching Annie's house (the second time her enthusiastic welcome shows that she has grown used to being his lover), we hear the aria 'Là ci darem la mano' ['There we'll take hands'] from Mozart's *Don Giovanni* on the soundtrack. It is from the scene in the opera where Don Giovanni tries to persuade the new bride Zerlina to be unfaithful with him on her wedding day. Hampton's musical reference is ironic. Don Giovanni is a seducer who is finally uncovered and dragged to hell for his crimes.

But Howard escapes any form of disgrace or condemnation, and the fact that he has nearly as energetic a sex life as the Don is taken by his friends as a good thing. When he first sleeps with Annie she insists that they make love in the dark but by the end of the story he has persuaded her to keep the lights on.

In the meantime discontent has been whipped up on campus over Professor Mangel's forthcoming visit, George's snooping has been exposed, and a confrontation with the authorities looks inevitable.

In the novel the scenes dealing with the student demonstration and the expulsion of George Carmody are dealt with in a few pages, but Hampton expands this material to take up most of the episode, which gives the series a more dramatic climax. The students hold a strike and demand that George be sent down, which he is. The protesters also stage a sit-in in the hall where Mangel is due to lecture. Henry knows that Mangel has died of a heart attack on his way to the university but he doesn't tell the students in case they laugh. Instead he stands on a table and asks them to leave. Their response is to pelt him with rubbish, causing him to fall and break his arm.

Although Henry is an absurd figure, his behaviour at this point shows that he has a sense of decency. Howard visits him in hospital but Henry asks him not to come back. He says that he doesn't object to the causes that Howard stands for but believes that the danger is in "those that ride on the backs of those causes". Bradbury makes Henry rather less perceptive about Howard in the novel but a more open condemnation was perhaps needed for the television version so as to counteract the viewer's natural inclination to empathise with a charismatic leading man.

The series ends with another party. It is the end of term, Christmas is approaching, and Howard is the campus hero. Melissa Todoroff, the obnoxious visiting lecturer, praises him as the 'radical's radical'. But his victory is not without its price. Felicity, who had begun by adoring him, comes to understand just how devious and exploitative he is. She leaves the party early, telling him that she intends to switch tutors the following term, and warns him not to get in her way. Flora has also finished with him, though whether this is because she is disgusted with him or because she is afraid of becoming too emotionally involved is left ambiguous.

Howard still has his relationship with Annie and down in the basement where they are making love she prompts him to reveal how he had engineered the demonstration against Mangel and George's expulsion. He claims that what he did was historically inevitable and so he cannot be held personally responsible. But Annie will not accept this.

> ANNIE: You did it for the sheer pleasure of the plot.
> HOWARD: It's the plot of history. There's a process. It charges everyone a price for the stand they choose to take.
> ANNIE: You seem to travel free.

At the party in the first episode Howard makes love to Felicity in the basement while Henry cuts his wrist by putting his hand through the bathroom window. At the end-of-term party Howard makes love to Annie in the basement while Barbara cuts her wrist in the same way. Hampton often uses this kind of symmetry in his own work but in this case the structure and pattern of events were already there in the novel.

The idea of suicide has been in Barbara's mind from the beginning. In Episode One she tells Howard that an acquaintance of theirs has killed himself, leaving a note that read: "This is silly". Howard is not particularly interested and he fails to notice that Barbara is growing more and more unhappy. Just before she injures herself she writes the message "This is silly" in red lipstick on the bathroom mirror.

We don't know whether or not Barbara survives and we are not shown what Howard's reaction is. In the final shot he is still in the basement with Annie while a caption on the screen tells us that at the last election he voted Conservative.

This last piece of information is Hampton's own but it would be wrong to interpret his updating of the novel as an attempt to imply either that Howard was never a real radical or that all radicalism is tied up with youth. In 1981, when the series was transmitted, "the last election" referred to is the one in 1979 that brought Margaret Thatcher to power. She represented a new style of Conservatism where the old ideas of social stability and order were rejected for a species of "enlightened self-interest". To see Howard as a Tory voter was not necessarily to accuse him of selling out but could be viewed as the natural outcome of his philosophy of total selfishness.

At an event at the National Film Theatre in August 1981 (reported in that month's *Broadcast* magazine) the series was screened in its entirety and Bradbury spoke about it afterwards. He explained that he was afraid that it may have provided ammunition for those who wanted to knock the new universities, and in Britain in the 1980s education was being attacked as something that had nothing to do with 'the real world', by people who seemed to believe that 'the real world' was somehow represented by Milton Friedman. He was also concerned about the explicit sex scenes. In his novel Howard and Flora's affair had been "a seminar continued in the bedroom" and he felt that their relationship had become a springboard for the fantasies of "lusty cameramen". Hampton, who was in the audience, spoke up during question time, saying that he "failed to see how naked ladies might distract from the flow of intellectual discourse".

One of Bradbury's worries was that the television version, with its inevitable depiction of 1970s clothes and furniture, would look as if it was ridiculing a past era that everyone had outgrown. There is always a risk that setting something in an earlier decade will turn it into a vehicle for nostalgia. Hanif Kureishi's novel *The Buddha of Suburbia*, which he dramatised for television with his director Roger Michell in 1993, treats the 1970s with a great deal of nostalgic affection, for example, and also ends with a reference to Margaret Thatcher's 1979 election victory. But the superficial trappings of tank tops and platform heels in *The History Man* do nothing to disguise the fact that there are ambitious cynics like Howard Kirk at all times and in all walks of life and they are just as dangerous now as they ever were.

Although he was generous in his praise of Hampton's dramatisation, Bradbury disagreed with the sentiments of the updated ending, saying that it was likely that Howard would have gone further to the left, and might even have masterminded the Toxteth riots.

Clive James, writing in the *Observer*, enjoyed the programme but accused it of making Howard too horrible: "The series offered a false reassurance. It said that snakes can't have charm." But Anthony Sher's outstanding performance gives Howard a shrewd reptilian carnality which, although repulsive, gives off an air of excitement and danger. It is entirely credible that even women who see through him might still be attracted to him.

The History Man is highly articulate and intricately structured. It is probably Hampton's best dramatisation for television and the only one to capture fully the astringency of his stage work. In addition the performances invest the exaggerated characters with life without destroying the series' overall satirical intent. Geraldine James as Barbara, Laura Davenport as Annie, Veronica Quilligan as Felicity and Paul Brooke as Henry are flawlessly cast, and Isla Blair pulls off the remarkable feat of portraying Flora's coolly detached view of other people's suffering without losing our sympathy.

Amongst the smaller parts there are good cameos from Michael Hordern as the ever-weary principal, Professor Marvin, Peter Hugo-Daly as the socially inept George Carmody ("the only student in the university with a trouser-press", as Annie remarks), Miriam Margolyes as Melissa Todoroff, a bumptious radical (a part similar to the one she would play in Hampton's later film version of *The Good Father*), and Maggie Steed as Myra Beamish, the sort of woman who can be relied upon to turn up and tell you about her marital crisis at the wrong moment.

Like all of Hampton's best work, *The History Man* refuses to be comforting yet it is not despairing. The vigour, intelligence and wit of the writing stimulates the mind even when the message is bleak.

HOTEL DU LAC (1986)

Actress Anna Massey and freelance producer Susan Birtwhistle asked Anita Brookner, a novelist they both admired, to write a television script for Massey to star in. Brookner turned down the opportunity, feeling that television was not her medium, but was happy to sell them the rights to *Hotel du Lac*, which was about to be published. This was in August 1984; in October that year the novel won the Booker Prize.

Hampton was chosen to write the screenplay and the film went into production in Switzerland the following summer. "Since it was a BBC production," he noted wryly in an interview with the *Sunday Telegraph*, "the writer had to stay at home." The film was broadcast in March 1986 on BBC2.

Anna Massey plays Edith Hope, a writer of romances (under the pseudonym of Vanessa Wilde), who takes a holiday at a Swiss hotel called the Hotel du Lac She has left England in rather mysterious circumstances; she refers to a 'crime' she has committed which has outraged all her friends. We see brief shots of her riding in the back of a Rolls-Royce somewhere in London, but we don't learn of the significance of this until much later on in the film.

The hotel, with its tinkling piano forever pouring out light romantic melodies such as 'Wouldn't it be Luverly?', is the epitome of middle-class gentility. But the lives of most of the other guests are far from 'luverly'. When Edith first arrives she invents life-histories for all the people she observes but as she makes contact with them one by one she discovers that she has not guessed correctly for any of them.

The Puseys, an English mother and daughter who indulge in shopping trips of enormous greed, turn out to be twenty years older than Edith had thought, and not nearly as aristocratic. Monica, the woman she takes for a dancer, is the wife of a high-ranking European official who has sent her to Switzerland for treatment for infertility, and an old lady whom she imagines to be the widow of a Belgian confectioner is actually a countess who has been forced out of her chateau by a jealous daughter-in-law. "So much for the novelist's famed powers of invention," remarks Edith self-mockingly.

Non-communication is one of the film's main themes. The Puseys feel sorry for Edith as she looks so lonely; they make a point of talking to her but are too wrapped up in themselves to listen to what she says. The Countess is deaf, and the hugely snobbish Monica, although she speaks to Edith as she can't stand most of the other guests, can be extremely rude and tells Edith that "sometimes you strike me as being a bit thick". Monica despises Mrs Pusey, whose wealth comes from trade, and is persistently unpleasant to her. At one point she begins to talk seriously about her own barrenness but Mrs Pusey, who had introduced the topic by revealing that she had had trouble conceiving her daughter Jennifer, then blithely changes the subject.

We see events only through Edith's eyes and on the whole she is a reliable narrator. We soon learn that she has a great capacity for the role of confidante but has no confidante of her own. The only way she can express her emotions is by writing letters to her lover, David. Heard in voice-over, these letters comment on the goings-on at the hotel and reveal her innermost thoughts and feelings. It is only at the end of the film that we discover that she has not actually sent any of them.

Interspersed with scenes at the hotel are flashbacks that show us what Edith's life was like before. She meets David, an auctioneer, at a party given by her man-eating friend Penelope, and begins an affair with him. He can only spare her the odd evening (he is married) but she puts up with the situation without complaint. Knowing that she can never have him exclusively, she accepts a proposal of marriage from Geoffrey, a single man who has been living alone since the death of his mother. But on the way to her wedding she orders the chauffeur to drive on past the church, to the dismay of everyone waiting on the steps for her. She finally returns home to find that her friends have gone ahead with the reception party though it is naturally a rather low-key affair. She returns her engagement ring to Geoffrey, who complains that she has made him a laughing stock. It is after this 'crime' that Penelope sends her off to the Hotel du Lac. Edith hopes that she can resume her relationship with David but as her stay at the hotel lengthens she is increasingly disappointed that he has not taken the trouble to write to her. And then she meets Mr Neville.

At first sight Mr Neville is a figure straight out of one of her own novels; he is suave, handsome, urbane, and he takes an unexpected interest in her. Like Heathcliff or Mr Rochester, he is referred to only by his surname, which makes him into a mysteriously remote masculine figure.

In a flashback we hear Edith explain to her agent that in her books there is usually a 'mouse', an ordinary, unglamorous woman who sees off a sultry temptress to win the hero for herself. Edith sees her books as updated versions of the myth of the tortoise and the hare. In real life, she explains, the hare always wins, but in her books she makes sure that the race goes to the overlooked. She sees nothing wrong in perpetuating what she takes to be comforting lies. Her agent wants her to write for a new market, the executive woman spending "lonely nights in the hotel" (as Edith herself will soon be doing). Edith is sceptical, saying that if the new women were that liberated they would go out and pick up a man in a bar. But she feels that the reason they don't do this is that deep down every woman still believes in the old romantic fantasy of a man 'discovering' her.

Now it is Mr Neville who has 'discovered' Edith. He identifies her as Vanessa Wilde (presumably recognising her from publicity pictures) even though she hadn't told him her *nom de plume*. He takes her out to lunch and she is flattered that he actually listens to what she says. But Mr Neville, it turns out, is not a true romantic hero for he advocates a philosophy of selfishness that is completely unromantic. He tells Edith that he has reached the conclusion that there is no such thing as perfect compatibility and so denies that a relationship between a man and a woman can ever be ideal. He is still smarting from the humiliation of his wife's leaving him for another man. If one is selfish, he declares, one need never be unhappy again. "Or entirely happy either," Edith adds. She knows that there is something sterile about this view of life and is not convinced by his arguments.

Mr Neville is as accurate as the devil at locating people's secret discontent. Over lunch one day he accurately summarises what Edith's life is like: she goes to publishers' parties but leaves early; she has had a few lovers but her friends think that she has had none. He then proposes marriage to her in the most blunt and unromantic manner imaginable. She is taken aback and says it feels as if he is interviewing her for a job. He admits that he doesn't love her but says that their marriage would be "an enlightened partnership". Both would be free to have affairs if they were discreet. He doesn't expect her to love him but they would enjoy a union based on companionship and shared interests. The relationship he describes is rather like that of Ann and Patrick in *Treats*—joyless, passionless and painless. Edith, lonely and fearful that she has lost David for good, later accepts his proposal.

Like Geoffrey, Mr Neville has a fear of being made a laughing stock. He chooses Edith because he can be certain that she will never embarrass him. But he does also admit to having some feeling for her. "You got under my guard," he tells her. "You've touched and moved me in a way I no longer care to be touched and moved. I'm sure it won't last."

Just as she is about to give him her answer, Edith breaks down in tears. To begin with Mr Neville's response is that of a conventional romantic hero. He says, "Don't. I can't bear to see a woman cry", a cliché straight out of a romantic love story, but then he adds, "It makes me want to hit her." Whether he means it or not, it is a brutal thing to say and it displays a total lack of compassion, and here we see the core of his personality.

In spite of this Edith sticks to her decision. The holiday season is coming to an end and her future seems assured. The Countess is packed off by her son to a hotel in Lausanne. Monica's hopes of curing her infertility are dashed. She is upset, not only because she feels her marriage depends on her having children, but she actually wants to have a baby. Only the Puseys, with their colossal selfishness, seem unchanged, still blind to the suffering or cares of anyone else. Yet there is one hint of discord in their lives. Mrs Pusey accuses a waiter of sneaking into Jennifer's room. Jennifer is entirely unperturbed by the fuss and seemingly oblivious to her mother's desire to desexualise her and keep her in a state of childlike dependence. Mrs Pusey is right to suspect something, but the truth is not revealed to her—it is revealed to Edith.

Edith explains in a letter to David—"the last I shall ever write, and the first one I shall send"—that she has agreed to marry Mr Neville. She goes on to tell him that he had been wrong to assume that when they were together she was doing "the same thing, with the same degree of selfishness" as he was. For her it had been no casual fling. He was wrong to assume that she wrote her stories with a cynical detachment. "I believe every word of them," she writes, "I still do." But now she has decided to face up to things squarely and honestly as far as her own life is concerned. "For the first time I feel like an adult with adult concerns," she says. She will have her 'adult' home life, her affairs, her bits of gossip, and her comfortable but loveless marriage.

She is on her way to post this letter to David when she sees Mr Neville coming out of Jennifer's room. As he steals away down the corridor Edith tears up the letter. She goes immediately to reception and sends David a telegram. At first she puts "Coming home" but then changes her mind and writes just one word: "Returning". "Coming home" implies that she would be going back to where she belongs but she knows that isn't right. What she really wants is a quietly contented home life that she can share with someone she loves. Unfortunately, neither David nor Mr Neville can offer her that so she decides, like a true romantic, that unrequited love is better than bloodless contentment.

It is not clear why her discovery of Mr Neville's affair with Jennifer should prompt her to make this decision. After all, he had warned her that he had no intention of changing his habits. But it seems that while she could tolerate his behaviour in the abstract, to have the evidence of it thrust under her nose is a different matter. She now has an image in front of her that has given her a foretaste of what life with him would really be like. And so she takes advantage of her last chance of freedom. Having turned down one opportunity of a respectable marriage to Geoffrey, she will now turn down the prospect of an unrespectable one to Mr Neville.

Hampton's dramatisation, and the direction of Giles Foster, successfully capture the flavour of the novel, and Anna Massey is absolutely right, subtly suggesting Edith's intelligent gaucherie with every embarrassed half-smile. She is helped by a well-chosen supporting cast, including Denholm Elliott as Mr Neville, whose charm does not hide his streak of malice, and Patricia Hodge as the arrogant yet strangely likeable Monica. Googie Withers and Julia McKenzie offer a delightful double act as the innocently horrendous Puseys. The film won the BAFTA Award for Best Television Drama.

The pain that people suffer when they are not compatible with those they love is something that Hampton analyses in his own original work, in *Total Eclipse*, *The Philanthropist* and *Carrington*, for example, and some, like Verlaine, are romantics who are not in touch with their true selves. With *Hotel du Lac* Anita Brookner gives us something slightly different: a romantic idealist who is self-aware and recognises that she has the power to choose. Edith knows that she may not necessarily be happy but at least she can decide what sort of unhappiness she can live with.

THE GINGER TREE (1989)

In a *Time Out* interview in October 1986 Hampton described *The Ginger Tree* as "a kind of Madame Butterfly's revenge". As with *Hotel du Lac*, it features a strong female leading role; both heroines are British women abroad who learn to assert themselves in an alien culture, and both are in love with men who prove to be, in different ways, untrustworthy. The story is dramatised from a novel by Oswald Wynd, which was first published in 1977. Wynd was born in Tokyo in 1913 of Scots parents and grew up speaking both English and

Japanese. He also writes thrillers (under the name of Gavin Black), many of which have Far East settings.

The rights to the novel were originally bought by Marilyn Hall and Juliet Gitterman, two Canadian producers who were based in Los Angeles and New York. They eventually bowed out of the series, having been, in Hampton's words "no doubt battered by years of delay and disappointment".

In the 1980s Hampton seems to have had more luck with the notoriously difficult world of international co-productions than he had with Hollywood. The project, which was jointly funded by the BBC in Britain, NHK in Japan and WGBH in Boston, took a comparatively speedy four years to reach the screen. Hampton wanted the series shot on film, which gives a better quality picture than the cheaper and simpler to use videotape. But NHK, the Japanese television company that was to be responsible for all the location work, said that they had not used film for ten years. *The Ginger Tree* was finally made on Japanese high-definition videotape and became the first drama to be seen on British television using this method.

Arranging a production that spanned three continents was not without its difficulties and in a production diary that serves as an introduction to the published screenplay Hampton outlines some of the problems he encountered.

He altered the novel far more than he had changed any of the other books that he has dramatised. With only four one-hour episodes he had to tighten the structure and streamline the plot, which takes a fairly leisurely course. The original is written in the form of a journal that the heroine, Mary Mackenzie keeps; the first half of the book covers two years in her life while the second half covers thirty-seven, as the journal entries become more erratic. Hampton dispenses with the idea of a narrator and smooths out the time-span by setting the first three episodes in the years 1903-1909. Episode four starts in 1935 and ends in 1942, the year after Japan entered the second world war.

Most of the early scenes in the novel are set in Peking but the Chinese authorities had an absolute ban on any film relating to the late imperial period, a policy, as Hampton points out, they conveniently overlooked in the case of Bertolucci's film *The Last Emperor*. Permission was finally given for the filming to take place on location in Manchuria, a decision that pleased Hampton as it meant that he could begin the screenplay in the period leading up to the Russo-Japanese war of 1904-05. When he was told at one point that the whole series was scheduled to run at 260 minutes rather than 240, he added a lot more material explaining the background of the Russian-Japanese conflict. Unfortunately, the producers changed their minds again and so all the new scenes he had written were ditched.

The second, third and final episodes are set in Japan, and Hampton went there to meet the film's co-producers and to look for suitable locations. His trip also provided him with some useful cultural references. When he was in Nagoya he kept hearing the word 'gaijin', which means 'foreigner'. In Episode Two he shows Mary hearing the word 'ijin' (the old Japanese word for 'foreigner') so often that she thinks that it means 'hello'. Another incident that found its way into the screenplay happened after a television executive showed Hampton a game of *shogi*, the Japanese version of chess. When Hampton asked which piece was the Queen he was told that there wasn't one as it is regarded as a soldier's game. He uses this information in the script: Mary explains to a friend that she had asked her lover the same question about the Queen in *shogi* and had received the same reply.

The series begins in Manchuria in 1903; Mary is preparing for her marriage to Richard Collingsworth, an English army officer. A brief flashback shows us how the couple met at Mary's home in Edinburgh the previous year. One of the guests at the wedding is Kentaro, Count Kurihama, a Japanese nobleman and solider, who will later become Mary's lover. Hampton introduces the character of Kentaro earlier on in the plot than Wynd did and also invented a role for him as a spy in Manchuria in order to explain his presence there.

Right from the beginning Richard is shown to be an insensitive husband. On the wedding night he leaves Mary's bedroom, saying calmly, "Goodnight, Mrs Collingsworth", as if having sex with his wife were some sort of rubber stamp that marked her as his property. And in a way this is totally in character because Mary's mother had offered him £300 a year if he would agree to the marriage.

Hampton makes Richard an altogether less sympathetic and a more mercenary character than Wynd does although we do learn in both the novel and the film that he is interested in getting his hands on the Mackenzie family business. Hampton adds a scene where Richard steals a lapis lazuli dish from a temple which Mary secretly returns later on. This incident establishes the often casual attitude that most British colonists had towards the culture of other nations while indicating at the same time that Mary is more honest and sensitive.

A few weeks after the wedding Richard announces that he is being posted to the front line as an official observer and will be away for several months. Again Hampton reduces the time-span. In the novel Mary and Richard have a daughter, Jane, but this is omitted from the film.

Shortly before she marries Richard, Mary meets Kentaro for the first time at a banquet hosted by Armand and Isabelle de Chamonpierre from the French Embassy. And later, while she is on holiday in the mountains with Armand and Isabelle after Richard's departure, she meets Kentaro again.

In the novel Kentaro's seduction of Mary takes place after a hundred pages but in the screen version the affair has started by the end of the first episode. As it appears that Mary surrenders her virtue rather quickly it was perhaps necessary for Hampton to show Kentaro giving her more encouragement than he does in the book (and for Richard to appear to be that much colder in his treatment of her), so that she shouldn't appear to be acting totally out of character. Also omitted from the film is Wynd's description of Mary's struggle with her faith and her sense of shame before God, which removes another obstacle to be overcome before she begins a relationship with Kentaro.

Richard returns home to discover that Mary is pregnant. She refuses to tell him who the baby's father is and he orders her to return to Edinburgh. She starts on her long journey home but while she is waiting for the ship she is approached at the dockside by a soldier, Yoshio Nomura, who tells her that Kentaro has made arrangements for her to live in Japan.

Episode Two opens with Mary's arrival at the port of Shimonoseki en route for Tokyo. On the train she is befriended by Baroness Aiko Onnodera, who explains that she is an old friend of Kentaro's. At first Mary is excited at the thought of seeing her lover again and imagines that he intends to marry her now that she is expecting his child. But Aiko tells her that Kentaro is already married and has four children. Mary is installed in a house in the Tsukiji district of Tokyo and is shocked to learn that her status is to be that of Kentaro's concubine.

Aiko is not a typical Japanese woman of the period. She is divorced, has travelled widely, wears Western clothes, and has served time in prison for her political activities in support of women's rights. She helps Mary to understand her position in her new culture. They go to a Kabuki theatre to see a performance of the play *Shigenoi's Parting from her Son.* All of the actors are men and Aiko explains that women are even more repressed in Japan than they are in the West.

Mary gives birth to a son, whom she names Taro, and for a few brief months she is happy. But one day her servant Misao takes the baby out and fails to return. Mary finds out that Kentaro had planted Misao in the house to spy on her and that he has now placed Taro with a Japanese family. She is distraught to discover that she has no recourse under Japanese law and that she would be committing an offence if she took her son back without permission. Kentaro is posted to Korea as a diplomat but aside from leaving her some money Mary has to fend for herself.

Apart from Aiko, the only friend Mary has in Japan is Alicia Bassett-Hill, an English missionary. She has given up trying to make converts of the Japanese but still tries to help people when she can.

At the beginning of Episode Three Mary goes to the Festival of the Dead, a ritual based on the belief that the dead return to visit the living every year. People release tiny wooden and paper boats lit by miniature lanterns so that their ancestors can return to their own world for another year. It is a poignant scene as Mary grieves for her own lost son.

In order to support herself on her own in Tokyo Mary finds work as a dress designer in a department store. Her Western-style clothes prove very popular and she becomes a valued member of the company. When Kentaro's wife opens an account at the store Mary is able to find out where she lives and learns that Kentaro has returned from Korea. One night she goes to the house in order to confront him about Taro. Kentaro refuses to tell her where the boy is and although she threatens to create a scene and involve his wife she cannot bring herself to do so.

Unknown to Mary, Kentaro continues to follow her progress in secret by sending a young student called Suzuki to make contact with her. She agrees to give Suzuki English lessons in return for help with her Japanese. They become friends but Mary turns him down when he proposes marriage.

She continues to work at the department store and is offered promotion, which entails a move to the city of Nagoya. She is reluctant to leave Tokyo and decides to take a holiday in Kamakura with two American friends, Bob and Emma-Lou Dale, in order to think things over. While they are away they are caught in an earthquake and for some reason that she cannot explain Mary takes this experience as a warning that she should turn the new job down. Her manager at the store makes it clear that her decision is not appreciated and she begins to make plans to set up in business for herself.

At the end of this episode Kentaro visits Mary to tell her that he is leaving for England. He says that he thinks of her every day and she replies: "And every day I think of him." Taro is now four years old and she still has no idea where he is.

By the start of Episode Four Mary, now 52, is a well-established business-woman in Yokohama. She meets Kentaro again and he tells her that his wife is dead. They resume their affair and Kentaro asks her to marry him but she refuses because he is still denying her any information about her son.

When Mary asks Kentaro to intercede on behalf of Aiko's new husband, a reckless socialist campaigner who has been arrested, he explains that although he is now a general he no longer has any influence. Hampton added a scene to show just how much Kentaro is hated by his contemporaries. While he is in bed with Mary two assassins break into the room to try to kill him. They fail but because of his reluctance to go to war Kentaro is edged out of any position of responsibility within the army. He is barely tolerated by a younger generation anxious for blood.

Kentaro is a more thoughtful soldier than Richard, and one who is more critical of the role that his army is playing in world affairs. He believes that the army should serve the state, not decide its policy. In the novel he refuses to answer any of Mary's questions about Nanking, where invading Japanese soldiers raped thousands of Chinese women but Hampton does explore this. Kentaro says to Mary: "It was as if we had learned . . . your barbarity, and were trying to make it perfect." This is unconvincing as it makes the Japanese seem weak-minded and easily influenced by British example. Hampton, understandably, did not want to criticise Japanese imperialism without also condemning Britain's immoral and disastrous foreign policy, but it seems unlikely that any nation has to learn brutality from another.

When it becomes clear that Japan's involvement in the second world war will make it dangerous for Europeans to remain, Kentaro arranges for Mary to leave the country. She is reluctant to go but realises that she has little alternative and in August 1942 she is deported. She leaves her shop in the hands of her long-serving assistant Minagawa and her home to Baroness Aiko, whose husband is still in prison. Alicia, who has been struggling with her faith, finds her purpose in life in going to an internment camp with other European prisoners. She says that she is near death and does not mind, and feels that she can be of help to people who do mind.

One thing that Mary has to leave behind in Yokohama is a tree that grows in her garden. She didn't know its proper name and it is not native to Japan, but its leaves smell of ginger. It had survived an earthquake and she admired its resilience. Like her, it had overcome disaster and had learned to flourish on foreign soil. In the novel Mary has her daughter Jane in England to return to but Hampton offers her a less secure future, with only her own courage and resilience to rely on.

While Mary is on board ship at Singapore a Japanese officer comes to see her. She fears arrest but he turns out to be Taro, now in his mid-thirties and serving as a pilot in the air force. He explains that his father had told him where she was and that he had wanted to be sure that she is safe. One question that Kentaro wants him to ask is whether she has forgiven him. Her answer is ambiguous: "Let us say that, as always, I understand his position."

Taro asks his mother to go the Festival of the Dead after the war is over to pay tribute to him. Soon after the ship leaves Singapore for England Kentaro commits hara-kiri.

Kentaro's suicide is another of Hampton's own additions and it brings the story to a more rounded dramatic conclusion. It is also hinted at with Kentaro's very first speech in the opening episode. Richard is talking to Isabelle and scoffs at the idea of the Japanese being a threat to Russia, declaring that any attack on them would be "absolutely suicidal". Kentaro interrupts the conversation to explain that in Japan suicide is not considered to be a disgrace but is seen sometimes as the noblest course of action. "Our history is full of examples of suicidal gestures which have transformed the pattern of events," he says. But his own suicide, when it comes, is an expression of his powerlessness and inability to change events. It is the opposite of Taro's willingness to accept death as a patriotic gesture.

In an interview with Nicholas de Jongh in 1970 Hampton mentioned Albert Camus' idea (expressed in the essay 'The Myth of Sisyphus') that the first important philosophical question one had to ask oneself was whether one should commit suicide. Somewhat to his surprise Hampton found that de Jongh "got rather over-excited by this idea" and made what had been a casual remark the centrepiece of his interview. And yet Hampton's work does feature a great deal of suicide, both actual and suspected. Some of the attempts are intentional and successful (Dora Carrington and Nelly in *Tales from Hollywood*) while others may or may not have been accidental (Mrs Evans in *When Did You Last See My Mother*? and John in *The Philanthropist*). Valmont in *Les Liaisons Dangereuses* seems deliberately to invite his own death in a duel since he fails to kill his opponent when he has the opportunity, while others, like Barbara in *The History Man* and Norma in *Sunset Boulevard*, make suicidal gestures that are probably not meant to succeed. Plarr in *The Honorary Consul* goes out to help the injured Father Leon knowing that it is likely to cost him his life, which it does, and in *Total Eclipse* Verlaine asks Rimbaud to shoot him though the request is ignored. This recurring preoccupation is not one that Hampton has ever analysed and he is not able to explain it, except to say that he is interested in extreme situations.

The Ginger Tree has a broader scope than Hampton's other television work and it combines a poignant love story with the wide sweep of historical and political events in a fruitful way. By concentrating on a complex personal relationship between a Japanese man and a British woman it shows how Western and Oriental cultures interact.

The series proved very popular with British audiences and has been sold to many countries around the world. Samantha Bond as Mary subtly charts the course from naive and impulsive young woman to an experienced and shrewd if ultimately unfulfilled entrepreneur. Daisuke Ryu (best known to Western audiences for his role as the youngest son in Kurosawa's *Ran*) is equally subtle and restrained as Kentaro. Notable amongst the supporting cast is Joanna McCallum as the saddened but in the end courageous and dignified Alicia, finding, as in a different way does Taro, peace in sacrifice. And Fumi Dan as the refined, aristocratic Baroness Aiko, skilfully avoids all the clichés of the suffragette battleaxe. Co-directors Tony Garner (for the BBC) and

Morimasa Matsumoto (for NHK, Japan) blend their styles well, so that one is not aware that the series is the work of two people.

If *The History Man* is Hampton's best television series—it has more of the sharp brilliance that is his trademark—with *The Ginger Tree* he still pulls off the feat of making a novel work dramatically while retaining a great deal of its original atmosphere. As with many of his stage plays, the characters are finally almost helpless in the face of larger events, but they still win some personal victories by facing up to their situation with courage and intelligence.

CHAPTER FOURTEEN

FILMS (1983–96)

> You want them to pay you and appreciate you and shut up, right?
> I think this is fair, yes. Like any artist.
>
> *Tales from Hollywood*

For nearly twenty-five years Hampton's career has been littered with abandoned film projects. In the preface to *Tales from Hollywood* he describes screenwriting as "an enjoyable but in my case apparently fruitless pastime". The cliché of the struggling young writer who is sucked in by Hollywood and becomes rich and successful at the price of his integrity was almost completely inverted in his case. He was a rich and successful playwright who, in 1976, gave it all up to work in Hollywood for almost no money at all. He said in an interview with *City Limits* in 1989: "It is much more fun writing films than writing for the theatre, which is terrible torture. However, on the whole, once you've delivered the script, working in the theatre is rather enjoyable, whereas in the cinema . . . things get taken away from you, you get fired, the film doesn't get financed, some terrible mishap occurs. The process of filming is pretty horrible."

Hampton's favourite film-maker is the Spanish surrealist director Luis Buñuel, with Billy Wilder a probable second. Among the screenwriters he particularly admires are Paul Schrader, most famous for his work with Martin Scorsese on films such as *Taxi Driver* and *Raging Bull*, and Harold Pinter, who, amongst other things, has scripted three films for Joseph Losey: *Accident*, *The Servant* and *The Go-Between*.

But Hampton was always aware that there were many pitfalls in working for the movies. As he remarked when he appeared in a television documentary on *Sunset Boulevard* in 1993: "I began to wonder if there was a future for a screenwriter in Hollywood apart from lying face down in the swimming pool."

He couldn't say he hadn't been warned. His first brush with the film world came as early as 1970, when Harry Saltzman, one of the producers of the James Bond movies, invited him to America to write an outline for a film based on the life of Nijinsky. Hampton did this but was then told that he had to sign a release form agreeing that he wouldn't claim a fee for his work. If he hadn't signed Saltzman would not have paid his hotel bill or his return air fare, which would have left him stranded in New York. He had got as far as meeting Rudolf Nureyev, who was being considered for the title role. Nureyev told him that he wanted Edward Albee to do the script but when Hampton reminded him that Albee had already written one, back came the terse comment: "Too much Diaghilev". Saltzman did release a film of Nijinsky's life in 1980 , directed by Herbert Ross and starring George de la Pena in the title role, with Alan Bates as Diaghilev. There was no contribution from Hampton.

Abandoned projects include an adaptation of Ibsen's *Ghosts*, which was to have starred Vanessa Redgrave until she pulled out for reasons that were never clear to Hampton, and a version of Somerset Maugham's *The Moon and Sixpence* for which he was never paid. Malcolm McDowell expressed an interest in his script based on David Storey's 1973 novel *A Temporary Life,* but the project foundered for want of a backer. What was possibly Hampton's most painful setback occurred in 1979. He had been commissioned by 20th Century Fox to write a screenplay based on Nicholas Bethell's historical work *The Last Secret.* This is an account of the British involvement in the forcible repatriation of Cossack soldiers to their homeland at the end of the second world war. He had researched the period extensively and wrote a script that was accepted for production. But while he was in Austria choosing locations with the film's director, Fred Zinnemann, 20th Century Fox changed hands. The new owners cancelled the project.

In 1989 Hampton dramatised a novel by Laurence Thornton called *Imagining Argentina* about the effects of the country's fascist dictatorship. Columbia Pictures were taken aback to discover that the first draft of his screenplay ran to only 53 pages (the average being about 120) and they have since sold the property to the Disney Corporation. No film has yet been made.

Hampton has had some success with his versions of foreign plays. His translation of *A Doll's House* was filmed in 1973, directed by Patrick Garland and starring Claire Bloom, and he collaborated with Maximilian Schell on the screenplay for the West German/Austrian co-production of Horváth's *Geschichten aus dem Wienerwald* [*Tales from the Vienna Woods*]. (These films have proved unavailable for viewing.)

Early in the 1970s Hampton also gained some experience as an uncredited rewrite man, spending two weeks on Tony Richardson's *Ned Kelly* (1970), which starred Mick Jagger as the Australian bandit. He did the same for Jack Clayton's 1974 film version of F. Scott Fitzgerald's *The Great Gatsby*, starring Robert Redford and Mia Farrow. Clayton had been set to direct a screenplay that Hampton had written called *The Tenant*, based on a French novel, *Le Locataire chimérique,* by Roland Topor. The project fell through and the story was later filmed, with a different script, by Roman Polanski. In 1979 Hampton did some rewriting on Michael Apted's *Agatha*, a film by Kathleen Tynan and Arthur Hopcraft about Agatha Christie's mysterious eleven-day disappearance in 1926, which starred Vanessa Redgrave and Dustin Hoffman.

It was a long wait—from 1970 until 1983—before Hampton was to see his name on screen as a credit for anything other than a translation.

THE HONORARY CONSUL (1983)

In the early 1980s Hampton was hired by the freelance producer Norma Heyman to dramatise Graham Greene's novel *The Honorary Consul*. She had chosen him because she had seen *Savages* and thought that a book about a diplomat being kidnapped in South America would suit him perfectly.

He wrote the first draft of a script and, as usual, spent a long time waiting for something to happen. When Richard Gere agreed to take the leading role the project was sold to Paramount Pictures. Hampton was one of the many victims of a strange levelling process that is typical of the Hollywood studios. It seems that the producers buy in the unique talents of leading writers and then do everything they can to make sure that the films they release look no different from anyone else's. Hampton and *The Honorary Consul*'s director, John Mackenzie, who had recently had a hit with the Barrie Keeffe-scripted thriller *The Long Good Friday*, had agreed that they wanted to make a moody *film noir* but the editor, with the studio's approval, cut the film like an action picture. They made the most of the car chases and played down the characterisation.

The film was shot on location in Mexico, though the studio bosses had favoured Costa Rica, because, as one executive remarked, "we own it". They tried unsuccessfully to ensure that Argentina, which is where the novel is set, was not actually referred to in the film.

With Richard Gere already in place as Dr Plarr, Michael Caine was cast as Charley Fortnum, the Honorary Consul of the title. Charley—inevitably, as this is a Greene story—is a drunken lapsed Catholic who is losing his grip on life. He is a far more broken-down example of European liberalism than West, Hampton's British diplomat in *Savages*, and his official position as a representative of the Crown is a nominal one. He is kidnapped and held for ransom by guerrillas because they mistake him for a far more influential visiting dignitary.

Michael Caine is convincing as Charley, reminding us that he can act when he stops parodying himself, and Richard Gere, a much maligned actor, isn't actually at all bad as the man who seduces Charley's wife, Clara, played by Elpidia Carrillo. Hampton spoke highly of her performance and regretted that so much of it had ended up on the cutting-room floor. But she had previously only appeared in *The Border* (Tony Richardson, 1981) opposite Jack Nicholson, Harvey Keitel and Warren Oates, and so was not considered a star name. Bob Hoskins (the star of *The Long Good Friday*) was sadly miscast as the dour local Chief of Police, with no opportunity to display the warmth and humour that he brings to most of his roles.

In spite of its starry cast the film doesn't really work. The pace is too slack for a thriller but the characters are not portrayed in enough depth for a political drama. Greene's fiction has not always been successfully brought to the screen. Hampton feels it is a myth that the novels are filmic and he sees Greene's characters as figures engaged primarily in private, internal struggles. This makes it more difficult to portray them on film, especially when modern studios demand action and eschew philosophy.

On the day after *The Honorary Consul* opened, Greene vigorously denounced it in a full-page article in the *Guardian*. The impact of his attack was lessened only when it became clear that he hadn't actually seen the film. Perhaps he was upset that director Peter Duffel, whose version of *England Made Me* he had liked, had not been involved. It had been reported in the *Evening Standard* as far back as 1974 that Duffel, with Greene's approval, was planning to make *The Honorary Consul* with Trevor Howard (who had starred in *The Heart of the Matter*), Donald Sutherland and Laura Antonelli. But Greene was notoriously ungrateful to film-makers. His anodyne spiritual crises have rarely made good cinema, with the exception of *The Third Man*, directed by Carol Reed in 1949. This was an original screenplay that he wrote with the help of Orson Welles, who scripted his own dialogue, and he was able for once to confront the nature of evil without his usual sentimental evasiveness.

In the States *The Honorary Consul* was released under the meaningless title of *Beyond the Limit* as Paramount decided that "Only the first word would be understood by American audiences."

THE WOLF AT THE DOOR (1986)

Most of Hampton's screenplays have taken a long time to complete and have gone straight into turnaround but *The Wolf at the Door* took him eight days to write and went into production immediately. Needless to say, it was not a Hollywood project.

The commission came from the film's leading actor, Donald Sutherland, who had been offered the role of the French painter Paul Gauguin by Danish director Henning Carlsen, best known in Europe for his 1966 film *Hunger*, starring Per Oscarsson. *The Wolf at the Door* was a Danish-French co-production and Carlsen worked on the original scenario with veteran screen-writer Jean-Claude Carrière, who had collaborated on Buñuel's last six films. Sutherland was not happy with their efforts so he contacted Hampton for a rewrite. "I said I'd do it if I could start entirely from scratch," Hampton told an interviewer from *Time Out* in 1986. "Donald said: 'Well you can't quite. They've already built all the sets'."

Working at high speed, and helped by the fact that he had already dramatised *The Moon and Sixpence*, Somerset Maugham's life of a fictional artist modelled on Gauguin, Hampton did in fact come up with an entirely new script. On the Monday after he finished it *The Wolf at the Door* went into production.

The story concentrates on a brief interlude in Gauguin's life between the end of his first visit to Tahiti in 1893 and his return just over a year later. The wolf at the door stands for both Gauguin himself and the poverty he endures so that he can pursue his art. One can see why such a theme would appeal to Hampton, who is here able to continue his investigations into the role of the artist in society. He re-uses a technique that he had first employed in *When Did You Last See My Mother?* of having a character tell a story twice, once near the beginning of the action and again at the end. Early on in the film Gauguin tells the daughter of a friend Aesop's fable about a fat domesticated town-dog who offers warmth and comfort to a starving wolf. The wolf is tempted but when he sees the dog's collar he opts for freedom in the wilderness even though this might mean death. At the end of the film Gauguin uses the same story to explain why he is going back to Tahiti, deciding that he may as well starve there as anywhere else.

Gauguin is romanticising his poverty, of course. He will not starve in Tahiti, but it is a cheap place to live and it doesn't frown on his penchant for young girls.

The film's French title, *Le loup dans le soleil* [*The Wolf in the Sun*], more clearly identifies the wolf as Gauguin, although we never see him in the sun, only longing for it. The action of the film, in fact, takes place entirely in France, where it always seems to be raining or misty. Tahiti is evoked only by Gauguin's paintings and by his persistent references to it. The only time we ever see the place is in a long shot behind the end credits.

Gauguin paints his room in Paris yellow and this not only gives it a sunny ambience but also serves as a tribute to his friend Van Gogh, whose use of the colour he had admired. He has three of Van Gogh's paintings and at first he refuses to part with them but he finally sells them to a dealer when he is desperate to raise money for his passage back to Tahiti.

Like Rimbaud in *Total Eclipse*, Gauguin is drawn to the vibrant colours and smells of the tropics. He claims that the Tahitians are infinitely more civilised than the Europeans and praises their innocence and spontaneity. In Hampton's play *Savages* the anthropologist makes fun of "the noble savage boys", those Westerners who hark back to Rousseau and think that the native life is one of untainted bliss. Gauguin has gone one stage further: not only does he believe that the primitive culture of Tahiti is superior to his own, he has embraced it whole-heartedly and 'gone native' himself.

August Strindberg, whom Gauguin meets a few times, agrees that family life can be stifling but believes that suffering is unavoidable wherever one goes. "Top hats or naked savages," he says, "where there is man, or more especially woman, there is destruction."

Hampton is careful to emphasise that Gauguin cannot shake off his bourgeois values that easily, however, and shows that he is every bit as much of a colonialist as the French government officials he despises; this is demonstrated by the fact that he has taken a thirteen-year-old Tahitian girl as a bride. Fourteen is the age of his own daughter, and it is also the age of Judith, the stepdaughter of his friend Molard, a man who is forced to work in an office when he would really like to be a composer.

Judith poses in the nude for Gauguin and begins to fall in love with him. She is furious when she discovers that he is only using her as a stand-in for his regular model but by the next time they meet she has forgiven him. Gauguin tells her that he is leaving Paris and she begs him to make love to her, saying "Anything you like . . . Anything." (These are the same words that Hampton gives to Carrington when she is in bed with Lytton Strachey.) As Gauguin embraces Judith he has a sudden vision of his daughter running towards him and he pulls away. Having earlier told her that he sees himself as a father-figure towards her he realises that sex with her would seem like incest. Judith is upset and confused and later gives him a clipping of her pubic hair in a locket as a keepsake.

Gauguin speciously invokes his special status as an artist to justify his behaviour. "All artists are criminals," he says. It is an opinion that Hampton also gives to Thomas Able in *Able's Will*. *The Wolf at the Door* is weakened by the fact that no one ever challenges Gauguin on this point. He is allowed to get away with his hypocrisy and exploitation of young girls. Only Annah, his Javanese mistress in Paris, displays any real anger. When she learns that he intends to return to Tahiti she rips up one of his canvases and takes all his money. But even she does not confront him face to face.

With a mother who was a half-Peruvian Creole, one of the things that Gauguin recognises is wrong with France is its racism. In one scene he is seen with Annah and a party of friends walking through a fishing village. A group of children starts to taunt them, calling Annah a nigger and a monkey. Gauguin slaps one boy's face and this leads to a fight. The boy's father and some other fishermen attack Gauguin and he falls and breaks his leg.

Another thing that hurts him about his country is the public reaction to his paintings. He has returned to France to exhibit the work he has done in Tahiti and we see him suffer in silence as people make philistine remarks about his pictures, not appreciating that his bold use of colour and his attempts to abolish perspective are deliberate. His rediscovery of primitive painting was to have an enormous influence on the development of twentieth-century art.

One of the visitors to the gallery is Degas, whose paintings have already brought him fame, and it is he, the arch-bourgeois, who appreciates the genius of the work. He buys one of the pictures, declaring that Gauguin "paints like a wolf". And he later buys another one, thus helping Gauguin to return to Tahiti.

In spite of its promising subject matter, the film suffers from a lack of dramatic tension. *Total Eclipse* has the affair between Verlaine and Rimbaud to give impetus to the story, but Gauguin isn't shown in any developed relationship. None of the women around him is sufficiently well characterised and they become little more than stooges. There is a great deal of argument but no real conflict, and so the overall effect is rather diffuse. Rimbaud despairs at what he perceives to be the futility of existence but Gauguin never rages over anything more specific than his Romantic notion of making his escape from bourgeois conformity into primitivism.

The film would perhaps have been better if the script had expanded more on Gauguin's techniques and aims as a painter; a work that doesn't explain *why* an artist is a relevant figure often seems to say that one can only judge him by the number of temper tantrums he has. Robert Altman's 1990 film *Vincent and Theo* (scripted by Julian Mitchell) concentrates on the relationship between Vincent Van Gogh and his brother, and so gives the story a dramatic focus that Hampton's treatment of Gauguin lacks.

The Wolf at the Door is a minor film but an underrated one. Donald Sutherland brings an intelligent, slow-burning reserve to the part of Gauguin and there are strong performances from Max von Sydow as Strindberg and Sofie Grabøl as Judith. It has been fairly successful in America but was not given a general release in Britain. The only time is has been seen in London was in September 1995 when it was screened by the National Film Theatre as part of a season of films on impressionist and post-impressionist painters. It was shown with Italian subtitles as this was the only print (the director's personal copy) that was available.

THE GOOD FATHER (1986)

Hampton turned Peter Prince's 1983 novel *The Good Father* into a film for the Channel 4 'Film on Four' slot. The novel explores what happened to the generation who went through the campus radicalism of the 1960s and shows how the men of that era tried to adapt themselves to the demands of the feminist movement. Their world is filled with broken relationships, through which they flounder uncertainly. In *The History Man* we see how radicalism could be twisted by one of its most vociferous exponents to suit his own self-serving ends, but in *The Good Father* the focus is on the victims of radical politics, the dazed people trying to live decent lives within a shifting social environment.

The main character, Bill Hooper, has become openly hostile towards women. He blames the ethos of the sixties for the break-up of his marriage to Emmy. "We gave each other total freedom," he says, "and we hated each other for taking advantage of it."

He has been given access to visit his young son, Christopher, but resents the fact that Emmy has custody. He finds an ally in Roger, whom he meets at a party. Although Bill is sympathetic towards Roger, who has also lost custody of his child, he fully intends to exploit the friendship to act out a vicarious form of revenge for himself. He urges Roger to fight for his son Richard through the courts, persuading him that he has a good chance of success because his wife, Cheryl, is now cohabiting with another woman. Roger is uncertain at first but decides to go ahead when he finds out that Cheryl is planning to move to Australia with her girlfriend, taking Richard with them.

Bill takes Roger to see an expensive lawyer and promises to help out with the fees. Roger gradually becomes more ruthless. Although Cheryl had told him about her lesbian relationship, which had started while they were still married, he tells Bill that he will swear in court that he didn't know about it until the divorce. Bill is shocked at such dishonesty.

Roger gets a court order giving him custody of his son and both men go that same afternoon to fetch the boy from his playgroup. Cheryl watches in tears and Bill smiles in triumph as he and Roger take Richard away. She contests the court ruling but loses the appeal. When Bill sees her breaking down for the second time, he realises how cruelly he has behaved. He confesses to Roger his real motive for helping him. He faces up to his own misogyny and accepts that his one-time support for feminism had been a sham.

Bill and Roger are both examples of what their oily lawyer, Mr Varda, dubs the "forever young generation", implying that they cannot face the demands of maturity. Instead of trying to see their situation in terms of its wider social context, they hold women personally responsible when their lives collapse. These men, who had once supported female equality, are upset to find that they are still the same old chauvinists underneath. "They really piss me off, women," Bill says at the beginning, going on to explain how he regretted the amount of time he had spent going to a men's group and listening to their "endless whingeing".

Later Roger shows Bill an article Cheryl had written in a magazine published in the 1960s by a Women's Collective, where she claims that the image of women would no longer be the victim cringing in the back alley but the sniper on the rooftop. Roger laughs it off as a 'period piece', but Bill takes it seriously, and it serves to reinforce his misogyny.

In spite of his feelings about women Bill starts an affair with Mary Hall, a young colleague at work. But he is not used to having sex so easily and says that when he was at university, despite the free love ethic, sexual relationships had been a matter for continual bargaining. He realises that this relationship too is doomed, especially when Mary talks about having a baby.

Several times during the film Bill has sudden, unexplained visions of Christopher screaming. The first time this happens he is so shocked that he crashes his motorbike and injures himself. In the last of these visions we see him strangling the boy. He explains later to Mary that his feelings about his son were what ruined his marriage: "That's when it started to go wrong. They take it all. I couldn't stand living with him any more. It wasn't Emmy I was leaving, it was him." Children, he explains, demand so much love, more than he felt he could give and it used him up emotionally. He had not admitted this to himself before but perhaps it explains why he didn't fight for custody of his own son. He still loved him but was afraid of his feelings.

In the end the problems are resolved. Cheryl and her girlfriend separate and she and Roger agree to take it in turns to look after Richard. Emmy and Bill become more friendly towards each other and she agrees that he can have Christopher to stay with him at weekends.

In the film's final shot we see Bill, alone in the new house that he has bought for himself, listening to the sounds of children playing. Although he is still trapped between his desire to be a father and his fear of being one, he has achieved a kind of catharsis, and his bitterness against women is gone.

Peter Prince is an experienced screenwriter—he wrote the prize-winning series *Oppenheimer* and the script for Stephen Frears' thriller *The Hit*—but he told Hampton that he didn't want to go through the pain of reworking his own novel as it was based on his own experience. He gave him *carte blanche* to make whatever changes he saw fit and declared himself happy with the final version.

The film is fairly faithful to the novel. Hampton gives Bill a greater insight into his own motivation, and the ending, though very similar, is a shade more optimistic. Prince leads us to believe that Bill will retreat into himself once his anger is spent, but Hampton, unusually for someone who has so often written about the descent into apathy, rejects the implication that Bill has given up on other people. But he couldn't resist bringing in one of his own preoccupations. At one point in the film Bill, who works in a downmarket publishing house, tells Mary that he had once written several novels but had burned them all because they were always being rejected for publication. In the novel the manuscripts are stored away in a tea chest. It seems that Hampton couldn't resist making Bill a writer who made a deliberate decision to give up rather than one who still harboured lingering hopes of success.

The director of *The Good Father* was Mike Newell, who has since scored an enormous hit with *Four Weddings and a Funeral*. He captures the authentic seediness of South London in a way usually seen only in gangster thrillers. Anthony Hopkins' performance as Bill is sensitive and intelligent in its credible portrayal of a basically decent man who becomes cruel and vicious when driven by circumstances. Jim Broadbent displays a subtle mixture of rage and vulnerability in the role of Roger. The excellent supporting cast is filled with the names of actors who have gone on to bigger things: Harriet Walter is Emmy, Joanne Whalley is Mary, and Bill's boss at the publishing house is played by Stephen Fry. Hampton was also reunited with two old associates: Simon Callow as Mr Varda, and Miriam Margolyes as Jane Powell, another knee-jerk radical similar to Melissa Todoroff in *The History Man*.

In a way the film is a companion piece to *Treats*. Both deal with people's failure to create personal relationships and both have as a central character a rampant misogynist. *The Good Father* is a well-made and absorbing film that makes quite a number of incisive points about how relationships can go wrong, but it lacks the remorselessness of *Treats*, which is more extreme in its depiction of mental cruelty.

Hampton's ability to deal lucidly with deep emotional states is muted on television. The work of Dennis Potter shows that it is possible to depict the extremes of pain and bitterness on the small screen but somehow Hampton has never responded to the medium with the same fervour. He has said that he sees television as a half-way house between the theatre and film. With the current disgraceful neglect of original drama on TV, it may be some time before another project comes along that will really stimulate his imagination.

DANGEROUS LIAISONS (1988)

The success of *Les Liaisons Dangereuses* on stage led to many offers from film companies. However, as American theatres usually demand a share of the proceeds from the sale of film rights of any work they produce, a deal could not be negotiated until the play had opened on Broadway.

In the audience on the opening night at the Music Box Theatre in April 1987 there were three executives from the Lorimar film division. They made a bid for the rights and suggested that Hampton himself should co-produce with Norma Heyman, the producer responsible for *The Honorary Consul*. Stephen Frears was chosen to direct. Events were complicated when Miloš Forman, the Czech director best known for *One Flew Over the Cuckoo's Nest* and *Amadeus*, put in a rival bid through Orion. Hampton went to meet Forman at a London restaurant but he never showed up. There were rumours that Forman was planning go ahead on his own, using a different script, and after Lorimar had tried unsuccessfully to contact him they decided to tighten the schedule so that their film would be released first.

Hampton and Lorimar won the race but it was a close thing. Forman's film, *Valmont*, went into production more or less at the same time as *Dangerous Liaisons* but was not premiered until 1989. The two leading roles were played by Colin Firth and Annette Bening, and the screenplay was written by Jean-Claude Carrière, who had written the original scenario for *The Wolf at the Door*.

Hampton produced the first draft of his screenplay in less than a month but it went through several rewrites before Frears was satisfied. To begin with Frears had not read Laclos' novel and, according to Hampton, he "had found no reason to break the habits of a lifetime and go to see the play". The two men embarked on a series of exhausting script discussions, most of which seemed to take place on transatlantic flights. They were anxious to get the running time down to two hours—an enthusiasm that they noted was shared, not surprisingly, by the production company. Some of the longer speeches were trimmed, and though one misses some of the finer details from the play, the plot is still clear.

Lorimar insisted that the cast of the film should be entirely different from that of the play. (Alan Rickman had yet to score his success in *Die Hard* and *Robin Hood, Prince of Thieves* that would make him one of Hollywood's most popular villains.) Hampton reluctantly agreed. During the casting discussions the name of John Malkovich kept cropping up. In the week before Christmas 1987 Hampton went to see him in Lanford Wilson's play *Burn This* and was impressed enough to go backstage, knock on his door and hand him the script of *Dangerous Liaisons*. Malkovich accepted the role of Valmont at once.

Glenn Close had the previous year been selected to play Mme de Merteuil on stage when the RSC actors had finished their allotted twenty weeks on Broadway. Although she was disappointed by the theatre's decision not to continue the run when the RSC went home (despite the fact that box-office records had been broken during the final week) she accepted the chance to take the role for the film. Michelle Pfeiffer was offered the part of Tourvel. Forman had meanwhile asked her to play Merteuil in *Valmont*, and for a while she was driving to work with both scripts on the seat beside her. Pfeiffer finally opted for Hampton's version even though she didn't have the leading role.

Dangerous Liaisons is in some respects more faithful to the book than the play was. This is most noticeable with the film's reinstatement of the novel's original ending. Merteuil (like Célimène in *Le Misanthrope*) is revealed in her true colours when her letters are made public. In the play Merteuil never writes any letters to her lovers for fear that they might incriminate her. But it is plausible for her to break this rule with regard to Valmont, as he is the only man she loves.

Towards the end of the film we see her at the opera where she is booed by other people in the audience; she is a performer who has lost her public. *Dangerous Liaisons* crams a great deal into its last few minutes and events are more compressed than in the play. After Merteuil's declaration of war we see the duel between Valmont and Danceny. This is intercut with the nuns' doomed attempt to save Tourvel, who is ill with fever. As Valmont lies mortally wounded he gives Danceny Merteuil's letters and warns him not to trust her. He also instructs him to go to Tourvel with a message: "Tell her her love was the only real happiness I've ever known." Danceny goes straight to the convent and is able to deliver these words of comfort to Tourvel just before she dies.

Hampton and Frears had many discussions about the final image for the film. Laclos wrote only in vague terms about what actually happens to Merteuil after she leaves France, except to say that she had the crown of all her misfortunes while in exile, though he doesn't specify what this was. Frears shot half a dozen different scenes for the ending, including one where Merteuil is beheaded. But he decided that this was too much, saying that such an ending would be like the giant foot that descends from the sky to squash everything below in Terry Gilliam's credits sequence for *Monty Python's Flying Circus*. In the end they scrapped all of the versions they had experimented with and finished with what was to have been the film's penultimate scene. This shows Merteuil on her own and near to tears, wiping her face-powder off. Having seen her in the opening scene being elaborately made up by her servants, we now see her stripped of all pretence and protection. She has nobody to turn to and nothing to hide behind.

A lot of the film is shot in close-up and by concentrating on the actors' faces Frears creates an intimacy that is almost claustrophobic. This technique also meant that he was able to avoid producing the kind of period costume romp where any moment a dashing young Errol Flynn may appear brandishing a sword and swinging from the chandeliers.

While it is true that an American accent in a classical piece can seem incongruous to British cinema-goers (a criticism that some people made about Forman's film *Amadeus*) it does have the advantage of underlining the point that human nature is the same now as it was in France two hundred years ago.

Like any other artistic activity the process of film-making is subject to many arbitrary factors. The lower-class characters in *Dangerous Liaisons* all speak with Scottish accents, and this was done to match the natural voice of Peter Capaldi who plays Azolan. The part was originally offered to Stephen Rea and if he had taken it then the peasantry would have become Irish.

Malkovich and Close bring just the right kind of serene, intelligent malice to their characters and Michelle Pfeiffer is radiant as Tourvel. The film proved to be almost as big a hit as the play and Hampton was able to add the 1989 Academy Award for Best Adapted Screenplay to his collection of prizes.

CARRINGTON (1995)

For many years Dora Carrington was an unjustly forgotten artist. If she was remembered at all it was because she had known some of the leading novelists of the 1920s and '30s: she was pilloried as Minette Darrington in D.H. Lawrence's *Women in Love*, as Mary Bracegirdle in Aldous Huxley's odious lampoon *Crome Yellow*, and as Betty Blyth in Wyndham Lewis's *The Apes of God*. The only sympathetic treatment of her was as Anna Cory in Rosamund Lehmann's *The Weather in the Streets*.

It may be that Carrington's paintings and drawings were overlooked for so long partly because she was a woman but her self-effacement and lack of interest in promoting her own work was also a factor. Although she had won many prizes while at the Slade Institute in 1910–14, it was only in the 1970s that her work began to receive a long overdue critical reassessment.

Some time after Michael Holroyd's exhaustive two-volume biography of Lytton Strachey was published in 1967-68 the literary agent Barry Krost gave Hampton a copy of the book. Krost had already suggested to John Osborne, a friend of his who was later to become a client, that the material would make a good play. Osborne decided against the idea but he was certainly influenced by the story of Strachey's life when he came to write *Watch it Come Down* in 1976.

Gore Vidal once expressed an interest in dramatising Holroyd's book, and in the late 1960s Ken Russell started to explore the possibility of directing it on television. On 2 December 1968 Noel Carrington, Dora's brother, wrote to the BBC to complain that Russell had suggested Oliver Reed, an actor not generally associated with effete homosexual roles, for the part of Strachey. But these projects came to nothing.

Hampton was involved in rehearsals for *Able's Will* in 1976 when he heard from Krost again, who told him that an executive from Warner Brothers was in London and was eager to commission a film about the Bloomsbury Group. The executive, Marty Elfand, invited Hampton to lunch but whoever took the message had written his name down as 'Mr Elephant', which was how Hampton addressed him throughout the meal. (The restaurant they went to was called 'The White Elephant', which probably added to the confusion.) Hampton told Elfand that he wasn't interested in writing about the Bloomsbury Group per se but would like to do something on Carrington and a deal was agreed.

At his Oxfordshire cottage, in an area that Carrington knew well, Hampton started work on the screenplay. He took six months to plot out the structure and a further three to complete the first draft, finishing in the middle of September 1977. Although he didn't appreciate it fully at the time, being able to spend the best part of a year on a single project was a rare luxury and one that he has seldom enjoyed since.

By the time the screenplay reached Warner Brothers Elfand had moved on but his successor sent it to Herbert Ross, who was Neil Simon's regular director. Hampton went to Los Angeles for a meeting with Ross but was unable to secure a firm commitment (Nora Kaye, Ross's wife, dismissed the script as a story about "a lot of pissy English people") so he flew home. He didn't hear any more about it.

In 1980 Michael Holroyd presented an edition of the *South Bank Show* to mark the centenary of Strachey's birth. With Warner Brothers' permission around eight minutes of Hampton's screenplay was performed, with Edward Petherbridge and Joanna David playing Strachey and Carrington. Holroyd also used extracts from Peter Luke's stage play, *Bloomsbury*. The programme won an award in America and was seen by Peter Gill, Hampton's director on *Tales from Hollywood*. In 1984 Gill decided to present a staged reading of *Carrington* as one of his studio nights at the Cottesloe Theatre. The next day Thames Television offered to buy the rights to the script.

The plan was that Euston Films, the film-making branch of Thames, and best known for some very un-Bloomsburyite programmes such as *The Sweeney* and *Minder*, should shoot the script. Not long after Linda Agran at Thames Television had paid Warner Brothers the equivalent of seven times Hampton's original advance she lost her job. Her successor, Andrew Brown, brought in director Mike Newell and arranged for two French companies, Pyramide and Noréa, to help fund the project. Thames then announced that they were not going to put up any of the finance themselves. By this time Newell was busy editing his film *Enchanted April*. Without consulting anyone Brown decided to appoint another director so that they could get on with the pre-production work on *Carrington*. At this point the two French backers withdrew and soon afterwards Thames lost its franchise. It was now 1992.

That year, Ronald Shedlo, an independent producer, discovered the script while he was staying at Hampton's office in Notting Hill. Shedlo, who began his career in films at the age of fifteen as Errol Flynn's secretary, had been a friend of Hampton's since buying the rights to *When Did You Last See My Mother?* in the 1960s. Undeterred by the script's apparent capacity to destroy everything it touched, he brought in another friend of Hampton's, the writer-producer John McGrath. Shedlo and McGrath spent ten months negotiating with Euston Films to buy the rights back only to find out after they had done so that their original finance package had fallen apart. It is an indictment of the state of the British film industry (if such a thing can be said to exist) that the project was finally rescued by two French production companies—Cinea & Orsans and Le Studio Canal Plus—and the Dutch firm PolyGram.

Having signed Emma Thompson (who had impressed Hampton when testing for the role of Carrington in the early 1980s) and Jonathan Pryce to star, McGrath contacted Newell to tell him they had a start date. "That's the good news," said Newell. "Here's the bad." He had just finished shooting *Four Weddings and a Funeral* and didn't want to make another "little English film".

Carrington now had the backing but no director. Philippe Carcassonne, one of the executive producers, told Hampton that in France it was not unheard of for writers to direct their own work, and when Emma Thompson made the same suggestion to him a couple of days later he gave way. He realised that if he refused the project might find its way back onto the shelf and so he "sort of backed into it, really".

The first screenplay that Hampton wrote had a projected running time of three and a half hours (Warner Brothers had certainly not been happy about that) and over the years he had produced eleven drafts, gradually reducing it to a more manageable two hours. "In the end, I needed some drastic re-ordering and compressing in the film's final section," Hampton said. "But essentially the script that was filmed was the same one that I wrote in 1977." Altogether it had taken seventeen years, the length of time that Carrington and Strachey knew each other, to get the film into production.

The story begins with the couple's first meeting in 1915 and ends with Carrington's suicide, six weeks after Strachey's death, in 1932. The structure of the film is a straightforward chronological narrative and is divided into six sections, each one indicated by a caption on screen.

The opening section, which is the shortest and acts as a sort of prelude, is called 'Lytton and Carrington 1915'. When Strachey first sees Carrington she is playing football with Vanessa Bell's children. "Who on earth is that ravishing boy?" he asks. As in *Total Eclipse*, this important initial encounter takes place at dusk and one character, lit by the glow of the setting sun, is watched, unobserved, by another.

Carrington sees her femininity as an encumbrance (she never used her first name) and wishes she were male. As Strachey finds out, she dislikes the idea of sex and when he tries to kiss her she repulses him. Her frigidity causes friction in her relationship with the painter Mark Gertler, which is dealt with in the second part of the film. When we first see the couple they are in a passionate embrace but every time Gertler puts his hands on Carrington's breasts or legs she brushes them off. She fears that he is only interested in her sexually and he fears that she doesn't appreciate his talent as an artist. He reasons that if he can get Strachey to tell her how good his work is she will agree to go to bed with him.

Part Two also shows Strachey's appearance in front of a tribunal for conscientious objectors. He mocks the proceedings by inflating a rubber cushion while explaining "I'm a martyr to the piles." When asked what he would do if he found a German soldier raping his sister he says that he would "attempt to come between them", a joke that is not lost on his friends and supporters in the court room. Hampton rather needlessly coarsens Strachey's actual response, which was: "I should try and interpose my own body."

Strachey is a regular visitor at Garsington, the home of the artistic patron Lady Ottoline Morrell, and with Gertler's encouragement he takes Carrington to meet her. Morrell tells him that at the age of twenty-two Carrington certainly ought to have lost her virginity and when Strachey points out that he too was still a virgin at that age, she replies: "But that's the whole point, don't you see, so was I. Is there to be no progress?"

At Garsington Carrington has an opportunity to be with Strachey and to talk to him. She realises that she is in love with him but as she knows nothing about homosexuality she doesn't yet understand why he will never be able to offer her a sexual relationship.

The only real intimate contact they have is when they share a single bed while they are on holiday together in Wales. Carrington, who has shyly undressed behind the wardrobe door, gets into bed and says: "Anything you like Lytton. Anything." He cannot bring himself to have intercourse with her but he does allow her to masturbate him. It is during this trip that Strachey suggests that they should set up house together, although it won't be as man and wife.

When Carrington sees Gertler again she finally agrees to go to bed with him but he is rough with her and she is disgusted. She leaves him and goes to stay with Strachey at Tidmarsh Mill, the house in Oxfordshire that he has rented. Gertler is extremely jealous and attacks Strachey in the street after causing a scene at a party in London where he has seen them together. Carrington stands by powerlessly as Strachey is rescued by some of the other guests from the party. The two men then walk away from each other. This is the start of what will become a recurring pattern in her life: to be helplessly trapped between different men.

The millhouse at Tidmarsh from 1918-20 is the setting for the third section of the film, which introduces the character of Ralph Partridge. He becomes a frequent visitor to Tidmarsh and Carrington seems at ease with him although she declares at one point that like "some Norwegian dentist" he is a dull conversationalist. He is a soldier with a distinguished war record and on one occasion he berates all conscientious objectors as slackers who ought to be shot. After he has gone Carrington apologises to Strachey, who surprises her by saying that he thought Partridge was "wonderful".

A painful triangular relationship develops: Partridge wants Carrington, while she loves Strachey, who has fallen in love with Partridge. She agrees to marry Partridge so that Strachey can continue to see him and he even joins them on their honeymoon in Venice.

All three return to live at Tidmarsh. It is not a true ménage à trois as Strachey never sleeps with either of the other two. In the film Partridge never comments on the relationship between Strachey and Carrington but he is portrayed as an intelligent man who is likely to have had a shrewd idea of the situation.

The fourth section of the film moves on to Carrington's relationship with Gerald Brenan between 1920 and 1922. Brenan, a novelist and travel writer, is a rather shy man who had fought alongside Partridge during the war. He and Carrington conduct their affair in secret. In one shot we see Partridge calmly fishing in front of the barn which conceals the two lovers in the hayloft and in another scene Carrington watches anxiously while Brenan walks away from the house while she and Partridge are making their way back along another pathway. When Partridge does discover the affair he confronts Brenan and gets angry with him, a somewhat hypocritical response, given that he himself has not stayed faithful to Carrington. In the end it is Carrington's lack of commitment that ends things. She tells Brenan that they should meet for a picnic at a special place on the South Downs on the anniversary of their first meeting but she forgets to go.

The longest span of time—from 1922 to 1931—is covered in the fifth section of the film, which is captioned 'Ham Spray House'. This is the property that Strachey bought with the profits from his book *Eminent Victorians*.

Once more the giddying partner-changing goes on. A young man called Roger Senhouse comes into Strachey's life and Partridge falls in love with Frances Marshall. Carrington is pregnant by a man called Beacus Penrose, who seems to offer her very little except for sex and the use of his yacht. This last relationship falls apart after he tells her (as Philip tells Araminta in rather different circumstances in *The Philanthropist*) that he doesn't find her attractive.

At the beginning of this section we see a tracking shot of Carrington riding a white horse though the spacious gardens of Ham Spray House. It is summer and the landscape is lush and green. Later on we see her on the horse again, in the rain, and learn that she had hoped to cause a miscarriage by riding recklessly. She is unharmed but decides to have an illegal abortion in London. She can't bear the thought of having a baby that isn't Strachey's.

Carrington's inability to fit in and find contentment is memorably underlined at the end of this section. She is seen seated in the garden at Ham Spray. It is night and she looks up at the house. In one room Strachey and Senhouse embrace, in another Partridge and Frances Marshall (later to become his wife) kiss, and in a third Penrose stands alone at the window. Carrington belongs in none of these rooms. As Strachey says earlier: "I don't know what the world is coming to. Ladies in love with buggers and buggers in love with womanisers—and what with the price of coal . . ."

But this rather self-consciously bohemian life comes to an end for Carrington as it becomes clear that Strachey is dying. The last section of the film,'Lytton and Carrington', covering the years 1931-32, shows his painful death from stomach cancer. Realising that he hasn't long to live, Carrington attempts suicide by carbon monoxide poisoning from the fumes from her car but Partridge finds her in time and she survives. She devotes her time to nursing and caring for Strachey. It is winter and the bare trees in the garden outside emphasise her desolation.

While they were in Venice Carrington had asked Strachey if he was afraid of dying and he didn't reply, but his final words to her on his deathbed are: "If this is dying then I don't think much of it".

Carrington, it seems, doesn't think much of it either. After Strachey's death she burns his Panama hat and his spectacles and throws away her paints. For six weeks she is distraught with grief. She borrows a shotgun on the pretext of wanting to shoot the rabbits on the land around the house. On 11 March, she gets up, puts on Strachey's dressing gown and prepares herself some breakfast. Then she goes upstairs, gets out the gun and rests the barrel under her heart. The film cuts to the same tracking shot around the garden that had been used before and the final image is the front of Ham Spray House as we hear the sound of a gunshot.

In writing about Carrington and her relationship with Strachey Hampton was able to show a woman who, unusually for an artist, gave no thought to her reputation. Certainly Carrington paints and draws all the time but she shows no inclination to show her work to a wider public. She dismisses Strachey's suggestion that she should exhibit her work and continues to fill the house at Tidmarsh with her paintings and decorations.

Strachey, on the other hand, earns his living as a writer, although he professes not to enjoy what he does. His output was certainly not prodigious —he wrote only six fairly short books in his lifetime, one of which was published posthumously. Neither of them is interested in creating art for the future. "What's posterity ever done for me?" Strachey says. He comes to the conclusion, rather regretfully, that he is better at living than writing.

Some people have criticised the film for its historical inaccuracies. Frances Partridge, Ralph's widow, was the only person depicted in the film who was still alive when it was released. She wrote an article in *Modern Painters* objecting to the portrayal of her husband as a bigot. But although it is perfectly understandable that someone would want a personal experience to be recorded faithfully, absolute fidelity to the facts should not be allowed to stifle creative freedom. If all drama had to do was to be historically accurate then most of Shakespeare's plays would be totally worthless. In the film Brenan observes that Partridge often expresses opinions that he thinks other people will disagree with in order to play a joke on them.

If one were to criticise along merely historical lines then one could certainly object to the portrayal of Strachey. At his tribunal hearing he is shown as a highly principled conscientious objector. This is true up to a point but the film ignores a letter that he wrote to his brother in early September 1914 that reveals a rather more personal interest in being exempted from military service. Strachey implies that artists such as himself should not be called up as they would make weak and useless soldiers. "If we weren't we'd still be too intelligent to be thrown away in some really not essential expedition, and our proper place would be—the National Reserve, I suppose. God put us on an island, and Winston has given us a navy, and it would be absurd to neglect those advantages—which I consider exactly apply to able-bodied intellectuals." When it came down to it Strachey wanted to spare everyone but himself most of all.

Soon after the tribunal scene we see Strachey at Garsington expressing his distaste that people should be enjoying themselves dancing on the lawn.

"Thousands of boys are dying every day to preserve this, did you know?" he says indignantly. This scene actually *is* a distortion of the facts. The Morrells were opposed to the war and Philip Morrell effectively ended any prospect of advancing his career as a Liberal MP by forcing a debate in the House of Commons over it, which the film doesn't mention. To show Strachey as some sort of campaigner for justice is most debatable; in real life he sneered at reformers like Bertrand Russell, accusing them of being glad that the poor existed just so that they could be helped by people like him (a dubious assertion and unlikely to be of much interest to the poor anyway). Typically, Strachey was incapable of seeing that the same argument applied to him: that he was glad the poor were there so that he could actively ignore them.

Strachey also gets off lightly in his treatment of Ottoline. He was well-known for accepting her hospitality for weeks at a time and then making spiteful comments about her behind her back. In the film this is reduced to just one snide comment: "I'm devoted to Ottoline. She's like the Eiffel Tower. She's very silly but she affords excellent views." But Hampton at least errs on the side of generosity, which is something that Strachey never did.

Another objection that came from some critics was that Hampton makes no mention of Carrington's bisexuality in the film, but the web of her relationships was tangled enough already and none of her lesbian attachments (if she ever had any, which is not certain) detract from Strachey as the central figure in her life.

As far as Strachey's sexuality is concerned the film does throw up one or two puzzling moments. In the first section he tries to kiss Carrington but she pushes him away. Later on, of course, he rejects her advances, making it clear that he would never be interested in having a sexual relationship with her. When he is on his deathbed he doesn't seem to know that Carrington is in the room and asks if she is there. He then refers to her in the third person, saying that he loved her and should have married her. Holroyd suggests in his biography that Strachey was conscious of her presence at the time and was trying to comfort her but in the film this is not indicated.

Because of the period setting, and the casting of Emma Thompson and Samuel West, who both starred in *Howard's End*, *Carrington* inevitably drew comparisons with the Merchant-Ivory films and was accused by some of being a piece of 'heritage cinema'. Many critics reject films that are about middle-class, artistically inclined characters, dismissing them as snobbish and insular. But a film should not be dismissed simply because it deals with people of a particular class or background. There is no such thing as a right or wrong subject and the success or failure of any work of art depends entirely on the talent of the people who create it. Any set of characters, if approached with insight and artistic energy, can enhance our understanding of what it is to be human.

Hampton sees *Carrington* more as a French film that happened to be English, one by a director like François Truffaut or Eric Rohmer, and he is one of the few writer-directors writing in England who would be capable of making the sort of fiercely intellectual films associated with the French *auteurs.* Unfortunately, *Carrington* is a less integrated film than one might have hoped for.

The script's main weakness is that it enters into Carrington's emotional confusion rather than attempt to reach an understanding of it. The film identifies with her so strongly and is so wedded to the facts of her relationships (with much of the dialogue taken directly from the real characters' actual correspondence) that it is incapable of assessing her. There are individual moments of wit and perception and it is full of incidental pleasures but this is not the same as having a closely argued script.

Hampton wanted to deal with each one of Carrington's love affairs in depth but this is difficult in a two-hour film and the narrative becomes diffuse and some of the figures are less sharply drawn than they should have been. Brenan, for instance, is never fully developed as a character, and Penrose seems to arrive out of nowhere and disappear before we have a chance to discover anything about him.

Many of the scenes (including the final one) in the film end with a blackout and this makes the overall construction seem slightly disjointed.

In *Total Eclipse* the relationship between Verlaine and Rimbaud is no less complex than that between Carrington and Strachey and yet we end up with a clearer picture of them as individuals who represented two opposing ways of looking at the world. In *Carrington* the motivation of her character is less clear. There is no attempt to analyse why she seems incapable of functioning independently of others, for example. Shortly before she marries Partridge she writes a letter to Strachey explaining that her love for him is one of the most self-abasing that it is possible to have (she tells him at one point: "I am your penwiper") but she never questions why she should feel like this. At one point Gertler asks her if she has no self-respect and she responds "not much". In this scene his expression of his disgust at the thought of her living with a homosexual brings the response: "You always have to put up with something", which seems to encapsulate her overall philosophy.

Even with these reservations, there is no doubt that *Carrington* represents a major turning point in Hampton's career. His handling of the cast is well-nigh faultless. For once he has created a female leading role and Emma Thompson is superb as Carrington, bringing out her unsentimental approach to life with skill. Jonathan Pryce as Strachey, looking like Carrington's portrait of him come to life, delivers a scene-stealing performance that veers brilliantly between realism and caricature and pulls off the near-miraculous coup of making the man seem likeable. The supporting cast are all strong: Rufus Sewell as Gertler is neurotic and petulant; Steven Waddington portrays Partridge with a reserved yet brutal intelligence when he could so easily have slipped into the caricature of a mindless English hearty; and Samuel West is appropriately low-keyed as the enigmatic Brenan.

Few of the cast had worked with Hampton before but Stephen Boxer, who played Alfons in *Faith, Hope and Charity* and Albert Etheridge in *White Chameleon*, has a small part as one of the officers at Strachey's tribunal and Penelope Wilton (the original Araminta in *The Philanthropist* and the reporter in *Able's Will*) has a splendid cameo role as Ottoline Morrell. Although Morrell is undoubtedly eccentric—she has an erratic dress sense and has a habit of going everywhere with at least six dogs who appear to be pulling her along on an invisible chariot—and tends to interfere in other people's affairs, she shows a genuine concern for Carrington's happiness. On the whole the film treats her more sympathetically than most people did when she was alive.

Carrington is Hampton's best film to date. Once again his career seems to be shaping up in the same way as David Hare's, who took to directing his own work with films such as *Wetherby* and *Paris by Night*. Screenwriters who turn to directing are often accused of making films that concentrate on dialogue at the expense of the visual imagination. This seems a small price to pay, especially now, when many films are just flavourless packages of special effects, but Hampton's cameraman, Denis Lenoir, who shot Bertrand Tavernier's *Daddy Nostalgie*, produces images that are subtle and fluent. He favours tracking and circling shots to keep the action from becoming static but this never becomes self-conscious. Much of the film is shot in a mellow, golden light, which makes it all the more surprising to see Strachey suddenly vomit into his beard at a tea-party or exclaim: "Fuck the upper classes". Distinction was also added to the film by Michael Nyman (Peter Greenaway's regular contributor) who composed a poignant score.

It was perhaps fitting that the film should have helped to kindle a general interest in Carrington's work, and a major retrospective exhibition was held at the Barbican throughout the summer and autumn of 1995.

In June 1995 *Carrington* was entered for the Cannes Film Festival where Hampton won a Special Jury Prize as writer and director, and Pryce won the Best Actor award. At Cannes Hampton made a very rare public statement on a political issue when he remarked that he couldn't remember when he had last seen a Heritage Minister at the cinema—a thrust at the then holder of the post, Stephen Dorrell, who made a brief appearance at the Festival, and one of those responsible for the moribund state of the British film industry.

A couple of other film projects that Hampton was involved with have been disappointing. In 1989 Volker Schlöndorff, best known in Britain for his screen version of *The Tin Drum*, asked Hampton if he was interested in writing a screenplay about the relationship between Verlaine and Rimbaud. He was interested to learn about *Total Eclipse* and agreed to start work on it. John Malkovich and River Phoenix were approached to play the leads but the project had fallen through even before Phoenix's sudden death in 1993. In 1995 the director Agnieszka Holland made a film of Hampton's play, starring Leonardo DiCaprio and David Thewlis. It played badly in America and has not been released anywhere else, although a novelisation has been prepared in Japan.

The film *Mary Reilly* reunited Hampton with director Stephen Frears and actors John Malkovich and Glenn Close but the result was not to be another *Dangerous Liaisons.* Hampton scripted the film from a novel by Valerie Martin which tells the story of Dr Jekyll and Mr Hyde from the point of view of a serving maid.

Mary, played by Julia Roberts, looks up to her employer, Henry Jekyll, as a surrogate father. Gradually she realises that Jekyll and the repulsive Mr Hyde are the same person and that he has been responsible for a series of murders. Like her own father he has two distinct personalities and is good when sober but bad when drunk.

Mary Reilly seriously lacks narrative drive—all the horror and subtlety of Stevenson's original tale has been lost—and the film is strangely insipid and lacking in tension. Glenn Close briefly livens things up with a high-camp cameo role as Mrs Farraday, a caustic madame, but when we see Hyde caress her severed head there is no terror.

Hampton's under-age sex motif reappears here. It is implied that Mary's father, as well as beating her and locking her in a cellar with rats, sexually abuses her. We see him in flashback calling her over to him. He begins to fondle her but stops when she accidentally breaks his bottle of gin. Later Hyde accuses her of enjoying her father's perverse attentions, thus hinting at the sexual desire he feels for her himself that he sternly represses in his persona as Jekyll.

Mary Reilly was beset by troubles. Hampton provided a variety of different endings and several months after filming finished the cast was recalled and a new one was shot. The final scene of the film as it stands is inconclusive and vague: Mary simply wanders off into the mist. We have no idea what effect the dramatic events she has just witnessed will have on her in the future.

Despite these setbacks Hampton is enthusiastic about his film career, which, helped by the success of *Carrington*, has taken off. He has said of directing that "like a virgin in a pornographic novel, having resisted so staunchly for so long, I found I couldn't get enough of it".

He has now directed his own dramatisation of Conrad's *The Secret Agent*, starring Bob Hoskins, Gérard Depardieu, Jim Broadbent, Eddie Izzard, Patricia Arquette and Robin Williams. The film had first been mooted back in the early 1990s. Hoskins was to direct (he directed his own original script of *The Raggedy-Rawney* in 1987) but this project, like so many others, had stalled. The novel has already been filmed, by Alfred Hitchcock in 1937 as *Sabotage*, with Oskar Holmolka and Sylvia Sidney. (The title was changed to avoid confusion with another film Hitchcock had made the previous year called *Secret Agent*, taken from a stage adaptation of Somerset Maugham's Ashenden stories.) A television play of *The Secret Agent* with David Suchet, Cheryl Campbell and Patrick Malahide was shown on BBC2 in 1992.

Hampton is a great admirer of Conrad. "He's sort of optimistic about individuals and pessimistic about history. That seems to be pretty much the way I feel," he says.

In 1995 Hampton signed a $2 million contract with 20th Century Fox to write two films, one of which he will also direct. He plans sometime in the future to direct a version of *White Chameleon* but has said that he felt it would seem self-indulgent to make a film about his childhood before tackling a few other subjects first. He hopes that his third film as director will be his version of *The Moon and Sixpence*, which was written before *Carrington*.

Hampton has completed a version of Donna Tartt's novel *The Secret History* for Alan J. Pakula. He has also dramatised *A Bright Shining Lie*, based on Neil Sheehan's eight-hundred-page biography of Vietnam War veteran Colonel John Paul Vann. Jane Fonda commissioned the script and HBO, an American television company, plans to film it.

Unlike many playwrights or novelists, Hampton doesn't consider producing screenplays is second-rate work to be done only when he has an overdraft. In fact it is his belief in film as a worthwhile form that has kept him going even when it seemed that nothing he wrote would ever reach the screen. That belief has now paid off.

CONCLUSION

> What now? Death, hell, destruction, madness, suicide, or will he come through smiling?
>
> *The Philanthropist*

Unlike many people who achieve success young, and despite his own early doubts about the validity of writing, Hampton has built a lasting career. He has made a virtue of versatility and he aims to make each piece of work stand or fall on its own merits. He has avoided being pigeonholed and now he is in the enviable position of having achieved huge success while remaining almost invisible to the media.

Hampton has yet to acquire as large a reputation in the cinema as he has earned in the theatre but this is most probably only a matter of time. Not only has his long-held ambition to be a screenwriter been fulfilled, he is , as he had never before thought he would be, a director. This will, at least in theory, give him more creative power to make the sort of films that he wants to make. It is not many artists who get a chance to start a whole new career in middle age but Hampton shows no signs of flagging. In an interview with Robert Butler in the *Independent on Sunday* he explained that he has now worked through his uncertainty at being a writer. Now all he worries about is what to write: "The task is to polish up your instinct—to be attentive to the things that seem to explode with the loudest pop when you first think of them."

With such a many-sided talent one might be tempted to ask who is the real Christopher Hampton, but this is a false question. A chameleon can change itself into any colour it wishes. Instead of having only one tone it can display the whole spectrum. All its colours are true colours.

Knowledge of the details of Hampton's personal life doesn't add very much to our understanding of the plays as he doesn't write directly about himself. This may in fact make him a more reliable writer. As Oscar Wilde said: "Give a man a mask and he will tell you the truth."

Hampton is decidedly a literary playwright (he became a Fellow of the Royal Society of Literature in 1984) and he sees drama as a forum where ideas are discussed even if conclusions can rarely be reached. His knowledge of the great European tradition deeply enriches his work. David Hare summed up

Hampton's outlook: "He has a more divine overview of things than the rest of us. Great literature is his real interest, it's real to him in a way that it isn't to the rest of us. His great passion is the French and German writers of the eighteenth and nineteenth centuries, so his attitude is that it doesn't matter very much what the rest of us are doing—there hasn't been a decent playwright since Molière."

Most modern plays fail because their language fails and most modern playwrights strive to evoke a mood or feeling without having the imaginative resources to achieve it. An excess of bland naturalism in the British theatre has brought on a sort of linguistic bankruptcy. Hampton's plays are dialogue-driven and his language is precisely crafted: the words, as in all the best plays, are what matter.

Even if Hampton gave up writing tomorrow and went to work on a building site in Africa it is reasonably safe to say that *The Philanthropist*, the 1981 version of *Total Eclipse* and *Les Liaisons Dangereuses* will be established in the repertory of 'classic' texts. For once that word is not misused.

NOTES AND BIBLIOGRAPHY

Sources for quoted material are given below. Unattributed quotations are from unpublished conversations between the author and Christopher Hampton.

CHAPTER 1

Hampton, Christopher *When Did You Last See My Mother?* (Faber and Faber, London, 1967, Samuel French, Inc., New York, 1967)

Osborne, John *Look Back in Anger* (Faber and Faber, London, 1957)

'Reps Clamour for Philanthropist' (unattributed, *Essex County Standard*, 10 May 1974)

Owen, Michael 'Who is Peggy Ramsay? And Why is She so Powerful? *(Evening Standard* Magazine, June 1988)

'When Did You Last See Your Mother?' (unattributed, *Observer*, 12 June 1966)

Norman, Barry 'My Ambition to be the World's OLDEST Playwright' (*Daily Mail*, 6 July 1966)

Butler, Robert 'Audience with the Invisible Man' (*Independent on Sunday,* 2 May 1993)

Hampton, Christopher 'Sloane Square Lessons' (Chapter in *At the Royal Court: 25 Years of the English Stage Company*, edited by Richard Findlater (Amber Lane Press, Ambergate, 1981)

Desert Island Discs (with Sue Lawley, BBC Radio 4, 7 January 1996)

CHAPTER 2

The extracts quoted in this chapter come from the 1981 version of the play first performed at the Lyric Theatre, Hammersmith. This is the text that Hampton chose to include in the 1991 edition of his collected plays.

Hampton, Christopher *Total Eclipse* (Faber and Faber, London, 1969, Samuel French, London, 1969. Revised edition Faber and Faber, London, 1981. Collected edition Faber and Faber, London, 1991)

Hampton, Christopher '*Total Eclipse*' *Radio Times* (26 April-2 May 1969)

Hampton, Christopher 'Two Children Free to Wander' (Talk on Verlaine and Rimbaud given on BBC Radio 3 after the broadcast of *Total Eclipse*: 1 May 1969, unpublished)

Starkie, Enid *Arthur Rimbaud* (Faber and Faber, London, 1961)

de Jongh, Nicholas 'Out of Eclipse' (*Guardian*, 7 September 1970)

Cushman, Robert 'A Tale of Two Poets' (*Observer*, 10 May 1981)

Hobson, Harold 'How Britain Can Repay Barrault' (*Sunday Times,* 15 September 1968)

'Milton Shulman at the Theatre' (*Evening Standard*, 12 September 1968)

Malcolm, Derek '*Total Eclipse* at the Royal Court (*Guardian*, 12 September 1968)

Callow, Simon 'Farewell, Henry the Great' (obituary of Victor Henry, *Evening Standard*, 6 December 1985)

Lahr, John 'She Who Must be Obeyed (*Sunday Correspondent*, 18 March 1990)

Hampton, Christopher 'Sloane Square Lessons' *op.cit.*

CHAPTER 3

Hampton, Christopher *The Philanthropist* (Faber and Faber, London, 1970, Samuel French, Inc., New York 1971. Revised edition Faber and Faber, 1985. Collected edition Faber and Faber, London, 1991)

Hampton, Christopher 'Sloane Square Lessons' *op.cit.*

Hawkins-Daly, Mark (Ed.) *International Dictionary of Theatre — 1 Plays* (St James Press, Chicago and London, 1992)

Hobson, Harold 'The Fatal Match' (*Sunday Times*, 9 August 1970)

Desert Island Discs op. cit.

CHAPTER 4

Hampton, Christopher *Savages* (Faber and Faber, London, 1974)

Lewis, Norman 'Genocide in Brazil' (*Sunday Times*, 23 February 1969)

Esslin, Martin 'Christopher Hampton's *Savages* at the Royal Court Theatre' and 'In search of *Savages*' Production Casebook no. 12 *(Theatre Quarterly*, October-December 1973)

Bryden, Ronald '*Savages*' (*Plays and Players*, June 1973)

Hobson, Harold 'Power Behind the Throne' (*Sunday Times*, 15 April 1973)

Wardle, Irving 'Documentary Polemic' (*The Times*, 13 April 1973)

Watts, Janet 'Hampton's Court' (*Guardian*, 5 February 1976)

South Bank Show (produced by Melvyn Bragg, London Weekend Television, 5 February 1989)

CHAPTER 5

Hampton, Christopher *Treats* (Faber and Faber, London, 1976, Samuel French, London 1976. Collected edition Faber and Faber, London, 1991)

Watts, Janet *op.cit.*

CHAPTER 6

Hampton, Christopher *Tales from Hollywood* (Faber and Faber, London, 1983)

Hampton, Christopher 'Hard Master' (obituary of Robert Kidd, *Guardian*, 19 July 1980)

Ratcliffe, Michael 'Sunset Waltz of the Emigrés' (*Sunday Times*, 21 August 1983)

Wardle, Irving 'Sparkle Without the Fire' *(The Times*, 2 September 1983)

Morley, Sheridan 'Hooray for Hollywood' (*Punch,* 14 September 1983)

Billington, Michael '*Tales from Hollywood*' (*Guardian*, 1 September 1983)

Owen, Michael 'Adolf on Trial in Hampton's Court' (*Evening Standard*, 15 January 1982)

CHAPTER 7

Hampton, Christopher *The Portage to San Cristobal of A.H.* (Faber and Faber, London, 1983)

Steiner, George *The Portage to San Cristobal of A.H.* (Faber and Faber, 1981)

Steiner, George *The Death of Tragedy* (Faber and Faber, London, 1961)

Steiner, George *In Bluebeard's Castle* (Faber and Faber, London, 1971)

'Steiner on Stage' (unattributed diary entry, *The Times*, 19 February 1982)

Nietzsche, Friedrich *Beyond Good and Evil* (translated by R J Hollingdale) (Penguin Books, Harmondsworth, 1973)

Wesker, Arnold 'Shylock and his Hitler' (*The Times,* 20 March 1982)

Gilbert, Martin 'Who Do You Think You Are Kidding, Mr Hitler? (*Jewish Chronicle*, 26 February 1982, reprinted in *The Times,* 6 March 1982)

Radin, Victoria 'Finding the Führer' (*Observer*, 21 February 1982)

Shulman, Milton 'Hitler the Accuser' (*Evening Standard*, 18 February 1982)

Billington, Michael 'The Portage of A.H.' (*Guardian*, 19 February 1982)

CHAPTER 8

Hampton, Christopher *Les Liaisons Dangereuses* (Faber and Faber, London, 1986)

Hampton, Christopher 'Are You Doing Any Original Work or is it Just the Adaptations?' (*Guardian*, 7 January 1986)

Grant, Steve 'Hampton Holds Court (*Time Out*, 1 October 1986)

Miller, Carl 'Cinéma de Complicité' (*City Limits,* 2 March 1989)

Quennell, Peter *The Singular Preference* (Collins, London, 1952)

Wardle, Irving *'Les Liaisons Dangereuses' (The Times,* 27 August 1985)

Platform Papers no 1: Translation (Royal National Theatre, London, 1992)

Peter, John 'Charades and Charisma' (*Sunday Times*, 29 September 1985)

Billington, Michael 'Sex and the Single Girl' (*Guardian*, 27 September 1985)

Coward, David 'Elegant Strategies' (*Times Literary Supplement*, 11 October 1985)

CHAPTER 9

Hampton, Christopher *White Chameleon* (Faber and Faber, London, 1991)

South Bank Show (1989) *op.cit.*

Lawson, Mark 'West of Suez' (*Independent* Magazine, 9 February 1991)

CHAPTER 10

Hampton, Christopher, Lloyd Webber, Andrew and Black, Don *Sunset Boulevard* (Faber and Faber, London, 1993)

Hampton, Christopher 'Twenty Years to Make a Sunset' (*Daily Telegraph*, 25 April 1993)

Perry, George *Sunset Boulevard - From Movie To Musical* (Pavilion Books, London, 1993)

Robinson, David 'Second Dawn on Sunset' (*The Times*, 5 July 1993)

CHAPTER 11

Hampton, Christopher and Clarke, Martha *Alice's Adventures Under Ground* (Faber and Faber, London, 1995)

Taylor, Paul 'The Trouble with Alice' (*Independent*, 10 November 1994)

Billington, Michael 'Absence of Alice' (*Guardian*, 10 November 1994)

Lewis, Peter 'Inspiring the Alice Band' (*Sunday Times*, 6 November 1994)

Peter, John '*Alice's Adventures Under Ground*' (*Sunday Times*, 13 November 1994)

With the exception of certain quoted material, Charles Lutwidge Dodgson is referred to by his pseudonym of Lewis Carroll throughout this chapter.

CHAPTER 12

Platform Papers op.cit.

Babel, Isaac *Marya* (version by Christopher Hampton from a literal translation by Michael Glenny and Howard Shukman) in *Plays of the Year 35* edited by J.C. Trewin (Elek, London, 1969)

Chekhov, Anton Uncle Vanya (version by Christopher Hampton from a literal translation by Nina Froud) in *Plays of the Year 39* edited by J.C. Trewin (Elek, London, 1971)

Chekhov, Anton *Uncle Vanya* (translated by Constance Garnett) (Chatto and Windus, London, 1923)

Chekhov, Anton *Uncle Vania* (translated by Elisaveta Fen) (Penguin Books, Harmondsworth, 1954)

Chekhov, Anton *Uncle Vanya* (translated by Michael Frayn) (Methuen, London, 1987)

Hope-Wallace, Philip '*Uncle Vanya*' (*Guardian*, 25 February 1970)

Wardle, Irving 'Chekhov Comparison' (*The Times*, 25 February 1970)

Grant, Steve *op.cit.*

Ibsen, Henrik *Hedda Gabler* (version by Christopher Hampton from a literal translation by Hélène Grégoire) (Samuel French, Inc., New York, 1971. Revised edition 1989) (version by Christopher Hampton from a literal translation by Karin and Ann Bamborough) (Faber and Faber, London, 1989)

South Bank Show (1989) *op.cit.*

Ibsen, Henrik *Hedda Gabler* (translated by William Archer and Edmund Gosse) (Charles Scribner's Son, New York, 1907)

Ibsen, Henrik *Hedda Gabler* (translated by John Osborne) (Faber and Faber, London, 1972)

de Jongh, Nicholas '*Hedda Gabler*' (*Guardian*, 26 April 1984)

Hiley, Jim 'House of Horrors' (*Listener*, 16 February 1989)

Hoyle, Martin '*Hedda Gabler*' (*Financial Times*, 25 April 1984)

Ibsen, Henrik *A Doll's House* (translated by Christopher Hampton) (Samuel French, London and New York, 1972, Faber and Faber, London, 1989)

Armitstead, Claire 'Cosy Chameleon' (*Guardian*, 28 April 1993)

Ibsen, Henrik *The Wild Duck* (translated by Christopher Hampton) (Faber and Faber, London, 1980)

Ibsen, Henrik *The Wild Duck* (translated by Michael Meyer) (Rupert Hart-Davis, London, 1962)

Ibsen, Henrik *The Wild Duck* (translated by Una-Ellis Fermor) (Penguin Books, Harmondsworth, 1950)

Higgins, John 'The Art of Finding English for Ibsen' (*The Times*, 12 December 1979)

Morley, Sheridan 'Duck no Turkey' (*Punch*, 2 January 1980)

Horváth, Ödön von *Kasimir and Karoline, Faith Hope and Charity, Figaro Gets a Divorce, Judgement Day* (translated by Martin Esslin) (P.A.J. Publications, New York, 1986)

Horváth, Ödön von *Jugend ohne Gott* (edited by Ian Huish) (Harrap, London, 1974)

Horváth, Ödön von *Jungste Tag* (edited by Ian Huish) (Methuen Educational, London, 1985)

Oakes, Meredith 'Unemployed Virtues' (*Independent*, 19 August 1989)

Kellaway, Kate 'Tales of a Viennese Hero in a Carrier Bag' (*Observer*, 15 October 1989)

Horváth, Ödön von *Tales from the Vienna Woods* (translated by Christopher Hampton) (Faber and Faber, London, 1977)

Ratcliffe, Michael 'Sunset Waltz of the Emigrés' (*Sunday Times*, 21 August 1983)

Grant, Steve *op.cit.*

Morley, Sheridan 'Vienna Cavalcade' (*Punch*, 2 February 1977)

Billington, Michael '*Tales from the Vienna Woods*' (*Guardian*, 27 January 1977)

Horváth, Ödön von *Don Juan Comes Back from the War* (translated by Christopher Hampton) (Faber and Faber, London, 1978. Absolute Press, Bath, 1990)

Barber, John 'Black Years Shown Through Witty Don' (*Daily Telegraph*, 19 April 1978)

Billington, Michael '*Don Juan*' (*Guardian*, 19 April 1978)

Wardle, Irving 'Conquests Resumed' (*The Times*, 19 April 1978)

Stewart, Ian 'Classical Theme in a Modern World' (*Country Life*, 11 May 1978)

Cushman, Robert 'Return of Don Juan' (*Observer*, 23 April 1978)

Horváth, Ödön von *Faith, Hope and Charity* (translated by Christopher Hampton) (Faber and Faber, London, 1989)

Hoyle, Martin '*Faith, Hope and Charity*' (*Financial Times*, 30 October 1989)

Billington, Michael 'Death of a Salesgirl' (*Guardian*, 30 October 1989)

Ratcliffe, Michael 'Fall into a Timeless Nightmare' (*Observer*, 5 November 1989)

Hampton, Christopher 'Heroes and Villains' (*Independent* Magazine, 31 March 1990)

Molière *The Miser and Other Plays* (translated by John Wood) (Penguin Books, Harmondsworth, 1953)

Molière *Don Juan* (translated by Christopher Hampton) (Faber and Faber, London, 1974)

Molière *Tartuffe* (translated by Christopher Hampton) (Samuel French, London and New York, 1985)

Molière *Tartuffe* (translated by Simon Gray) (Faber and Faber, London, 1982)

Morley, Sheridan 'Comedies Française' (*Punch*, 10 August 1983)

Platform Papers op.cit.

South Bank Show (1989) *op.cit.*

Reza, Yasmina *Art* (translated by Christopher Hampton) (Faber and Faber, London, 1996)

Hampton has another Molière translation, *Georges Dandin*, waiting in the wings. He was originally commissioned in the 1970s by BBC Radio and later did a version for an American theatre company but the text has not been published.

Hampton's version of *Le Mariage de Barillon* a farce by Georges Feydeau and Maurice Desvallières retitled *Signed and Sealed* was staged at the Comedy Theatre in 1976. It was directed by Patrick Garland, with Kenneth Williams, Peggy Mount and Bryan Pringle. The play came off within three weeks and has not been published. Williams mentions Hampton and this production briefly in his *Diaries* but he spares him from the often lacerating observations that he made about many other fellow professionals.

In 1979 Hampton translated *The Prague Trial* for BBC Radio. This was a documentary piece by Patrice Chereau and Ariane Mnouchkine based on the smuggled transcripts of the trials of some Czech dissidents arrested by the Communist dictatorship. The text has not been published.

CHAPTER 13

Newman, Charles 'Hampton—Luck and Talent in a Brutal Business' (*AIP and Co.*, January 1984)

Hampton, Christopher *Able's Will* (Faber and Faber, London, 1977)

Bradbury, Malcolm *The History Man* (Martin Secker & Warburg, London, 1975)

Selway, Jennifer 'Return of a Revolutionist' (*Observer*, 4 January 1981)

Bradbury, Malcolm 'The Celluloid Collar' (*Listener*, 28 April 1988)

Radlo, Nick 'Bradbury Airs His Doubts About *The History Man* BBC2 Style' (*Broadcast*, 24 August 1981)

James, Clive 'Mass in the Crevasse' (*Observer*, 1 February 1981. Reprinted in *Glued to the Box*, Jonathan Cape Ltd., London, 1983)

Brookner, Anita *Hotel du Lac* (Jonathan Cape Ltd., London, 1984)

Greenstreet, Rosanna 'Mantelpiece' (*Sunday Telegraph* Magazine, 19 March 1992)

Hampton, Christopher *The Ginger Tree* (Faber and Faber, London, 1989)

Wynd, Oswald *The Ginger Tree* (William Collins Sons & Co. Ltd., London, 1977)

Grant, Steve *op.cit.*

de Jongh, Nicholas 'Out of Eclipse' (*Guardian*, 7 September 1970)

CHAPTER 14

Miller, Carl *op. cit.*

Bergson, Philip 'Stage and Sceen' (*What's On*, 12 January 1984)

Omnibus: 'Sunset Boulevard' (BBC1, 21 December 1993)

Oakes, Philip 'Coming On' (*Sunday Times*, 18 March 1973)

Greene, Graham *The Honorary Consul* (Bodley Head, London, 1973)

Newman, Charles 'Against the Odds' (*AIP and Co.*, December 1983)

Prince, Peter *The Good Father* (Jonathan Cape Ltd, London, 1983)

Hampton, Christopher *Dangerous Liaisons* (Faber and Faber, London, 1989)

Hampton, Christopher 'Going for that Gut Feeling' (*Guardian*, 29 December 1988)

Hampton, Christopher *Carrington* (Faber and Faber, London, 1995)

Partridge, Frances 'Art and Film' (*Modern Painters*, Autumn 1995)

Hill, Jane *The Art of Dora Carrington* (The Herbert Press, London, 1994)

Holroyd, Michael *Lytton Strachey—A Critical Biography* (William Heinemann Ltd., London, 1967-68)

Holroyd, Michael 'No Need To Lie' *South Bank Show* (London Weekend Television, 7 December 1980)

Sweeting, Adam 'Less Dangerous Liaisons' (*Guardian*, 12 September 1995)

Gritten, David 'Bigger and Bigger' (*Telegraph* Magazine, 2 September 1995)

CONCLUSION

Butler, Robert *op.cit.*

Burn, Gordon 'The Hairy Times of a Smooth Man' (*Telegraph* Magazine, 25 November 1989)

Readers checking on the published work of Christopher Hampton should be aware that there is another writer with the same name, a Marxist poet, and author of the book *Socialism in a Crippled World*. Hampton tells the story of how his namesake once wrote a letter to the *Guardian* attacking Harold Pinter. "I got a very Pinteresque phone call," he said. "Very long pauses, and I said, 'Is this about the letter?' And he said, 'Yes, yes, it is, actually.' I told him it was another Christopher Hampton. I think he believed it was a particularly ingenious excuse."

INDEX

Where major characters in the works are mentioned for purposes of comparison, they are entered under the name of the character, not the title of the work.